COMMUNITY LIBRARY

D0354199

THE GOOD DEATH

The
GOOD
DEATH

AN EXPLORATION
OF
DYING IN AMERICA

———— • ————

Ann Neumann

Beacon Press
Boston

BEACON PRESS
Boston, Massachusetts
www.beacon.org

Beacon Press books
are published under the auspices of
the Unitarian Universalist Association of Congregations.

© 2016 by Ann Neumann
All rights reserved
Printed in the United States of America

19 18 17 16   8 7 6 5 4 3 2 1

This book is printed on acid-free paper that meets the uncoated paper
ANSI/NISO specifications for permanence as revised in 1992.

Text design and composition by Kim Arney

Many names and other identifying characteristics of people and facilities
mentioned in this work have been changed to protect their identities.

Library of Congress Cataloging-in-Publication Data

Neumann, Ann.
     The good death : an exploration of dying in America / Ann Neumann.
          pages   cm
     Includes bibliographical references and index.
     ISBN 978-0-8070-8062-7 (hardback) -- ISBN 978-0-8070-8063-4 (ebook)
1. Death—United States. 2. Terminal care—United States. 3. Thanatology—
United States. I. Title.
     HQ1073.5.U6N48 2016
     304.6'40973—dc23
                                                                    2015025729

For my sister, of course.

Contents

CHAPTER ONE

Terminal Restlessness

I placed the tiny, white pill on the US Army spoon my father had used to eat cereal for nearly forty years. From a white plastic bottle, about the size and shape of a small flask, I extracted five drops of pink liquid morphine. I released each drop one by one onto the spoon and used the tip of the dropper to push the Ativan in slow circles until it dissolved. Then I sucked the mixture back up into the dropper. *Morphine takes your pain away. Ativan calms you down.* I wanted to lick the spoon.

From where I stood, I could hear him move on the vinyl hospital mattress in the next room. He was only shifting, dropping his stiff, pinched hands onto the sheet beside him. Not trying to get out of bed. He had complained about the mattress until four days before, when he stopped complaining about anything. My bare feet on the cold tile in the hallway, the dropper in my hand, the acrid smell of stale coffee coming from the kitchen behind me, I stood listening to the empty house.

Perfectly cured, twenty-four-inch oak logs my father had cut, split, and stacked the previous spring now shifted with an ashy thump in the woodstove down the hall. I looked out the window to the bird feeder he had made twenty years ago. It stood firmly planted in the frozen ground. Juncos and phoebes chattered and picked at the seeds in the tray and then flitted and disappeared into the gray pines behind them.

I could not see his face, only his thin, white feet against the simulated wood grain of the footboard. The blanket had slipped to one side. He moved his right foot up and toward his body, then back to the footboard in a slow, kicking motion, trying to get the blanket back over his toes. He was awake. I looked at the watch on my left wrist, which I'd set to military time when dusk had begun to blur into dawn. It now read: 15:57.

Lifting my shoulders and working a smile into my eyes, I stepped from the hallway into his dark room.

The toilet in the downstairs bathroom wouldn't flush. My younger sister, Mindy, called the man who pumps septic systems to come clean out our tank. She and I took turns searching for the cap in the yard— another bit of necessary information we could no longer ask our father for. One of us kicked at the frozen sod, while the other tried to keep him from getting out of bed.

Terminal restlessness, the hospice doctor had told us. At the end of life, organs begin to shut down. Old ladies who hadn't left their beds in years suddenly rise up with unimaginable strength to move furniture. Frail, aged men who have been silent for months grow angry and yell profanity at anyone who passes by. They are agitated, violent. They want to go. Our father wanted to go home, and he was sure this was not it. I tried citing the evidence to the contrary. I pointed out the ceiling he had hung, the walls he had painted, and the carpet he had laid. I showed him photos of the house he was in, the same stone house we had built together three decades before, mixing mortar and gathering stone as a family. The same house in which he wanted to die and to which I had returned to help him do so. But he did not believe me.

When a nurse from hospice arrived, my sister and I cried with relief and exhaustion. We couldn't keep him calm. We hadn't slept in days. He kicked at us and swung his twisted arms—at us, his daughters, as if he didn't know us anymore. Even the house was against us, its plumbing gurgling and sputtering. We wanted the nurse to tell us what to do. We wanted more drugs, other drugs that would keep him calm. She insisted that we could no longer keep my father at home, even with regular visits from the hospice staff. We had to take him to the hospice facility thirty minutes away, where drugs stronger than our pink flask of morphine could be administered. We were his advocates, the ones charged with his final wish, to die at home, and we had failed. When the ambulance arrived, the septic pump truck was blocking the driveway. The EMT backed across the frozen yard as the workman searched for the tank cap with a metal rod. He stopped to watch us load our father into the ambulance, an extra in our family drama, then went back to stabbing the turf.

In the ambulance, I gripped the rail of the stretcher, feeling the familiar rise and fall and bend of the road to town. I imagined the hospice facility to be exactly what my father didn't want: rows of withering patients lined up along pastel walls, whispering middle-aged nurses, strangers in pink uniforms, their faces full of pity. My father's eyes rolled deep in his head. He struggled to get his right hand out from under the straps and turned his face away from me as I brushed the hair from his forehead.

The young EMT asked, "How was your Thanksgiving?" I looked at him without answering. Four days before, we had cooked a Thanksgiving turkey but not eaten it. The day before, I had passed my thirty-seventh birthday in my pajamas, with sleeplessness, dirty bedclothes, and the responsibility of giving care I wasn't sure I had in me. And now we had failed to let our father die at home. It felt like the greatest failure, and yet I no longer knew what I was doing any more than my father in his thrashing delirium did.

Hospice nurses ran to the back doors of the ambulance when we arrived. He was awake again, moaning and struggling against the straps of the stretcher. I followed them as they rushed the stretcher down the hallway and into a private room. He fought them; they jammed needles full of heavy doses of Haldol or Thorazine, hospice drugs of choice, deep into the waning muscle of his thighs to calm him. As he slipped into quiet, I understood that he was no longer my charge. I was no longer responsible for that body. The schedule that had kept me listening and feeding and dosing and restraining for three months was over, my responsibilities usurped by the uniformed and capable. That night, as I lay on the sofa at the foot of his bed, nurses came and went with syringes and incontinence pads in two-hour intervals. Then, after ten years of eating away at his body like a gluttonous parasite, his cancer finally destroyed them both.

In the lobby, family who had come to spend a moment with him, to touch the cooling skin on his hand, to whisper last thoughts to his deaf corpse, now sat silently with their spouses. Their coats smelled of cold winter air. Their eyes reflected the deaths of the past eight months: my grandfather, ninety-four, of old age; my cousin, thirty-seven, of Hodgkin's lymphoma; and now my father, sixty, of non-Hodgkin's lymphoma.

"What do we do now?" I asked my sister. She gave the exit door at the end of the hallway a faraway look; it opened onto the stubble of a sheared winter cornfield. Quietly, a mortician opened the door and pushed a stretcher inside. Another extra, like the septic tank man, come to clean up our mess. Without looking at us, he steered into our room with a wide turn.

The mortician unfolded a square of clear plastic—the stiff, heavy kind that painters use to protect floors. Nurses straightened my father's arms and legs and then, with a sheet, lifted his body onto the stretcher. "This is my Dad," I told the mortician as he wrapped the plastic, first over Dad's legs and then his arms and hands, taping the protective layers. The plastic crinkled like a tent. In less than two days, gases in my father's body would push fluids, fecal matter, and urine out of his orifices. Morticians call it the surge. Then, when his name or number came up in the queue, they would push his body into a furnace and reduce it to four pounds of ash in a white box that my sister would pick up and place in the corner of the rec room, where my father had always sat.

The mortician lifted Dad's head and removed our pillow, covered with green-and-brown wood ducks in flight, and handed it to me. "It's still warm," I said.

I came undone. The things that had once held me together now seemed unimportant. When a leave of absence couldn't be extended long enough to see my father through his illness, I had quit my job. I finally had to acknowledge the end of my marriage, which had been dissolving for a few years like paint under solvent. Nothing else—my friends, my flat in New York City, my own ambitions—could measure up to the rugged emotional pinnacles I'd just dragged myself across. Of course I was happy to be alive, as I was courteously and knowingly told that caring for the dying should make us. But holy hell, I'd seen *death*, and it was close and permanent. Final. What was I supposed to do with that?

For the first two weeks, I didn't leave my father's house, my memory-infested childhood home. I ate the canned beets he had purchased from the scratch-and-dent store, burned the wood he had neatly cut, and slept in his bed with a view of the bird feeder. I watched back-to-back reruns of *CSI*, a crime procedural that always concluded with a comforting definitive answer. Everyone brought food and left it on the porch; I didn't answer their knocks or calls. I returned their cookie tins, Pyrex dishes, and Tupperware at odd hours so I wouldn't have to see these dear neighbors and friends on their front porches in the daylight. What would I say?

Caring for my father before he died was no easier than caring for myself after. I was still lost. With haste, I knew I had to get myself up and out. I had to counter the shock of grief with the shock of change. I renewed my passport, handed the house over to my sister, raided my retirement account (what was I saving it for?), and booked a ticket to Japan. For a year and a half, I hurtled around the globe, from shabby guest house to broken-down bus, through Russia, down the Adriatic coast, across Cyprus, Egypt, and the rest of Africa. I was careless, reckless even, and haunted—barely dodging wild elephants, Russian crooks, thieves, thugs, and disorientation. Grief, I learned, is a journey.

Grief for a parent is also often terrifyingly messy. I spent three hours on the tiled balcony of a ramshackle hotel outside Nakuru, Kenya, comforting a middle-aged man from Baltimore. When I had told him I'd lost my father, he launched into his own story, the heartbreaking kind that chronicles the labor of caretaking because the work of mourning is easier to explain than the emotion of it. "The solemnest of industries," Emily Dickinson called it, "the sweeping up the heart." Only hours and tears into our conversation did I ask when his father had died. "Ten years ago," he told me. Ten years. I realized that I was in a club: those who knew what it was like to see the death of a loved one up close. We could almost recognize each other on the street.

It was something visceral that had sent us into a tailspin, something that had to do with caring for our loved ones' bodies. The way we watched, so closely and with such patient horror, as they fell apart— not just the dandruff and draping skin and sagging face, but the saliva and puke and soiled bedsheets. "Our brains light up in weird and remarkable ways at the sight of blood or fecal matter as if these weren't, in fact, perfectly mundane," wrote Florence Williams. My brain was lit up and I wanted to know why.

While my father and I had never seen eye to eye, we were close; we'd spent years together, working and hiking. I knew what he smelled like; I was used to his body. But caring for him, bathing him, brushing his teeth, and holding the basin for him as he vomited—those were altogether different acts. I'd never asked anyone else to do those things for me, and I could only imagine what it felt like for him to give up so much physical privacy. Loss of dignity is what the hospice people called it, the loss of the ability to physically care for yourself. He was slowly being evicted from his body; it wasn't his anymore. Whatever constituted him—his brain, his soul, call it what you want—was being pushed to the curb.

I had been in the examination room with my father when he told his doctor he didn't want to try the final experimental cancer treatment (a drug course with 5 percent efficacy and guaranteed nausea, shedding hair, disability, and depression). He just wanted to go home and die. What did I think was going to happen? Yet I had not imagined what was coming. I had never taken care of a dying person before. I had never even seen someone who was dying. Why didn't the hospice nurses, on their weekly visits to our home all those months, tell us what was happening? That dying is a process of functions, like digestion and circulation, slowly slacking off the job? Because it's difficult to explain? Because they see it all the time? Because the body is unpredictable?

The way we talk about dying and the way we die are two very different things. Death fills our books and movies, our music and our language, just as it has in every other human era. What's different today is that our experience of death is a simulacrum, a myth, a romance where our loved one gives us a last meaningful look, then slips into a long sleep. By the romance of death, I mean what you find in the genre of movie or novel that depicts death as noble, beautiful, or peaceful, like the 2004 movie *The Notebook*, which I caught while in a hotel room in Windhoek, Namibia. The husband reads the story of their relationship to his wife who has Alzheimer's. They're both old now and their story is nostalgic, full of vintage cars, simpler times, and well-worn family dramas. He's reading from a notebook she kept throughout their life together. Because their love is so strong, when the story is finished, her memory briefly returns and they're able to crawl into bed together, hold hands, and die peacefully in their sleep. You can find this pretty rainbows-and-butterflies motif on posters covering hospital and hospice walls, at doctors' offices, in cancer centers, on support websites. It's the Hallmark ending, exactly what I was hoping to get with my father. He'd go home, I'd make soup, he would tell me he loved me and hold my hand, and then he would close his eyes to sweet death. Deep down, we all hope for this, but we also fear that's rarely how it happens.

Part of the reason we don't know how people die is because we no longer see it up close. Plagues, basic infections, and childhood diseases have, for the most part, been eradicated. We've added an additional thirty years to the human life-span in the past century. In 1900, Americans could realistically expect to live to the age of forty-seven; by the 1930s, fifty-nine. By 2000, that age expectancy had reached nearly eighty. Infant mortality rates alone have dropped from fifty-six deaths per one thousand births in 1935 to seven per one thousand in 2000. This improvement in general health in the United States has prevented many of us from directly experiencing death in our homes, the way it often used to occur. Today, 80 percent of Americans die in facilities—hospitals, nursing homes, clinics. When we do see the dying or the dead, it's most often during an abbreviated visit to a hospital ward where doctors and nurses are taking care of the drugging, changing, and bathing. We're visitors. The aspects of dying that are deemed unpleasant (or not made-for-the-movies acceptable) take place behind a curtain. Death has been put off and professionalized to the point where we no longer have to dirty our hands with it.

It hasn't always been this way. Little more than three generations ago, death made frequent house calls, particularly in rural areas. In some ways, the story of medicine in my native Lancaster County is told through the story of my family, Mennonite farmers who arrived about 170 years before the first hospital was founded. My grandfather's father, Enos Harnish, was the first in the family to drive a car. He was also the first in the family to die off the farm, in a hospital, although he stayed at home until shortly before his death, his legs filling up with fluids from dropsy, what we now call congestive heart failure. His daughter, Elizabeth, died the same way. Ninety-year-old Aunt Biz sat in the Mennonite home with her legs propped up on a stool, her wavy hair a little grayer, her cackling laugh the same as ever, refusing to take medicine for the swelling. She'd had a good run of it, she was sure.

But it's another Elizabeth I think of when I think of a peaceful home death. This Elizabeth, the granddaughter of Harnishes by marriage, lived on a farm with her husband, Martin F. Witmer, less than a mile from where I went to high school. From my extended family's surprisingly well-documented history comes this story, handed down orally, then recorded on page 902 of the *Biographical Annals of Lancaster County, Pennsylvania*, printed in 1903 by J. H. Beers & Company: "The family are all Mennonites, and as the Witmers are among the oldest residents of the township, they are held in very high esteem by their neighbors." Elizabeth was Martin's second wife, the stepmother of two boys and the mother of three daughters, Mary, Fannie, and Lizzie. I imagine Elizabeth, eighty-two years and twenty-one days old, shuffling along the linoleum of the drafty farmhouse kitchen before morning light, fetching water for coffee. A dozen jars of pickles she canned the day before sit evenly spaced on a cloth on the counter. Zinnias, pink, red, and yellow, from the July garden are in a milk glass vase on the table. Elizabeth pauses to look at them for a moment and then collapses in a stroke that sends the kettle clattering. Fannie and Lizzie, unmarried and still living at home in their sixties, come running. Elizabeth is unconscious when they find her. They carry her up the stairs and place her in her bed, still warm from when she left it. Mary, the oldest daughter, is called from her home a mile away. The three daughters tend to their mother, a chore that is more emotional than physical. She never awakes. "She was sick but one day, having had a stroke of paralysis early in the morning," the *Biographical Annals* plainly states.

A doctor at the turn of the century, particularly a doctor in rural Lancaster County, was little more than a shaman, traveling from farm to farm on horseback with a rudimentary black leather bag lashed to his saddle. His tools were few and unproven; odd tinctures in small dark bottles, smelling salts, perhaps a flask of whiskey. While a vaccine for smallpox existed, along with various other treatments for scurvy or dropsy, antibiotics were still some sixty years away. Opium was recognized as a standard treatment for pain at the end of life in the mid- to late century, but its prevalence of use is hard to gauge. Elizabeth, because she was unconscious, most likely wasn't in pain. She was surrounded by her daughters and stepsons when she died. They laid her out in her best Sunday dress, and the next day they hauled her body to the grave.

Because of medical developments, we've gotten away from caring for our dying, from seeing death up close, just as we've gotten away from making our own pickles. Our contact with death has diminished so drastically since the turn of the nineteenth century that we desperately want to know more. As Michael Lesy writes in *The Forbidden Zone*, "The fictions we live [about death] only famish our craving." After my father's death, I was famished and I could tell by the questions friends asked that they wanted to know more too. I wasn't asked the metaphysical or religious questions—Where is he now? Did he believe in God?—but the concrete questions about dying—What did he die of? Was he sick for long? How did he know he was dying? And if I talked more about how his body changed, they listened intently, too abashed to ask their own specific questions about his organs, his skin, his last breath.

The only way for us to satisfy our shock or hurt, caused by the gaping disparity between what we say about death and how it actually arrives, is to spend more time with the dying. To know how death comes for others is to know how death could come for us. Knowing what death looks like strips away all the romance but makes it easier to understand and to live through. Yet the medical community's conduct around death continues to shield us from what we want to know—and what we would benefit from knowing.

Even in hospice settings, death is hushed. At an in-hospital hospice ward on Manhattan's Lower East Side, a sheet listing each of the patients is taped to the front counter for the nurses to keep track of who's alive and who's not. Names are frequently crossed out, with new ones scratched above in pencil. The binder that volunteers write notes in—"Mrs. Smith ate two spoons of applesauce. Enjoyed talking about her family. Showed me pictures of her grandchildren."—often contains a note from the hospice coordinator not to mention "hospice" to the patient or their family. Either they haven't wanted to hear the terminal news or they haven't been told what's happening. This practice of shielding patients from knowing their fate is not new, but it is controversial and varies according to region, patient age, class, religion, and ethnicity. When someone dies on the hospice ward, all the room doors on a wing are closed so that no one inside can see the dead body as it's rolled off the floor. Patient stays are short, a week or less, because until the time they've been moved to hospice, they've been in other wards of the hospital receiving treatments meant to cure, treatments that have nonetheless failed to cure.

To discuss dying with a patient is sad work. Doctors have to admit their inability to cure whatever disease is ending a patient's life. Directly discussing hospice means discussing death, and many avoid doing so. Into this fray, between the dying patient and the mute medical community, falls a patient shamed for not wanting to try another experimental treatment; a patient under pressure from family and friends to "not go gentle," to not give up the fight; or a family wrecked by incurable disease but too distressed or ill informed to ask the right questions or know their options.

Saying no to continued treatment, removing life support, regardless of its efficacy, can feel to family like deciding to end their loved one's life, like a betrayal. For patients, it can be understood as giving up, as being uncooperative or depressed, even suicidal. Yet the pain often caused by ineffective treatments can be debilitating, not to mention clinically depressing and bankrupting. If that's a good way to go out, unconscious, sick from chemo poisons, or under the pump of a ventilator, patients have begun to ask, what's the bad way?

For the first time in human history, the definition of death changed in the 1970s. Up until then, death had meant the almost simultaneous end of heartbeat, breathing, and brain function. But a revolution in medicine took place in that decade, developing innovations that could keep the lungs and heart functioning indefinitely. Respirators and defibrillators had winnowed the definition of death down to brain function alone. And nobody—not doctors, lawyers, patients, or families—knew what that meant. For centuries, the heart and its pulse had meant life and vitality; it was the rhythm of our cultures, our communities, our familial bonds. Ancient Egyptians removed all organs but the heart before mummification, thinking it was vital to the afterlife. In the 1600s, it was thought that the soul resided in the hollow muscle of the heart. William Blake depicted the heart as the "central-sun, the heart of the world." We get to the heart of a matter; we know things in our heart; we take serious matters to heart. And it was clear: either the heart was beating and you were alive, or it wasn't and you were dead.

The brain is a completely different matter, mysterious and complicated. It has three primary sections, each with unique and interdependent functions. How much brain function qualifies you as alive? The whole thing? What parts of the brain make you human, not just a body with biological properties? Where in the brain does your personality, your laugh, your ability to recognize your family reside? And how do you measure these things? These medical advances—coupled with cardiopulmonary resuscitation (CPR), 911 phone lines, and the population's shift to urban living where an ambulance team could readily reach the stricken in their homes or on the street—saved countless lives. But they also created a new area of ethics that was unexplored. No one even had a map. Sometimes a heart can be started by shocking the patient or pounding him on the chest (compressions that frequently break the ribs of the frail or elderly) and the lungs can be reactivated by forcing air into them, but if the patient has been without oxygen for more than four minutes, the amount of damage to the brain is hard to measure and often irreparable. In these cases, where technology had preserved "life," death often becomes a conscious decision: to stop the respirator or the pacemaker, to remove the feeding tube, to end the treatment that delivers no results. In her 2010 article for the *New York Times Magazine*, "What Broke My Father's Heart," journalist Katy Butler wrote about the excruciating—and ultimately impossible—task her mother asked her to complete: shutting off her father's pacemaker. He was eighty-five and had suffered dementia for several years, and his body was in full decline. "Sewn into a lump of skin and muscle below his right clavicle was the pacemaker that helped his heart outlive his brain," she wrote. Living without a brain wasn't living, Butler and her mother concluded. After fifty years of watching the definition of death be pulled apart by technology, society mostly agrees. Medicine and the law are another story.

A series of cases surrounding the shifting definition of death were brought before the public in the 1970s, including that of Karen Ann Quinlan. Quinlan was twenty-one when she collapsed after drinking alcohol and taking Valium. She had been unconscious and not breathing for more than fifteen minutes by the time paramedics arrived and resuscitated her. How much of her brain was still functioning was a mystery. After she had been kept alive on machines for a year, her parents "began to ask a question never really asked before in human experience: Should they turn off the respirator, which could not return their daughter to 'living' life, and allow their daughter, Karen Ann Quinlan, to die?" writes lawyer William H. Colby in *Unplugged: Reclaiming Our Right to Die in America*. The hospital feared homicide charges and refused. The Quinlan case, which flooded national and international headlines, was taken to the New Jersey Supreme Court, which side-stepped the "is Karen alive?" question. The court determined that a patient and her family had the right to privacy and could deny medical treatments, even if that denial meant certain death. Americans in their living rooms watched the media drama the Quinlan family lived through and en masse decided that being artificially kept alive on machines was not their idea of a good death.

In 1969, Elisabeth Kübler-Ross, a Swiss American, published a study on the five stages of grief, *On Death and Dying*. The book focused attention on patients at the end of their lives and began the grassroots movement to improve end-of-life care in the United States. The first modern hospice was opened here in 1971. Now, nearly 1.5 million deaths (out of a total of 2.5 million) occur in hospice each year. The number is misleading though. While patients can be admitted to a hospice program if they are diagnosed with six months or less to live, the average stay is less than two weeks. More than a third die after only seven days in hospice. One challenge is the requirement that patients' end curative treatment before being admitted; some are not ready to give up the hope for recovery. While the focus of hospice is to keep dying patients as comfortable as possible, financial, familial, cultural, and ethical variables continue to make the hospice experience different for every patient. Some have families with enough resources—money and time—to care for them as they die at home (Medicare typically only covers four hours of in-home care a day, not enough for those who are immobile or alone). Still others are moved to in-hospital hospice wards when they or their family finally acknowledge that their illness can't be cured. Others finish out their days in an elder home, with a hospice nurse paying visits to the facility. There are also designated hospice facilities, like the one my father died in.

Alongside the growth of the hospice movement came the autonomy movement, which pursued another route in its search for a good death: the law. Forms such as advanced directives, medical proxies, and living wills have been developed to help us make our final decisions; laws have been enacted at the state and federal levels to protect those decisions. After my father's death, I went straight to our family lawyer and had him draw up my own will and medical proxy. Everyone who knows me well knows where these documents are kept (in a manila envelope in the gray metal file box to the right of my desk, the numbers for my sister and my lawyer on a Post-it note stuck to the outside). Yet the existence of laws that protect my end-of-life wishes doesn't mean I'll get what I want should a bus hit me on the busy streets of Manhattan tomorrow. Routinely, law is thwarted by practice: an ambulance crew, say, that must resuscitate me and has no way of knowing what my living will says or even if I have one; an estranged relative showing up at my hospital bed to demand that everything be done to "save my life"; even my grieving family's inability or unwillingness to request that life support be stopped.

Depending on what factions of the hospice and autonomy movements you look at, they've overlapped and learned much from one another over the last forty years. An emphasis on community and family relations imbues each with a focus on support structures and joint decision making. The well-being of the patient is rightly primary. Yet both movements are still without power in the face of endless medical advancements, uninformed legislators who shape end-of-life laws, "pro-life" activists who eschew choice for saving "life" at all costs, and general ignorance of what dying is like. Neither movement has fully

grasped the meaning (and variability) of its own resounding principles: dignity and a good death. Dignity and a good death, just as death
itself, continue to be terms that are ill defined. They're concepts that
are unique for each one of us, depending on our age, culture, faith,
interests, and a host of other factors. How can hospice, with its intentional and specific idea of a good death, and how can the autonomy
movement, with stacks of legal documents, ever anticipate the variety
of death experiences?

Furthermore, because of the institutionalization of death—our
removal from it and our inability, through experience, to know how it
happens—and the numbing effects of grief, we often don't so much
make decisions as drift into passive indecision and acquiescence to
authority, whether it be that of doctors or nurses or a hospital board.
It's what Joanne Lynn, a geriatrician at the College of Medicine at
Ohio State University, called the "glide path." Patients are encouraged by medical staff to comply with a phalanx of tests and treatments that bring hope but don't improve their loved one's health,
and that often increase pain and suffering. The next thing they know,
ninety-five-year-old grandma is prescribed a new drug for her Alzheimer's (that costs the family's savings and may or may not react with
whatever drugs she's already taking) or eighty-two-year-old Uncle Ben
is headed into surgery for a new knee, his stage-four cancer notwith-
standing. Bereft families who are left feeling helpless look to medical
staff to do something. It's hard for them to know when there's nothing
beneficial left to do, particularly when hope is so often considered to
have benefits of its own.

Hope is prayer's second cousin, darkly dressed and hovering around
the outside edge of the family photograph. If prayer is a plea to the
Almighty for a precedented miracle—prayer's memory is long—hope
is a plea to nothing, to everything, to any possible refutation of the
facts. It is tethered to the dreadful single-digit percentage, the medical
equipment humming, the long sleepless night. Prayer can (or once

could) deliver a miracle; hope can only give a body another week, maybe another month. Sometimes the dying can set goals and reach them: *just let me see my son get married, my granddaughter turn ten, my family carve into the Thanksgiving turkey.* Hope can outlast dress fittings, gift wrapping, and potato mashing, but it can't deliver anything more. What hope does best is make plans. Sometimes those plans are to desperately avoid the worst.

Two years before he died, Dad mentioned that he was thinking of shooting himself or hanging himself out behind the shop. When things got bad, he hoped to find a painless way out. I was terrified I'd be the one to find him, his body swinging somewhere or bloody and mangled. I told this to a friend who brought me a copy of *Final Exit: The Practicalities of Self-Deliverance and Assisted Suicide for the Dying*, the *New York Times* best seller first published by Derek Humphry in 1991. Humphry, a brusque and controversial figure, was a principle founder of the Hemlock Society in 1980. *Final Exit* outlines the ways in which a person can kill himself, without legal ramifications. I read it and read it again, then gave it to my father. I was certain that, if I ever had to make the decision to end my life, I knew exactly how I would do so (sleeping pills, turkey basting bag over the head, loose rubber band around my neck to keep the carbon dioxide in), and my father would find his way, if he wanted to. I wanted him to know that whatever he decided, I supported him. Instead, he found death, good or not, in a hospice facility far from his beloved hollow.

When I finally left Africa for home, I quickly realized that all the hurt I thought I was working out on the road was still there, where I had left it. The divorce papers, the job search, the house that Dad built—my memory's catalog of images consistently fell open to the same one: my father, almost naked, pale, lean, and contorted. I realize that in many ways, my memory's recall of this image was my need for what Susan Sontag called, in her 2003 book *Regarding the Pain of Others*, "the pleasure of flinching." It's an easy memory to access because it hurts so much, but also because it made me feel close to him again. Yet it was crowding out all the good memories I had from our life together, like when we'd catch each other's eye some golden afternoon while cutting wood on the farm. Or the comforting intimacy of his voice when I'd call him out of the blue to talk about the rain. His twisted body, arranged in a way it never would have been had he been alive, was crowding out all the things I loved about him. I replayed the last hospice scenes in my head. Did everyone die this way, fighting with both arms and legs until the needles came? I wanted to know if his had been "a good death." And if so, might it come for me the same way?

It was clearly time for me to find another way to deal with my grief. Like my decision to get out of the country after he died. But this time, instead of running away from it, I had to get closer to it. I had been unmoored by my own grief for so long that I had no alternative but to finally make sense of it, to wrestle it to the ground and know it. To function in the world again, I'd need to understand what had happened to my father, to my family, to me—to all of us. I didn't grasp the nature of this work at the time, but I was doing what Peter Trachtenberg describes in *The Book of Calamities*: I was launching myself into an investigation with all the raw energies and emotions I had put into grieving. "Before suffering people can form a coherent picture of their suffering," he writes, "they must first ask questions about it, or maybe of it. In doing so, they are performing the work of science and philosophy, interrogating their reality in order to derive a thesis about it."

Finding a good death seemed about as likely as finding the fountain of youth. What was good about dying? I had no idea where to begin, but since my reality of death began with hospice, I became a hospice volunteer. Most anyone can volunteer, and training is fairly brief, but hospice programs are constantly in need of more willing participants. Volunteers are warmly welcomed. I learned how to sit with other peoples' dying. And I kept going. I followed my pain-filled curiosity to conferences and clinics, to academic lectures and to grief sessions in church basements, to isolated prison cells and to pale-blue hospital wards where every hushed word could be the last. I didn't care if it was a morbid inquiry or a vain self-improvement project. I asked questions, yes, but mostly I listened to the stories of others who were close to death, their own or a loved one's. I pursued an expert's knowledge of how we human beings, in this time and country, slide into death or thrash at the end, and how those of us left behind stumble around in the absence. I told myself that this investigation was something that my father, who never let a loose chair leg or a broken appliance go unfixed, would have appreciated, if not encouraged. Something was rattling around, and I was going to set it right.

From my very first days as a hospice volunteer, I learned that I could help individuals to have better lives and deaths by doing little things like listening, being present, and understanding their experience. But I also quickly found that improving deaths was not simply a matter of telling patients what their options were and letting them choose. Improving deaths involved more than the little things. Educating doctors to talk to patients about their ends is vital, yes, and so is educating patients on what to expect, but doing so will not better the way all people die, just the ones that message reaches. Helping one family to remove an unwanted ventilator wasn't going to prevent the next from having to make the same decision, nor was it going to change a process that had developed over time to default to ventilators. It wasn't going to address the complicated needs of a vast number of elders approaching end of life in the next few decades, an elder population we aren't prepared to care for. It wasn't going to correct the desperate financial challenges that individuals and the country face, that particular demographic groups—economic and financial minorities, for instance—struggle with every day. And it wasn't going to answer the question of how we got here, to a place and time where the dying are misunderstood, ignored, underserved, and ill informed.

A larger understanding was necessary: of *why* we die the way we do today; of the development of medicine and concepts of choice, autonomy, informed consent; of how hospice and hospital cultures were formed and perpetuated; and of what our regard for the dying has become in broader society. Too, the laws that regulate what is available to the dying had to be considered, along with their purpose and origin. As well, the financial systems that had locked us into the untenable way we currently die. Religious and other cultural forces also play a role in how we die. I had to ask myself how all of these interactions influenced end-of-life care. By focusing on individual lives and deaths, it became clear to me that changing the way we die would be a project of depth and breadth, one that involved loving care for patients as well as a fearless examination of the social, legal, and institutional systems that governed the end of our lives.

CHAPTER TWO

Mortality Parade

Avenue House is a tidy, nondescript brick building on the Lower East Side of Manhattan. A large ramp sloping left and right from the elevated front door takes up most of the facade, but otherwise Avenue House blends in with food distributors, apartment buildings, and delis. Fresh out of hospice volunteer training, I thought I'd find myself in an elder home, quiet graying folks with the distance in their eyes. What I found was a cross between a hospital and a halfway house, filled with busy, lively people of all ages whose life experiences were completely unlike my own. Avenue House was an education behind glass doors. I was sent there by my hospice organization because a patient named Marshall was depressed and lonely. I knew he was dying because I was sent to see him, but I knew nothing else.

I found him in a tidy two-person room, in the bed closest to the door. He was wearing forest-green sweats, tops and bottoms, and a baseball cap. Mets. He was a small black man, lean and wiry, with graying, close-cropped hair. He didn't look particularly sick. More worn out than deathly. His sweats were about two sizes too big. His eyes were heavy and slow. Marshall was watching a small TV on a long adjustable arm that reached from the wall behind his head. Judge Judy was dressing down a pimply-faced kid in an ill-fitting sports jacket. "I hear you might like some company," I said after introducing myself, carefully leaving "hospice" out of my bio as I was told to do. Sometimes patients prefer to look at their mortality askance. Marshall nodded shyly. "Can I watch *Judge Judy* with you?" He pointed to a stained chair at the foot of his bed. A ruffle of get-well cards covered the wall behind it. Families aren't always able to accept that their loved one is dying, the cards reminded me, or they think that doing anything other than hoping for a miracle is the same as giving up.

Marshall shared a room with a man named Timothy who, unlike Marshall, was always talking, always a little dirty, and a little strung out. More than once I watched Timothy trade food items that he had hoarded from the cafeteria on his own facility-wide black market. Cups of dry cereal, cookies in cellophane. Residents of Avenue House came and went, poking their heads inside the door and then moving into Marshall's line of sight to wave hello and ask how he was doing. They came to see Marshall as much as they came to see Timothy. Room 210 was a popular stop on their social rounds.

People of all ages, genders, and colors moved around me as I sat at Marshall's side. Children of visitors waddled in the halls, shabby down-and-outers sat in wheelchairs, relentless years showing on their hollowed-out faces. Staff in stain-resistant uniforms, solid colors, and comfortable shoes. I was pushing forty, and I thought I was living, but here, where everybody was sick and some were dying, was a bustling life I had otherwise never had access to.

I sat beside Marshall for two hours that first visit, trying to talk about the weather and the plaintiffs showing deference to TV judges, before I realized that company didn't mean conversation. Getting to know Marshall was going to take time. Just being next to him was what mattered.

That evening I went home to my computer to learn more about Avenue House. Why were all these people, young and old, *living* there?

Avenue House, I quickly discovered, is an all-HIV facility. A panic hit me. Hospice training had taught me to be a good hand-washer before and after visits, but I'd taken a sip of Marshall's orange soda out of his cup, I'd shaken his hand and removed his shoes, I'd used the toilet in the room. Wasn't my hospice coordinator obligated to tell me my new patient was dying of AIDS? In a flash I knew that my fear was totally irrational. I was of the generation best educated about AIDS prevention. I was aware of the ways in which HIV patients were wrongly shunned as dirty, not to be touched, contagious. There are only two primary ways that one can contract HIV, the virus that causes AIDS: from use of dirty needles and from unprotected sex. My little ripple of fear was nonsensical. But there it was. And in that moment, for the first time, the stigma of disease was suddenly real to me.

Hospice volunteer. Whoever the patient is, whatever her illness, whatever she needs, you give. There's something satisfying in that, in having a purpose that involves little negotiation of boundaries. I've fetched flowers, Twinkies, and magazines. I've wiped butts and pushed wheelchairs, watched TV and held hands, dialed estranged daughters and read the entire Psalms. Hospice work asks that you care without condition—personality traits, life choices, diagnosis, physical appearance, race, class, everything is irrelevant. There's a person in front of you who is dying. And you're going to fetch and love, then lose and hurt.

A preacher and some Avenue House patients would periodically come by Marshall's room to lay hands on him and pray. I would move away from the bed and stand with my back against the wall. They would encircle Marshall, their hands in the air or on his legs and feet, shoulders and head. They would speak in tongues and entreat God to make Marshall walk again, to take away his illness, to make him whole. A second preacher came, dapper, clad head to toe in purple, from his brimmed hat with a purple band to his purple pinstriped suit and purple handkerchief, to his metallic purple shoes with purple laces.

He swayed and bobbed and growled out God's love. He told Marshall about God's bosom and right hand, and I saw that Marshall relaxed when he heard this. I imagine it's not that he thought his sins were absolved, but that he was worthy, despite them. I wanted the man in the purple suit to lay a hand and a prayer on me.

Marshall had "accepted the Lord into his life" two weeks before I met him. Much as the care of his body had been placed in the hands of the nurses of Avenue House, the care of his soul was in the hands of the Lord. And it calmed him. I could see he was still scared to die—he hovered somewhere between wide-eyed shock and drowsy depression—but he clutched his tiny Bible and embraced his new praying friends. His wife and adult son lived in New Jersey and seldom visited. But Avenue House gave Marshall a friendly, accepting community. If he felt abandoned, he also felt adopted. They were a comfort to him. In a very different way, I learned how to keep Marshall comfortable too. He was ashamed of his pain, too timid to tell the nurses what he was feeling. He would tell me what his pain was—he couldn't go to the bathroom, his stomach was distended, he couldn't sleep—but when the nurses came around, he would force a smile for them, for their authority. He didn't like taking medications of any kind. He also had excruciating breakthrough pain, the kind that comes when one dose of medication wears off before the scheduled next dose. For the hospice office, I kept a notebook. On Friday, April 9, I wrote:

> Oh a horrible day of pain. As soon as I walked into his room, I knew it had been a rough day so far. M was literally doubled over in pain—an expression I didn't fully understand until seeing him—with his head on the railing of his bed. The room was in disarray, a large sticky mark was on the floor by his bed; his nightstand littered with overturned cups and cans. Timothy, M's roommate, greeted me when I walked in with, "I'm glad you're here. He needs you. They threatened to kick me out today for

getting him pain meds at the drugstore." It seems that he's been in pain for some time. He tells me that the meds last two hours and that the nurses tell him he can't have more for another two so he lies awake, calls his wife to tell her to call the doctor or he sends Timothy out for Advil.

"I just want to die," he whispered to me. I asked the nurses to come, to bring the doctor with them. The obstacles to making him comfortable were many: the nurses had directions they had to follow; Marshall wasn't explicit about how he was feeling; he once told them he didn't like being drugged out; and he didn't like to take the Maalox for constipation because it tasted bad. His hands were cold, and I held them, rubbed his head as he rested it on the railing, told him the doctor and nurses were coming, that he was going to feel better soon. We both watched the clock.

A second time I pleadingly told the nurses at the front desk that we needed help. I stayed with Marshall until the doctor, the floor manager, and the primary nurse finally came to the foot of his bed. They spoke about him, not with him. They discussed what the challenges were and what new course of medication they could prescribe. After much resistance, they discussed switching him to Methadone, a drug that carried a particular stigma in Avenue House. It's a junkie drug, what heroin addicts take to get off heroin. "Well," the nurse said, "Methadone is highly addictive." "He's dying," I whispered at them, an impatient tone in my voice. I listened to everything the doctor and staff said, then bent down to hold Marshall's hand and tell him the translation: "You have to tell them when you hurt. Making pain go away takes some trial and error. They want to try Methadone, but you may have some side effects like constipation and feeling groggy, but do you agree that that's better than being in pain?" He nodded his head.

Cicely Saunders, a British nurse who founded the first modern hospice in the United Kingdom in 1967, often claimed that her program (and philosophy) was directly descended from the shelters set up by monks across Europe in the Middle Ages. Monks cared for soldiers returning from the Crusades, for travelers, and for the poor and sick.

How Saunders came to develop the modern idea of hospice is famous among hospice workers, particularly volunteers. It's a love story, really. Saunders was a nurse in a cancer ward during the mid-1940s when she met a patient, a Polish Jew named David Tasma, who was dying from inoperable cancer. Saunders had recently converted to Evangelical Protestantism and was looking for a way to live her faith, to "say thank you and serve," write Fran Smith and Sheila Himmel in *Changing the Way We Die*. Saunders and Tasma talked for long hours about faith and mortality. He made Saunders aware of how abandoned and lonely dying patients were. Saunders read two Psalms to Tasma, hoping to comfort him. Write Smith and Himmel: "I only want what is in your mind and your heart," he replied. That simple desire came to represent everything she believed hospice should offer: the best therapies the mind could conceive along with the kindness, attention, and friendship of the human heart.

Saunders conceived of hospice as a way to address all the suffering a person was experiencing as he or she faced death, not just the physical pain but the emotional pain, the discomfort of being in a bed for so long, the loneliness, and the loss of control of one's body, environment, and future. She completed medical school and later founded St. Christopher's Hospice in London. Saunders was commanding, over six feet tall and able to speak passionately about end-of-life care. Her ideas, and her ability to captivate an audience, directly influenced American hospice development. Saunders's relationships with Elisabeth Kübler-Ross, author of the classic *On Death and Dying*, and Florence Wald, a nurse who opened the first US hospice, in Connecticut, inspired the birth of hospice care in the United States in 1974.

Saunders, later made *Dame* Cicely Saunders by Queen Elizabeth II for her hospice work, is a compelling figure in the hospice movement, but her philosophy owed much to another early founder, an American with surprisingly literary roots. Rose Hawthorne Lathrop, daughter of the author of *The Scarlet Letter*, Nathaniel Hawthorne, married young and traveled in a distinctly literary circle. Her husband, George Parsons Lathrop, later became editor of the *Atlantic Monthly*, and Lathrop had her own literary ambitions. She published short stories, poetry, and a book, *Along the Shore*. She and her husband converted to Catholicism together, but after the death of their infant son, slowly drifted apart.

Lathrop became a nurse at New York Cancer Hospital in the late 1890s when she was forty-five. She saw the horrible deaths of the poor from cancer and decided to open Sister Rose's Free Care. "I set my whole being to endeavor to bring consolation to the cancerous poor," she wrote in her diary, write Smith and Himmel. She took up residence in the Lower East Side of Manhattan, buying a tenement to house the sick and dying. She was later encouraged by a Dominican priest to establish an order of nuns and, in 1900, became Mother Alphonsa in the new order Dominican Sisters of Hawthorne.

In photos taken after joining the order, Lathrop is wearing a large black-and-white wimple that sits high off her head and drapes broadly across her shoulders and down her back. Her face is broad and she wears large glasses that make her look stern. "Lathrop forbade proselytizing and welcomed patients of all religions, or none," write Smith and Himmel in *Changing the Way We Die*, "but she believed that she was preaching the gospel through nursing, and she rejoiced when someone came to the faith."

In 2003, Cardinal Edward M. Egan proposed Mother Alphonsa for sainthood. In March 2014, according to the Dominican Sisters of Hawthorne website, the "Decree of Validity for the Diocesan Acts in the Cause of Mother Rose Hawthorne" was signed by the Vatican.

The next step in beatification requires a miracle. The Dominican Sisters of Hawthorne ask that if you experience a miracle when praying to Mother Alphonsa, you contact them immediately.

The day after Marshall started Methadone, I stopped to say hello to the desk nurse on my way to his room. She told me that Marshall had been nauseous all morning, most likely from acclimation to the new drug. When I got to his room, he looked resigned to discomfort, no longer fighting against doubling pain. I let him know that it would take a while to adjust the dosage and that some of the side effects might not be pleasant, but that at least the pain was under control. The change in him was striking and wonderful. We watched TV for a while. I cleaned up his nightstand. He commented in a low tone that he had lost his voice, and I said that he didn't need to talk. I was happy to sit with him quietly. "But I want to talk," he croaked. In my journal, I wrote:

> When I was preparing to leave and arranging with him for my next visit, he hanged his head and again apologized. "I'm sorry I've been so much trouble for you." I made small of it, saying that he needn't apologize to me ever again and that that's what we do—I was saying it to myself as much as I was to Marshall—we rely on others sometimes and there's no need to feel badly about it. On my way out, I spoke with his nurses—he's apparently had no breakthrough pain since they started the Methadone last night. He was set to have his next Methadone dose at 2 and still he was comfortable without breakthrough pain.

The change was almost unbelievable. Marshall and I began spending our time together talking about his life, his career as a welder, his family. As the weeks passed, I got to know him. We looked at photos of his family and watched his favorite movies, action flicks with heroes and bad guys and happy conclusions. I brought him whatever foods he was craving. Sometimes Marshall couldn't feel his feet. He could feel when I touched them, but he couldn't move them. He had the wide-eyed look of sedation, and I wondered at the inexact science of balancing his pain with medication.

After that week, I began visiting Marshall almost every day, far more than my hospice schedule required. I enjoyed sitting with him, hand in hand. We'd fallen into a routine. We'd watch TV, my head on the railing: *Judge Mathis* or *House of Payne*, daytime shows that I had never seen before. My coming and going became common on the second floor. I'd say hello to the regulars—the woman in the pink nightgown who first called me into her room to show me pictures of her new niece; the young black man who sat by the elevators staring at the doors; the old Latina woman who would doze in her wheelchair in the hallway, her head on her left shoulder; the nurses chattering at the front desk. Once on the street, at the bottom of the ramps, I would take a deep breath of the city's air. I could still smell Marshall on me, a mix of cocoa butter and the sour scent of a rotting body, an institutionalized, dying body.

Marshall's decline was obvious now. He no longer dressed in his sweats. He was constantly in a blue-and-white hospital gown. He never left his bed, and the nurses had put his small brown feet in special slippers to take the pressure off his heels. They rotated him from side to side to prevent bedsores. The room was quiet now; even Marshall's roommate Timothy kept himself away or read on his bed behind the curtain.

On my last visit, Marshall was in and out of lucidity. He would turn his head toward me and grin, then his dry lips would slacken and he would doze into sleep. He moved very little and the skin of his body seemed to have sunk into the bed, his bones a simple collection of small bumps under the smooth sheet. The nurses hovered around us for the hours that I was there; their knowing watchfulness alerted me. He was going. "Read him the Psalms," one nurse told me. I picked up Marshall's Bible and started at the beginning, "Blessed is the man that walketh not in the counsel of the ungodly, nor standeth in the way of sinners, nor sitteth in the seat of the scornful." And chapter 77: "I cried unto God with my voice, even unto God with my voice; and he gave ear unto me. In the day of my trouble I sought the Lord: my sore ran in the night, and ceased not: my soul refused to be comforted." Periodically, Marshall would wake up and look at me, then through me. He pulled his shaking hand out from under the sheet and pointed to a dim corner of the room over my shoulder. He saw his mother there, his wife, other friendly faces. By chapter 86—"Bow down thine ear, O Lord, hear me: for I am poor and needy. Preserve my soul."—Marshall was asleep.

That night I couldn't sleep. At 3:30 a.m., I was hanging out my kitchen window staring at the moon. It was so pregnant with light that the typically opaque New York sky was perforated with even fewer stars than usual. My area of Brooklyn was balmy, still and salty from the nearby open water, from the hum of air conditioners and eight million people breathing rhythmically in their sleep. I had a stiff neck. I was as weary as the heavy humidity, with a leaden anticipation of a sad blow. I was grieving. It was a familiar feeling, like an echo of the waves I'd ridden over the past five years, the wake from my father's death and dying. Hospice called the next morning to tell me Marshall had died.

I had completed hospice volunteer training a few short weeks before I met Marshall. When I walked into my first class, held in the middle floors of an office building a stone's throw from Wall Street, I was surprised to find more than two dozen people, ages nineteen to seventy-five. I expected a handful of dainty ladies, sitting with their ankles crossed. Women have always been the domestic caretakers of the dying. I was aware that my new volunteerism was gendered work—even volunteering we view as gendered—something that men are too busy to do, something that holds a particular stigma. Women's work. Hospice has changed drastically since the days of Rose Hawthorne Lathrop—it wasn't just for the poor, for instance, and it had become hypermedicalized—but the room still held a majority of women. Some volunteers, like a tall young man about twenty-two years old, had come to help prepare themselves for medical or nursing school. One young woman in a floral dress, perfect makeup, and platinum hair said she had time on her hands—"And I thought, why not volunteer for hospice?" A veteran of the AIDS epidemic in a bohemian skirt who had "lost too many friends" felt that hospice work made her a better person. "It makes me thankful I'm alive." One of the oldest women in the room, sitting primly on my left, was paying a debt. Jean had the puckered hands of a septuagenarian and full dark cups of skin below her eyes. She was mannered but feisty, like she was still every age she had ever been. Hospice had helped her care for her husband, Michael, when he died. That was twenty-five years ago. Her voice cracked. She finally felt ready to help others die.

Help others die. It's a weird phrase. It betrays our long-held standard of encouraging others to "not go gentle," to fight to the end, to never give up. On the one hand, helping others die acknowledges the limits of medicine and contradicts the denial of death prevalent in our culture. On the other, it embraces an ethic of charity and care that reaches back to religious orders like the Dominican Sisters of Hawthorne.

However secular we think our society, religion continues to be most overt at the deathbed. While contemporary hospice teams include chaplains among the social workers, nurses, and volunteers, American spirituality is the new nature of faith among hospice programs. Interfaith and all-inclusiveness are the tone of hospice today, a reflection of the changing religious landscape in the country.

I did not want to meet Mr. Cortez. Marshall had died only three weeks before. But hospice couldn't find anyone to sit with him while his wife attended Mass on Saturday nights. Who wants to hold hands with the dying on Saturday night? I didn't, but I said yes anyway, maybe to wipe Marshall out of my thoughts. Mr. Cortez would be my rebound patient. It was the middle of a heat wave. Lower Manhattan was the kind of July hot and humid that makes you angry, but too breathless to do anything about it.

The Cortezes lived in the projects below the Manhattan Bridge. Inside the main door, I found graffiti and trash, urine on the floor of the elevator. The hallway was dark after the bright summer sun. Would it be safe for me to come here in the dark, when the days were shorter, I wondered? I had no idea what Mr. Cortez was dying of or how long it would take.

Mrs. Cortez, a plump Latina woman with short hair and glasses, showed me into the bedroom, where Mr. Cortez took up little space on a hospital bed. "I'll be back after Mass," she said in a heavy Puerto Rican accent and slipped out the door, locking it behind her. Immediately Mr. Cortez came to life, as if the sound of the lock woke him up. I watched the lower half of his face, collapsed and nearly toothless, as he gummed words that I couldn't understand. He was bird-thin and active, fluttering his hands as if to take flight or to stir the thick air in the room. Our first task was to survey the collection of tweezers he had in the pocket of his pajamas, one, two, three, four, five. Each taken out, held before me, then displayed across the bedsheet in a row. "A tweezer for every occasion," I said. He smiled and clumsily gathered them up and put them back in his pocket. Mr. Cortez's motor skills were florid and unpredictable, a hand striking several places before it did what his brain told it to. I couldn't make any sense of what he was trying to tell me, half pantomime, half garbled sounds from an uncooperative mouth. Mr. Cortez was insistent. We were going to communicate! Frustrated, we both sat back and took a breath.

I decided to try asking yes-or-no questions, a sort of game that could help us make sense. "Do you want something?" I asked. With the most subtle of gestures, a slight blink of his eyes, he touched his chin to his chest. A yes. I had just caught it in the midst of other shakes, shifts, rhythms, and twitches. "Is it in this room?" Yes. With a pointing, jabbing arm, he accused the top dresser drawer. I touched it. Another yes. As I opened the drawer, Mr. Cortez chopped his flat right hand up and down in the air. I mimicked him and finally understood that he wanted me to find something in the front of the drawer, vertical, between the clothing and the drawer face. It was a red vinyl folder of papers. I brought it back to the bed for us to look at. Inside were Mr. Cortez's retirement papers from the city, his commendations for driving a limousine for seventeen years, a photo of his father, who had served in the military. Mr. Cortez didn't want me to see him as this frantic, birdlike person on the bed; he wanted me to know how he saw himself. As a person, not a patient. As a man who had had a rich life and a full history of accomplishments, not this waning body. He was proud. I put the file back in the drawer as Mr. Cortez closed his eyes and finally became still.

The next time I visited, I found Mr. Cortez sitting up in a chair in the living room, next to the white, plastic-covered sofa, with a TV tray in front of him. He was feeding himself with a spoon. Oatmeal, applesauce, and a blueberry muffin. His arms were all over the place, as though he were swatting flies or trying to get food into his own mouth by playing airplane, as we do with toddlers. Mr. Cortez was showing off for me, performing eating. He was smacking his lips as muffin crumbs flew, waving his spoon like he was conducting the Philharmonic, and slapping his gums at his juice cup. *Smack, smack, smack*, like he was going to eat the cup. Food crumbs floated in the juice and clogged the straw. It was a performance of pure joy in motion and sound—and impossible etiquette. He couldn't stop the shakes and tremors, but he could make them a flourish, a rhythmic show of remaining skill.

If he could use a spoon, I reasoned, he could write. Our frustrating charades could use a break. I pulled out a notepad from my purse and held it in the air as if it were a question. Mr. Cortez paused, then swooped it from me. He struggled to synchronize the tremors of his left hand with the tablet and the tremors of his right with the pen. I couldn't imagine what he'd first write to me.

"I used to play a Spanish instrument. I can't play it now because the bridge is broken." "Do you think you could play it now if it were repaired?" I asked. Yes, he nodded. He reached over to the little cassette player on the coffee table. The *la-chicka-chicka* of a happy Latin song filled the little room. We both smiled and danced in our seats.

In 1978, according to the history page of the National Hospice and Palliative Care Organization website, the US Department of Health, Education, and Welfare task force wrote that "the hospice movement as a concept for the care of the terminally ill and their families is a viable concept and one which holds out a means of providing more humane care for Americans dying of terminal illness while possibly reducing costs. As such, it is the proper subject of federal support." In 1982, Congress created the Medicare Hospice Benefit, allowing the terminally ill to receive federal coverage for end-of-life care, a development particularly important to those reliant on Medicare for their needs. While the Medicare Hospice Benefit will provide twenty-four hour crisis care when necessary, the burden of daily care—cooking, cleaning, bathroom assistance, bathing, sorting medications, bills—falls to the families of those still at home, or to staff for patients in facilities. For those who fall in the gap—between full coverage (the poorest of the poor in state-funded elder homes or places like Avenue House, where Marshall died) and those who can afford full-time caregivers at home—hospice isn't always enough. Four hours of care a day can leave many stranded and isolated for the other twenty hours.

The Medicare Hospice Benefit covers equipment, doctor and nurse visits, and medication, limiting the cost that a hospice can charge Medicare for a drug copayment to five dollars. Congress saw hospice as a way to keep end-of-life care costs in check, already a concern to the national budget in the 1980s. To ensure that savings, it required that anyone entering hospice end all curative treatment. Chemotherapy and other drug courses that aimed to cure cancer or another illness were no longer accessible to hospice patients. The reasoning was that those who need hospice, who are actively dying, have come to terms with dying. The provision fails to acknowledge the emotional challenges, for patients and their families, to accept that death is inevitable. Medicare coverage also limits the program to six months. It wasn't an arbitrary time frame, but it did ignore the inconsistency of diagnoses and the strength of the human will and body.

Multiple studies have shown that hospice patients can live up to two months longer than their peers who remain in standard (curative, hospital) care. That's two more months to get your finances in order and to make peace with estranged family members, two more months of birthdays, anniversaries, weddings, and births. A lot can happen in two months, even when you're dying.

From the days of Mother Alphonsa and Cicely Saunders, hospice was intended for those dying of cancer, but hospice has seen a large increase in other types of patients, such as Alzheimer's patients and Parkinson's patients, who can live for years with a diagnosis. Their deaths often come more slowly, a drama of physical decline and increasing frailty that plays out over years, even decades.

On the next visit, I found Mr. Cortez in the living room again. As soon as his wife closed the door behind her, he pointed to a walker in the corner. "Do you usually get around on your own?" I asked. He was so frail, his legs so thin, I couldn't imagine they would carry him. But he nodded his head yes and, using the technique I learned from Marshall, I spread my feet to bear the weight of another person and lifted him from under his arms. Every volunteer with a mobile patient fears a fall. One out of three seniors falls, and falls are the leading cause of senior injuries, fatal and nonfatal. I held Mr. Cortez so tightly I feared bruising his arms. But we were upright, embracing like family members or lovers, when I caught him looking at me closely. Not like an old man about to die, not like someone with flakes of skin clogging up the hair at his scalp, with brown and white spots mottling his hands and arms, but like his toothless, smacking mouth warranted kisses. "You're a devil!" I said, and he grinned ear to ear.

"Bedroom," he said with a cackle. Of course. "Pot," he said when we arrived. I maneuvered him to the pot, a sort of chair with a bucket for a seat and, when he pointed at his pajama pants, I pulled them down. Then his adult diaper. He had no butt, nothing but skin and bones. I was a little jarred by how comfortable it was for him to be naked in front of me, or rather how awkward his nakedness made me.

Now seated, Mr. Cortez shook his pointing finger at the dresser again. This time he wanted a vinyl folder of photos. He on the pot, me at his elbow on the bed, we began to look at snapshots taken decades ago. Family in Puerto Rico, panoramas of the island's countryside, then a photo of himself with friends standing in front of a white car, perhaps here in the parking lot by the projects. He pointed to a handsome man, late twenties or early thirties, with a bouffant hairdo and rolled-up shirt sleeves. There's a sexy jaunt to his pose against the car. The photo is black-and-white; it's the 1960s.

"Who is this?" I asked trying to conceal my disbelief. Mr. Cortez jabbed his index finger into his chest. "This is you, Mr. Cortez? You're handsome!" I meant it. He was stunning, filled with bravado and brashness. A thin mustache lined his upper lip, a full double chin, a thick torso. The photo breathed machismo. I pulled out another one, him with his band, holding his little guitar like a beloved dance partner. And then another, a series of three black-and-white images taken in a photo booth of Mr. and Mrs. Cortez, obviously in love, their heads together. I could feel the happiness. Full and ripe and proud. I was mesmerized by the photos—and haunted by them. These beautiful, swaggering, sexy people were now old. My eyes moved from the image of a full and vibrant, young and proud Mr. Cortez embracing his young wife, to the wasted and dying man on the pot a few inches from me, showing me not who he was but who he is.

After we got him off the pot (I'd never wiped another adult's butt before), dressed and into bed, Mr. Cortez shook his arm to a place beside the dresser. An instrument case. When I opened it, I found the same instrument, a *cuatro*, worn along the strings from years of use, that I had seen in the photos. The bridge was missing, the neck was loose, it had no strings, but Mr. Cortez took it from me and cradled it in his arms. "Strings," he said.

The next time I arrived I chirped, "Hello, Mr. Cortez." He was on the pot again and Mrs. Cortez was preparing to leave as if for a date, not Saturday night Mass. She preened in the hall mirror.

"He's been writing on a tablet for me because I can't understand what he's saying."

"Sometimes I can't either," she said and I felt better.

"He's also asked me to get strings for his instrument."

"Oh," she waved her hand. "He can't play anyway." We both knew she was right. "What illness does he have," I asked.

"Parkinson's. Twenty-five years." I shuddered at the patience and devotion of twenty-five years, watching your husband's physical and mental decline, getting away only a few hours each morning to work as a crossing guard. And on Saturday evenings to go to Mass.

Mr. Cortez pointed to my hair when I entered the bedroom. He was balanced on the portable pot, oblivious to the smell or any kind of embarrassment either of us might have. I looked in the mirror—the house was full of mirrors, floor-length ones in the hallway, two on dressers in the bedroom, a horizontal mirror in the living room—to see what he was pointing to. He looked into the mirror, too, at himself, studying his own face, slicking back his hair with a fluttering hand. Yes, my hair was still wet. "I rode my bicycle to the subway," I said. "I got caught in a downpour."

He took up our notebook and slowly wrote, *One of my sons died from a bicycle accident. Under the bridge.* He pointed out the window to the bridge that passed over the edge of Manhattan a block away. *He was 41.*

"I'm so sorry. That's too young. I'm forty-one."

You don't look that old, he wrote, and I was flattered.

I was born 1.15.36.

"So you're," I paused to do the math, "seventy-four?"

He nodded.

"You don't look that old," I said, echoing his compliment. His eyes twinkled, and he glanced at the mirror again, smoothing his long gray hair back over his scalp. He pointed to the picture of his father on the wall opposite his bed. *I don't want institution. My father in. He was 97 when he died.* More math. Twenty-three years to go, I thought.

When we got Mr. Cortez up from the pot, he demanded his walker and led me to a door in the hallway that was always closed. Inside, the walls were haphazardly painted red, with excess flicks of paint along the ceiling. A futon was against the left wall, and a few items of men's clothing were neatly folded and stacked on it. Not Mr. Cortez's clothes. On one side of the window, a small pair of nunchucks was hooked over the abandoned curtain rod bracket. A Slinky was hanging from the other.

Mr. Cortez shuffled to a tall dresser where a boom box filled the top surface area. The screen flashed a pattern of colors until he pressed the play button. The screen rolled through a colorful display, then flashed, *GOODBYE.* He lifted a plastic frame from a shelf. In it a man about my age was smiling and holding a four-year-old girl, her hair in braids.

"This is your son?" I asked Mr. Cortez. He hit his closed fist on his chest. A row of men's shoe—sneakers, boots, dress shoes—was at the foot of the dresser. On a shelf, there were a TV and DVD player, a few bottles of the pills that bodybuilders take, a clock, some knickknacks and books—Aristotle, Algebra, Business Math. Now I understood. For three years, this room, his son Johnny's room, had sat this way, virtually unchanged. Mr. Cortez pressed the boom-box panel again, *GOODBYE*, and opened the top dresser drawer.

Its contents were jumbled and messy, like a kitchen junk drawer, but Mr. Cortez fingered each item lovingly—wrinkled pay stubs, an overnight case full of condoms (the kind handed out free and marked with colorful designs), pictures of Johnny with his buddies and with women. Mr. Cortez worked his shaking fingers into the back left corner of the drawer and dug a folded letter out of a tin. I thought of how little privacy the dead have. *GOODBYE*. The letter was written on yellow lined paper, folded like a high school note. Mr. Cortez handed it to me.

"Do you want me to read this," I asked, uncomfortable because I was snooping through a dead man's possessions. He nodded his head, and as I began to read, I realized that it was to Johnny from a friend. It was a letter from prison. I read out loud to share with Mr. Cortez the guilt of this invasion of privacy. The slang sounded silly in my voice, in the abandoned, unchanging room.

Hey bro what up? Louis tells Johnny that he had better keep his head down and stay in school. Before they know it, Johnny will have his AA, his associate's degree. Working out is good, being healthy and getting ripped, Louis writes, but a degree is better. *Watch your step*, he writes, because any violation of parole will end with Johnny right back inside. Like an expert, Louis lists the years that Johnny will get for various parole violations. Then he tells Johnny to send more pictures. But not Polaroids, because they aren't allowed in prison (it's too easy to hide drugs between the photo's layers). *It's lonely in here at night,* he writes. *Get me some photos of hot girls to keep my mind busy.* I folded up the letter and handed it back to Mr. Cortez, still unsure why he wanted me to read it. He pushed it deep down into the papers and condoms and photos in the drawer like he was planting a seed. A seed with no chance of growing. He closed the drawer and again pushed the button on the boom box. *GOODBYE.*

The fall leaves had begun to turn as I walked down the street to Mr. Cortez's building. I'd finally found the right strings for his cuatro. He was in bed when I arrived, his blue-striped pajamas askew, a handful of crumpled paper towels shoved into the chest pocket. As had become our habit, I bent down in front of him to catch his eye and touched his chin with my hand.

"Hello, Mr. C," I said smiling. He raised his own shaking, fluttering hand to my chin to acknowledge me. He was no longer able to keep his mouth closed, his lower jaw hanging and wet with saliva. I pulled my other hand from behind my back to show him the strings. He clapped his hands with joy and pointed to the instrument case beside the dresser. I pulled out the cuatro and handed him a coiled guitar string. With one motion, so fluid, smooth, and practiced that it surprised me, he rolled the coil between his two index fingers until it opened into a long line. Mr. Cortez died the next week, two hours before Saturday night Mass.

I've known Evelyn Livingston for four years. Every Friday evening, I enter the finely restored deco lobby of her building on Central Park West. The doorman and I exchange friendly greetings; the man behind the desk hands me a white key card for the elevator without having to ask where I'm going. I've made a habit of noticing the fresh flowers that adorn the desk and the interior lobby, dramatic arrangements of protea and greens in the winter, allium and lilies in the spring. These days, Evelyn is a permanent resident of the white divan in her front room. It's a long and wide mass of furniture, taken up with magazines and medical journals, a burgundy vest for when it's cold, a basin for when her nausea is uncontrollable, and linen-covered pillows of various sizes that she uses to keep herself comfortable, an endless task. She used to use a walker to slowly go to the bathroom or back to her bedroom at night to sleep, but she's now sleeping on the divan. A portable toilet like Mr. Cortez's sits in the corner, covered with an elegant batik cloth. She hasn't left the front room in months. After washing my hands—the immune system of homebound patients often can't fight the germs picked up on the subway—I used to come into the room and greet her with a kiss on her papery right cheek, but we've begun to worry about my germs as well. I now touch her knee; I tell her it's for our good luck.

One-and-a-half-million patients, about the total number of residents in the state of Idaho, die in hospice care each year. Although the program is for patients with six months or less to live, one-third die or leave the program after only seven days. Mr. Cortez was in hospice for three-and-a-half months, likely because his family acknowledged that he was dying years—even decades—before. Evelyn is an anomaly. Four years is an eternity in hospice time. Every handful of months, a doctor comes around to recertify her, to send the federal government the reassurance that yes, Evelyn is dying. She's just taking her time.

She's a doctor, the hospice coordinator had told me. And she wants to write her memoir. From the address and the request for a writer, I knew that my experience with Evelyn would be unlike those with Marshall or Mr. Cortez. Class and wealth often determine how someone dies, with what medical care, comfort, and attention. As a doctor, Evelyn had the knowledge of how death comes and the means to make her last days comfortable. If a good death was possible, she was going to teach me what it looked like.

I already knew, after my experience so far as a hospice volunteer, that to answer the questions I had about how Americans die—to even know if I was asking the right questions—I would have to go outside the confines of hospice volunteering. I had to venture into the controversies with activists who felt hospice didn't go far enough or went too far, the bioethicists who were studying broader concepts like informed consent and autonomy. I had to talk to the lawyers who specialized in end-of-life jurisprudence. And I had to meet the patients and families who were caught not at home but in the challenging terrain that stretched, impassible for some, between the idea of a good death and the painful place where they found themselves in their last days.

CHAPTER THREE

Priceless Days

The hospice ward where I volunteer when I don't have a home patient is on the fourth floor of a hospital on the Lower East Side of Manhattan. It is on the same floor as the maternity ward. In the elevator on the way to my shift, I often watch exuberant new mothers, grandmothers, and aunts point to the directional sign—"4. Hospice, Maternity"—and gasp. "It's just not right, putting babies next to dying people," they say. But life's a cycle, I think, and the fourth floor is where two of its ends neatly meet. If I couldn't volunteer with patients dying at home and could volunteer only at the in-hospital hospice ward, I might have been tempted to quit long ago. I don't like the frenzy and clinical atmosphere of the hospital, the florescent lights and institutional paint colors, the drab blue curtains in each room. It's not possible to get to know patients because their stays are short; I rarely see patients more than once. They are unconscious or die before my next weekly shift comes around.

The reason for these short stays is sometimes because of an unexpected event: a stroke, a fall, a heart attack. But more often it's because the patient was elsewhere in the hospital fighting an illness that she couldn't beat. She was undergoing the effects of a treatment that could not cure death. In younger patients, that fight makes sense; their young bodies are strong and can withstand harsh treatment. The epic fight against death holds the promise of many more years for them. But for elders, chemotherapy, for instance, can be incredibly taxing. It damages the kidneys; it can cause nausea and vomiting, depression, mouth sores, sore muscles, "brain fog," and can weaken the heart. For an older body that most likely already has underlying conditions or has lost its resiliency, chemotherapy can make life unbearable; it can turn one's last days into painful endurance. When doctors finally accept that a patient is not going to live, she's taken upstairs to one of the beds on the hospice ward to waste away, her last days and weeks spent surrounded by machines, strangers, the haze of drugs, and banal decor.

The hospital where I volunteer is Jewish, and there are eighteen rooms on the floor; eighteen is *chai* in Hebrew: life. The ward is a stretch of gray linoleum in the shape of an *L* with the central desk where the two wings meet. I never know quite what to do with myself when I'm there. My shift is usually two hours long, and each of them crawls by. I start on one side of a wing and work my way around, popping my head into each room to see who's there. The ward is where patients end up when it's become obvious to their doctor that there's nothing more to do, and that the bed in the intensive care unit could better serve another customer. Sometimes, family members wander through; sometimes, there's weeping or small talk or a low TV garbling in the background. But usually, there are quiet patients in various states of need and fear, if they're conscious at all. When making my rounds, I find it's easy to hear when I'm approaching a patient on a ventilator. The huff and push of the machine echoes down the hallway.

A ventilator is a terrible sound. To see patients attached to one is jarring. They are *jarred* by the machine forcing air into their lungs. Their bodies are continually shaken on the bed. Typically, their mouths are filled with the respirator tube, isolating them from any communication with others. If they're unconscious, it's hard to tell if they have any awareness at all. In hospice, we're fond of reminding each other and families that hearing is the last thing to go, that we should watch what we say near patients. Volunteers are encouraged to speak to the unconscious, to abet their perceived loneliness with soothing conversation, but I suspect many on the hospice ward are quite past the point of wanting to hear my account of the weather.

When, one fall day, I wandered into a room filled with the huff of a ventilator, a stranger with a badge, a frantic woman, threw her arms around my neck. In the bed behind her was her husband, Jack. Morbidly obese, he filled the narrow hospital bed; the railing on either side marked his girth with vertical indentations. The taut skin on his face, neck, and arms shook with each pump of the machine inflating his lungs. Jack, who was in his mid-fifties, had had a heart attack. "What should I do," his wife, Amy, begged me. "He can't eat," she cried. Jack's mouth was filled with a breathing tube, white strips of tape, their sticky edges curled and dirty, stretched across his full, lax cheeks; his eyes were closed, sunken, surrounded by dark circles. The bed shook each time the ventilator pushed, and Amy couldn't look away. It seemed to raise her anxiety with each huff. She wanted the staff to give him a feeding tube. Their disabled daughter, about sixteen, sat in a motorized wheelchair next to the bed, her face expressionless as if she were in shock, a half-eaten bag of gummy bear candies in her hand. Amy's understanding of her husband's state—of his future, of their future—was clearly not the same as the hospital's. She still hoped, begged for his recovery.

Yet we were in room eight of a hospice ward. Who knows what damage Jack's brain had suffered when he collapsed and stopped breathing. Or how long his brain had gone without oxygen before the emergency paramedics found him and got his heart beating again, before they manually inflated his lungs to keep oxygen circulating through his large body. Eating was a sign of hope, Amy thought. Getting food into

Jack would help her feel like she was doing something; it would take away her helplessness. It would make her feel as if they could return to their lives as they were before. When she calmed down, she said to me in a half-whisper, "They want to take him off this machine," as if she was betraying him with the words. She was afraid that if she removed the ventilator, Jack would die. But she was also afraid of what would happen if she didn't. One looming answer—nothing—tortured her. Would he, could he, go on like this? For how long?

Medical overtreatment has long been cautioned against throughout history. In *Embracing Our Mortality*, Lawrence J. Schneiderman, a doctor and academic at the University of California, San Diego, notes Hippocrates's warning: "Whenever the illness is too strong for the available remedies, the physician surely must not expect that it can be overcome by medicine. . . . To attempt futile treatment is to display an ignorance that is allied to madness." *Futility* means vain, fruitless, serving no useful purpose, a severe disappointment and a futile treatment is a treatment that cannot save a life. It is "madness" to treat a patient who cannot be cured, according to the Hippocratic Corpus, a body of texts that are loosely attributed to, if not Hippocrates, the school of doctors he established, roughly 450 to 350 BCE. Schneiderman also notes Plato's example of a good doctor in *Republic*: "For those whose lives are always in a state of inner sickness Asclepius [who was a legendary, indeed divine, physician] did not attempt to prescribe a regimen to make their life a prolonged misery. . . . A life with preoccupation with illness and neglect of work is not worth living."

Avoiding overtreatment and a patient's prolonged misery got a lot harder as new ways to extend life were developed in the 1960s and 70s. In *Principles of Biomedical Ethics*, by Tom L. Beauchamp and James F. Childress, futile treatment is defined as one of the "conditions for overriding the prima facie obligation to treat." The book, published in 1977, is a landmark in the medical field and a comprehensive first attempt to establish consistent ethics for medical practice against the backdrop of racing technological advancement. "Typically the term *futile* refers to a situation in which irreversibly dying patients have reached a point at which further treatment provides no physiological benefits or is hopeless and becomes optional," they write. The concept of futile care as it's been defined throughout the ages may be simple; it is treatments, operations, and medications that are not (or are no longer) able to cure a patient of a fatal disease. But determining what care is futile is difficult and dependent on many factors.

One of those factors is our fear of death. Not just the physical pain of death but of everything surrounding it, too, like abandonment of loved ones, the loss of physical control, the end of the world as we know it. Like all mysteries, death scares even the strongest of believers, even believers in hope, in heaven, in a better life after death. I've rarely met a dying person, Christian, atheist, or other, who hasn't doubted her understanding of what death meant for her. (I've also rarely had a hospice patient who isn't, at some point, in enough pain and discomfort to say she wants to die.) While doubts and fears about death are common, even natural, they are abetted by decades of science's hopeful promise to "cure" old age or to mitigate death. We live in an era where death is not real to us; it's something that happens to other people, and so we kid ourselves that it can be avoided. A cure for cancer or Alzheimer's or kidney disease will be found before it finds us. Increasing life-spans have lulled us into thinking—if we think of death at all—that maybe we can dodge it, that maybe we can live forever.

We should be careful what we wish for. Ovid accounts the dangers that can befall one who wishes to live forever. The prophetess Sybil asked Apollo for immortality and he granted it, but she had neglected to ask for eternal youth. Over the years, Sybil grew older and smaller until she was so tiny that the people of her home city, Cumae, hung her in a basket above the town square. At last, only her voice remained.

According to the tale, when asked, "Sybil, what do you want?" she would reply, "I want to die." Jonathan Wallace, a lawyer and playwright, wrote, in 2009 in his paper "What Sybil Knew," that her desire for death can be attributed to two factors: she was burdened by her "limitless and despairing knowledge of human affairs," and "she found herself becoming more decrepit than she could bear; the continuing degradation of her body, projected across the unlimited bounds of time ahead of her, was a terrifying prospect." On the hospice ward, I see countless Sybils, their stares long, even their voices gone.

Jack, who had suffered a heart attack, was likely taken by surprise; his wife, Amy, and their daughter surely were. They had no idea how to deal with their sudden situation; even the hospital staff was unable to convince them that a feeding tube and ventilator would not bring Jack back to them. Any emergency, an infection, a hernia, a stroke, the flu, a fall can dash even well-made plans on the rocks of panic and hope. Every new medical advance can become a decision and presents unanticipated challenges for patients and their families.

Katy Butler, in *Knocking on Heaven's Door*, a memoir of her unsuccessful efforts to turn off her father's pacemaker as he descended into dementia, physical frailty, and his eighties, describes how hope, even unfounded, colors medical decisions. Her book beautifully chronicles the challenges of avoiding medicine's inclination to treat, not care, for patients. After a stroke, her father suffered a hernia in rehab and was told that, despite his age and underlying diseases, a pacemaker was necessary for a hernia operation. "My parents were contemplating more than a pacemaker," writes Butler, they were "contemplating how much suffering they would bear in exchange for more time together on earth. And they did not know it." A cascade of procedures, on top of daily care requirements, engulfed the family.

As family members who are often responsible for advocating or directing our loved one's care, how can we not hope for more time? As philosopher Adrienne M. Martin writes in *How We Hope*, "Hoping for an outcome is a distinctive way of treating one's own attitudes toward the outcome. Specifically, one treats them as reasons to engage in various feelings and activities, and thereby *incorporates* them into one's rational scheme of ends." We build hope into our plans and we devise the future out of it. Hope staves off fear and grief and helps us to act when we must. Sometimes it binds us to immediate actions in the face of crisis, even as it clouds our perception of a real future.

In "God Will Find a Way," an essay in the anthology *On Moral Medicine*, Margaret E. Mohrmann, a doctor and professor of biomedical ethics, describes the power of hope and how it clashes with medicine in challenging ways. A child in the pediatric intensive care unit at Mohrmann's hospital is diagnosed with a fatal degenerative neurological disease. Jermaine is a "miracle" child, Mohrmann tell us, born twenty years after his sister and desperately wanted by his parents, who decide to take Jermaine to the National Institutes of Health for a second opinion. While there, Jermaine stops breathing and, because how to proceed with his care has not yet been discussed, NIH doctors intubate him—run a tube through his mouth into his trachea—and attach him to a ventilator. Not long after, Mohrmann finds out that the parents want to transfer Jermaine back to their local hospital where Mohrmann works so they can be closer to home, surrounded by their family and church community.

The staff at Mohrmann's pediatric intensive care unit don't want the child and his family to return. They are still recovering from the long, slow death of another young boy whose parents, at the advice of their lawyers, refused to remove him from machines, despite his deteriorating health and certain pending death. The staff felt "helpless in the face of powerful forces—legal, economic, egotistical, pedagogical, scientific, and so many others—that seemed to care about everything but the welfare of the child and the well-being of the workers," Mohrmann writes. The ward dreaded experiencing the long and painful death of yet another child so soon.

But Mohrmann finds that Jermaine's family is not just hopeful that their son will live; they are waiting for God to make the decision for them. They knew their child, though slowly approaching death, was not in pain. They were giving God the chance to heal just at the time when there seemed no hope of healing. Mohrmann writes, "The quality of *their* survival—what the rest of their lives would be like after the critical event, with or without a surviving child—had something to do with how I worked with them during the crisis." She was able to ask more specific questions of the parents about what they would consider to be a sign from God. An overwhelming infection? Heart failure? Yes, they told her, they would see these as a sign from God that he was ready to take Jermaine. "It was of central importance to his parents' future that they be able to remember that in the midst of the struggle they had remained faithful to Jermaine and to God, according to their understanding of what such fidelity required," she writes. Jermaine died of heart failure a few days after their conversation.

Mohrmann's story demonstrates why there is no consensus on the definition of futile care. When we consider the needs of everyone surrounding a patient, our understanding of the benefits of care is extended to a family, a community, and medical staff. But Mohrmann's broad interpretation of futile care is only possible because Jermaine is young ("do everything" is justifiable) and because he is not in pain.

What happens when we calculate pain and suffering into the costs of futile care? How does our goal of a good death—for everyone—change when we consider the cost of pain? We arrive at a new math, one that accounts for both the financial expense of end-of-life care and also the physical and emotional expense. But there's another issue here to consider: not only are precious medical resources being used to torture dying patients. That would be bad enough. But that use prevents applying their benefit to patients who are not dying, whose lives can be improved and saved. In many ways, by pushing dying patients into futile tests and treatments, by avoiding difficult conversations, by ignoring the costs of pain, we are denying those who need these resources a chance to live.

Journalist Lisa M. Krieger's story of her father's death anchored a special insert in the *San Jose Mercury News* in 2013. Krieger tallies the costs of her father's final ten days and comes up with $323,658. Kenneth Krieger was an eighty-eight-year-old former engineer with dementia when he contracted septicemia, a bacterial infection. He had done everything he thought necessary to plan for the end of his life: he had drawn up legal "do not resuscitate" and "desire for a natural death" orders. But, alarmed by her father's disorientation one Saturday—"he was shaking, dehydrated and speaking gibberish"—Lisa rushed him to the nearby emergency room. So began ten days of tests, drugs, and X-rays. Everything confused her father; he was distressed by the hospital environment. At the time, she wasn't thinking of the financial costs; how could she? But she was watching the pain and disorientation that it caused her father. "Could an 88-year old with weak bones, an irregular heartbeat and dementia survive?" Krieger asks herself after she's taken her father to the intensive care unit and approved a battery of tests and procedures. "And if he survived, then what?" Staff suggested her father undergo surgery. "When all the specialists left, I summoned my strength and stopped the attending physician: Please, tell me what's ahead of us." His assessment was grim. Krieger finally said no. "It is easy to get quick access to world-class treatment. It's much harder to reject it," she wrote.

In our collective effort to avoid death at all costs, we are all complicit in a painful and costly phenomenon that has developed over the past five decades: a funneling of medical resources away from those who need them. According to the Centers for Disease Control and Prevention, the ten current leading causes of death, in order, are heart disease, cancer, lung disease, stroke, accidents (unintended injuries), Alzheimer's, diabetes, kidney disease, influenza and pneumonia, and suicide. Because the American population's average age is rapidly rising, health-care resources are increasingly spent to stanch successive ailments that come with old age. In 2009, the number of those sixty-five and older was 39.6 million; by 2030, that number will double to 72.1 million. Suicide and accidents aside, death is increasingly becoming a series of treatments, therapies, drug courses, and experimental trials that address—or prolong— the remaining illnesses. Americans may now live three decades longer than they did at the turn of the nineteenth century (an average that accounts for the decrease in childhood deaths and deaths from curable, basic infections and disease), but many of those extra years are not the golden retirement we expect.

What all these numbers add up to financially is a looming economic catastrophe: in 2010, Americans spent nearly $2.6 trillion on health care, more than 17 percent of the US gross domestic product. And twice what was spent in 2000. Half that total was spent on just 5 percent of Americans; about one-third of Medicare dollars goes to the last year of life.

It's hard not to consider what the needless $323,658 spent on Kenneth Kreiger's last ten days could have otherwise been used for. Like one year of health coverage for more than 250 people (when you calculate health insurance at $100 a month when subsidized through the Affordable Care Act). Like 170 days in a New York nonprofit hospital's intensive care unit (when one day of stay is calculated at an average of $1,906). Like the births of thirty-two new babies (calculated at $10,000 for a vaginal birth with no complications, in New York). As Daniel Callahan of the Hastings Center told Kreiger, "We have to realize that this endless fight against aging can't go on."

Even as our fear of death prevents us from looking at it head on, from talking about the pain that it causes patients and families, and from applying its costs to beneficial purposes, medical ethics and lawyers have contested overtreatment for decades. One court case in particular marked a new era in the public's thinking about end-of-life pain and futile treatment. In 1983, Nancy Cruzan was on her way home from work on a road near her home in Missouri when she had an accident. She was thrown from her car, and when paramedics found her, she was face down in a ditch full of water. They resuscitated her and rushed her to the hospital. She was twenty-five at the time, with a healthy body. They were able to restart her heart and her lungs, but after three weeks in the hospital, her doctors determined she was in a persistent vegetative state, "a profound or deep state of unconsciousness," according to the National Institute of Neurological Disorders and Stroke. Her parents were hopeful that she would recover; after a few weeks, because she was unconscious and could not eat, Joe and Joyce Cruzan signed a form that allowed a feeding tube to be inserted, first through Nancy's nose and later through an incision in her stomach. "We didn't read anything," Joe said. "If they said we needed to do it, we signed."

After four years, the Cruzans came to the conclusion that Nancy would not recover, that she was no longer in her body and that she wouldn't have wanted to live by artificial means. They consulted their priest. When Joe asked about removing Nancy's feeding tube, the hospital told him it would take a court order. When he asked if they could take Nancy home and remove the tube there, they were told that they could be charged with murder. What followed were years of litigation. PBS's *Frontline* filmed Nancy and her family in their hospital room, for the first time allowing Americans to see what challenges the Cruzans faced. In June 1990, the Missouri Supreme Court ruled that the Cruzans could remove their daughter's feeding tube, but the case was appealed. After the Missouri Supreme Court ruled against the Cruzans, the US Supreme Court took up the case on appeal. William H. Colby, the Cruzan's lawyer and author of *Unplugged: Reclaiming our Right to Die in America*, writes that dozens of amicus or "friends of the court" briefs were filed for both sides, but the two primary briefs opposing the Cruzans came from the United States Conference of

Catholic Bishops, which argued that feeding tubes were comfort care and compulsory, and the solicitor general of the United States, Kenneth Starr. Protesters, both right-to-die advocates who supported the Cruzans and "pro-life" groups who considered the removal of a feeding tube to be immoral starvation stood outside the court and outside Nancy's hospital room.

"I sympathize with the hardship of caring for a helpless woman, but I have no sympathy for a family who solves their problems by starving their daughter to death when there were hundreds of bona fide offers to care for her regardless of her condition," the Reverend Joseph Foreman, an antiabortion activist, said in a statement at the time, as reported by Tamar Lewin in the *New York Times*. "Even a dog in Missouri can not be legally starved to death."

Foreman's "dog" statement was ridiculous but compelling to his allies, who considered the "starvation" of a young woman to be inhumane. His position disregarded medical analysis of Nancy's status and prevented many from anticipating or thinking deeply about the challenges the country faced as more and more patients were placed on physiological support. But his characterization of the case was powerful for another reason: it discredited the love and devotion the Cruzans had shown their daughter and considered their decision to be selfish, even evil. Foreman and others felt that the decision to remove the tube was the same as killing, that it proved the Cruzans were not fit to make their daughter's medical decisions. Foreman and others used the Cruzan case to set the blunt, scorched-earth tone for future culture-war clashes that were to come.

The court ruling was the first of its kind, establishing that patients had the autonomy to make their own medical decisions, to remove "life support" machines, even if doing so meant certain death. The Cruzans successfully proved to the court that they had "clear and convincing" evidence that Nancy would not want to continue living in her present state. Legal jurisprudence had finally caught up with medical technology and the new category of life—or death—that it created. Nancy died twelve days after her feeding tube was removed, her name forever attached to the right to weigh prolonged life, pain, and suffering against medicine's futile machines.

In Judeo-Christian tradition, pain begins at the beginning, with original sin, when Adam and Eve are expelled from Eden. Pain was a sign of guilt. It was just punishment for criminal behavior; it brought us closer to God. "Suffering was—and still is—regarded by many as something that can, must, or ought to be endured," writes Melanie Thernstrom in *The Pain Chronicles*. It made us better. Thernstrom tells us that, in the mid-nineteenth century, the president of the American Dental Association condemned the use of anesthesia for tooth extraction, saying, "I am against these satanic agencies which prevent men from going through what God intended them to go through." Relief of pain during childbirth was also controversial: women were intended by God to suffer during labor. Even when the twentieth century ushered in modern medicine, vestiges of earlier concepts remained. "The remedy for pain seemed plain: treat the disease or injury, and the pain should take care of itself," writes Thernstrom. Medicine focused on curing underlying illnesses and disease, instead of alleviating pain.

Ideas of pain as unavoidable, if not redeeming, are particularly prevalent at the end of life. When combined with medical culture's focus on curing illness—what journalist Katy Butler in *Knocking on Heaven's Door* calls "the tyranny of hope"—patient care has taken on a *try everything* fervor. One more round of chemotherapy, one more course of an experimental drug, without regard for the pain and suffering of the patient, without consideration of his discomfort or the searing trials of recuperation. Life, it is thought, no matter how wracked with pain, how old, how disabled, is always preferable to death. Treatment, however futile, is the default. French sociologist Émile Durkheim tells us that pain itself "has nothing desirable about it," and yet it is a "normal function of physiology." Pain is an indicator of bodily problems; its function is to warn us that something is physically wrong. However, physical pain is never just physical. It is psychic as well or, in hospice phraseology, "existential." Pain can be the result of confronting one's existence, not just a body that hurts, but a loss of love, grief for a deceased parent, the loss of a job, debt, regret, impending death. Pain, when persistent and untreated, causes depression; it wrecks relationships, takes away security, and alters how we see the world. Emotional pain has physical effects: when a love ends, we say our heart is *broken*; we become *blind* with rage; we *languish* in despair. Pain also removes us from ordinary existence; it transports us to a new world we had not known before. Isolation.

We know our own pain exists, but we often fail to believe or accept the pain of others. "'Having pain,'" Elaine Scarry tells us in *The Body in Pain*, can be "thought of as the most vibrant example of what it is to 'have certainty,' while for the other person it is so elusive that 'hearing about pain' may exist as the primary model of what it is 'to doubt.'" This is, she tells us, because we are incapable of expressing pain when we experience it. Pain takes our words away; it makes us resort to "the sounds and cries a human being makes before language is learned."

In hospitals across the United States, nurses often wear placards around their necks that show a series of faces, their expressions ranging from "0, NO HURT," to "10, HURTS WORST." The "0" face is smiling, the eyes are wide and happy, the eyebrows pleasantly arched. The "10" face is frowning, the eyes are half closed as three tears fall from them, the eyebrows are low and heavy. Donna Wong, a pediatric nurse, and Connie Baker, a child life specialist, developed the scale in the 1980s to address what they saw as a challenge to treating pediatric patients' pain: children don't have words to describe what they are feeling. But I first encountered the scale in hospice where the patients were adults who also didn't have the necessary words. Another pain scale, the McGill Pain Questionnaire, was developed in 1971 by

Ronald Melzak, a psychologist at McGill University in Canada, and his colleague W. S. Torgerson. Words like *lacerating, stabbing, pricking,* and *throbbing* are arranged on the McGill Questionnaire in twenty rows, two to six words each. The questionnaire is meant to help patients find words for how they feel, writes Scary, because the "act of verbally expressing pain is a necessary prelude to the collective task of diminishing pain." More than forty years after the development of the McGill Questionnaire and the publication of Scarry's *The Body in Pain,* after the rise of hospice programs across the United States, it's difficult to conclude that we've made much progress in the "collective task of diminishing pain." One effort, inside and outside the medical community, to address patient pain is to place medical decision-making power in the hands of patients.

The idea of medical autonomy—that patients have the right to decide what medical treatments they do and don't want—has existed for decades. Ethicists cite its first appearance in 1891 when a woman who had been injured in the sleeping car of a train refused a medical examination. In *Union Pacific Railway Co. v. Botsford,* the court ruled that the woman, Clara L. Botsford, could refuse the exam on the grounds of privacy. The Missouri court, when deciding *Cruzan,* cited *Union Pacific Railway.* As the US Supreme Court did in its 1973 decision on abortion, the Missouri court determined that a person's medical privacy was tantamount. Medical advancements, emergency resuscitation, ventilators, and feeding tubes had changed the way society, the courts, and the Cruzan family understood death. No longer was it a natural process that proceeded after a fatal trauma, illness, or elderly decline. It allowed patients and their families to consider the emotional and physical price they were paying for more days on earth.

Yet the ideology that pain is natural and that death can be deferred is still embedded in the economic structure of health care. "The system rewarded nobody for saying 'no' or even 'wait,'" Katy Butler tells us in *Knocking on Heaven's Door.* Doctors' conversations with patients about physical and emotional pain are not reimbursed, but treatments that cannot cure—and will only increase suffering for patients, their families, and their caregivers—are. The "tyranny of hope" is also then a tyranny of profit.

Over the past five decades, as medicine has advanced and cases like *Cruzan* have spurred national debates, a movement has formed to combat overtreatment's relentlessness, its insistent plague on the last months of life. Legalization of aid in dying, some say, is a way for patients to take their own medical decisions into their hands, to hasten death and therefore skip the needless pain and suffering—to skip the loss of their body, their mind, and their environment. "Death with Dignity," as the state initiatives are called, gives those with six months or less to live the legal right to get prescriptions for lethal medication from their doctors. Politically sophisticated, couched in current ideas of personal choice, dedicated to the need to give patients silenced by pain a voice, and gaining ground across the country, proponents of aid in dying believe that there is nothing worse than emotional and physical pain. Not even death.

CHAPTER FOUR

Double Effect

"What brings you to Montana?" the clerk at the rental car counter asked after looking at my New York driver's license. I waited for him to make eye contact with me, but he didn't. He was young, about twenty-five, and doughy, with corn-silk hair and light-brown eyes.

"Assisted suicide," I deadpanned. "I hear it's legal in Montana now." He lifted the corners of his mouth in a friendly way and nodded. Then, processing what I said, stopped and lifted his eyes from the computer monitor. He looked at me about a half second too long.

"I'm writing about it," I said, shrugging. Writers could be trusted with rental cars. Potential suicides, maybe not.

"I'm in nursing school," he said. "I haven't heard anything about it. They can make it legal to kill yourself?" Now I had his attention.

"Well, it's already legal in two states," I told him. "Montana's the third."

He came around the counter to hand me my paperwork and took the handle of my wheelie bag. As he walked me to my car, he asked more questions. That "assisted suicide"—a term he reacted negatively to—was legal in Montana came as a surprise to him, but as I defined what the law allowed, he nodded in approval. It was early morning, mid-December; a dusting of snow covered the ground. I had arrived in Billings the night before and stayed in a shabby Motel 6 near the airport. I felt terrible. A head cold had come on a few days before I was scheduled to leave New York, but because my flight, car, and interviews were all confirmed, I mustered. I took a bunch of cold medicine and hoped for the best. The early morning air, the snow, the curious rental car clerk all cheered me. I had been in New York for too long without a break. It was liberating, despite the dragging head cold, to be in a new landscape, one that was so vast and open. I thanked the clerk for pulling my bag and settled into the little rental car for the five-hour drive to Missoula. I could have flown to Missoula, but the chance to drive thrilled me and gave me time to think about the questions I would ask my interviewees that day. The sun was just coming up as I pulled out onto Route 90 and headed west. It cast a long shadow off the car ahead of me and made the grasses of Montana's plains a golden red. I found a local radio station that played old country, heartbreak songs, interrupted by advertisements for grocery stores. Truck drivers raised two fingers at me when I passed them on the left. Red-tailed hawks sat on weathered fence posts to watch the traffic go by; in the distance, black cows dotted the tall grass. I thought of Willa Cather's description of western prairies in *My Ántonia*: "There was nothing but land: Not a country at all, but the material out of which countries are made." I popped another DayQuil in my mouth and washed it down with gas station coffee.

Almost exactly two years before my plane touched down in Billings, Lewis and Clark County District Judge Dorothy McCarter had decided that the "constitutional rights of individual privacy and human dignity, taken together, encompass the right of a competent terminally-ill patient to die with dignity." Her decision was announced on December 5, 2008, on what would have been my father's sixty-fourth birthday. The case was brought on behalf of a man named Robert Baxter, who, like my father, had been diagnosed with cancer for ten years. Immediately after Judge McCarter's ruling, the state attorney general appealed the decision to the Montana Supreme Court, which heard arguments in September 2009. I was drawn to Baxter's case; he seemed familiar to me. In the photo I have taped by my desk, Baxter is wearing sand-colored canvas overalls and a teal blue T-shirt. He looks out from the shadow of a trucker's hat marked with a bull's eye and the outline of Montana stitched in white thread. His hair, beard, and mustache are white as snow. A marine during the Korean War, Baxter had settled in Montana to drive long-haul trucks. The state suited him: he was an outdoorsman who camped, fished, and hunted. At the age of sixty-six, he was diagnosed with lymphocytic leukemia, a cancer that attacks the white blood cells in bone marrow. Baxter went through several rounds of chemotherapy, but his leukemia marched on. After nearly ten years of hoping to beat it, he realized he had done everything possible. He was ready to die.

I had a 3 p.m. appointment with Mark Connell, the Missoula lawyer who had represented Baxter. Before I had gotten on the plane for Montana, I had watched a YouTube video of Connell arguing before the Montana Supreme Court. In it, Justice Jim Rice asks Connell how aid in dying would affect important laws intended to protect citizens.

Connell's voice is calm, almost buttery, authoritative without being too assertive. In the video, he's wearing a dark suit and tie, the model of a small town lawyer. He answers,

> Statutes in Montana, the Montana Rights of the Terminally Ill Act, cross that line over and over and over again. We're not working on a blank canvas here. Montana law recognizes multiple situations where it's all right for a doctor to hasten death. This happens every day in our hospitals. This double effect doctrine is when a doctor goes to a patient and his family and says, "You're suffering, I'm gonna put you out of suffering. Here's the extra morphine

that will do the job." This is done deliberately so. And so our law recognizes there are certain situations where, because of the paramount duty doctors have—and the state recognizes—to alleviate suffering, medicine can proceed to the point where death is hastened. Our contention, as you know, is that there's not much difference between that and aid in dying. It takes a small step further.

"Double effect." An action that has two outcomes. Connell was referring to the medical principle that a doctor may medicate a patient to alleviate pain and suffering, even to the point of death, so long as the doctor's intention is to relieve suffering. In *Principles of Biomedical Ethics*, Tom L. Beauchamp and James Childress write, "This rule incorporates a very influential distinction between intended effects and merely foreseen effects." The principle traces back to St. Thomas Aquinas, a Dominican friar and Catholic theologian who died in 1274. In *Summa Theologica*, his seminal, foundational work, Aquinas writes, "A single act may have two effects, of which one alone is intended, whilst the other is incidental to that intention." Aquinas says that the nature of an act depends not on its outcome but on the "agent's" intention, and he gives an example of how the double effect works. He says that when we protect ourselves from an attacker, our intent is self-protection. If we happen to kill the attacker, our action of self-defense is justified because "the agent intends to save his own life." Double effect has been a principle in Catholic moral theology for more than a century; later, it was taken up by philosophy and applied ethics. The double effect was ultimately enshrined in medical ethics by Beauchamp and Childress in 1977 as medical technology was quickly complicating the dying process and clear ethical principles became necessary. But the double effect has always been accompanied by controversy. Some don't place the same emphasis on intent that Aquinas did (or the Catholic Church continues to), particularly when the second outcome is foreseeable, even predictable. Even, perhaps, hoped for.

Missoula is a small town with just over sixty-eight thousand residents and a reputation, similar to Austin, Texas, as a bastion of liberal thinking in the middle of a politically conservative state. The Clark Fork River, which collects in the Rocky Mountains and runs northwest to Idaho, bisects the town. Connell's office is a colorful, well-kept Victorian on Spruce Street, two blocks from the river, four blocks from the county courthouse, and directly across the street from St. Patrick's Hospital.

I asked Connell, a tall, affable man with a firm handshake and brown eyes, why he took the Baxter case. "I thought it was an issue that needed to be decided, in Montana and elsewhere," he said. He had experienced the long and painful deaths of his father-in-law and other family members. It was a personal issue for him. "It involves a broader set of questions that our society needs to deal with. Who gets to decide these things? Should it be the government or the person?" he continued. I detected the strains of a libertarian argument running through his explanation. Government, he felt, should have no say in such personal matters: matters that should be private between a patient and her doctor. "Whether it's a hospital or a medical association or whomever, we all know that when we get very sick and our lives are about to close, typically we don't have control of what's happening," he said. Once upon a time not so long ago, patients consulted with their trusted physician; they decided together how the end would come. Extraordinary measures didn't exist. Doctors could keep patients comfortable; they could make patients in pain unconscious. Now, with most people dying in hospitals and institutions, often divorced from both their family doctor and the natural, unmedicalized way of dying, they are subject to imposed laws and ethics. Death has become a decision to remove machines that only make the dying process longer. Connell said, "Whether you like it or not, you may have the end of your life decided by somebody else."

Connell became interested in end-of-life issues in college when he read Jessica Mitford's *The American Way of Death*, a searing, sharp, and often funny takedown of the funeral industry. Later, he'd come across Sherwin Nuland's best seller, *How We Die*, in which Nuland describes, with a doctor's physiological detail, what happens when we die of cancer, stabbing, heart attack, and other causes. Nuland demystifies the dying body by explaining how various systems—the circulatory system, the respiratory system—shut down. Over the years, Connell watched law and medicine change as new medical technologies were introduced. These new technologies could prop up individual failing systems, but they couldn't stop death; they could only prolong pain and suffering. "I saw the Baxter case as one that concerned important social policy issues, but also one with enormous personal dimensions. Death is a universal experience, but almost universally in our culture we don't want to talk about it," Connell said.

Efforts to legalize aid in dying in some states have amplified the public debate about how Americans die. In 1994, Measure 16 was passed by Oregon residents; 51.3 percent voted for the law and 48.7 voted against it. Called Death with Dignity, it established a framework for those terminal patients who wanted their doctors to give them a lethal dose of medication. The law is very specific. Patients have to request the medication orally and in writing, their diagnosis has to be corroborated by two physicians, and patients are required to wait fifteen days between requests. If there is any question of depression or delirium, a third professional has to determine whether the patient is mentally competent or not. Patients are required to be residents of the state, to be eighteen years of age or older, and to take the medication themselves (doctors and family members are prohibited from directly dosing the patient). An explicit tracking and reporting mechanism was put in place, and the law requires that death certificates of those who use Death with Dignity list the underlying illness as cause of death, not "suicide" or even "Death with

Dignity." Insurance companies are prevented from retaliating against the families of those who use the bill.

While the law has stood for twenty years, it hasn't been without challenge. Another measure was brought before Oregon voters in November 1997, a few years after Death with Dignity passed, that would have repealed the law. It was defeated by majority vote. Not ready to let voters have the last word, US Attorney General John Ashcroft challenged the law on the grounds of the Controlled Substances Act in 2004; he tried to rescind the licenses of doctors who participated in Death with Dignity by making prescriptions. His case was blocked by a lower court. The decision was appealed by incoming US Attorney General Alberto Gonzales, but the US Supreme Court decided in January 2006 that the law could stand.

In 2008, Washington became the second state to legalize aid in dying. Initiative 1000, bolstered by fourteen years of standing in Oregon, was approved by 57.82 percent of the state's voters. The law, also called Death with Dignity, looks a lot like Oregon's. In Montana, after Connell argued Robert Baxter's case before the Montana Supreme Court, a decision was issued on New Year's Eve, 2009. It stated that a doctor's prescription for lethal drugs did not defy the state constitution. And with that, Montana became the third state to legalize aid in dying and the first to do so via the courts, albeit without the strict checks and balances of the prior two Death with Dignity laws.

That the first three states to legalize aid in dying are all in the general northwest of the United States has not gone unnoticed by observers. Physical and ideological distance from the country's center of power on the East Coast, strong political ideas about independence and personal liberty, even inclusion of the right to dignity in the constitution—as in Montana—have made the aid-in-dying movement's early successes possible there. Yet, the states that have since legalized aid in dying, Vermont, California, and New Mexico (where it is on appeal in the courts), make it difficult to generalize about political inclinations and the law's proponents.

"Before you leave," Connell said to me, "remind me to show you Bob's picture. I have it upstairs on my wall." It was the same picture I had hanging by my desk, the teal blue T-shirt, the overalls, the trucker's cap with "Montana" stitched on it.

Roberta King was named after her father, Robert Baxter. She is tall and lean with short blond hair and a ready laugh. After Bob's death, she wrote and spoke publicly about his quest to make aid in dying legal. It was a role that she took on with reluctance, only after she grasped the bind that her ill father was in: dying painfully, legally unable to get to death when he wanted. Baxter wasn't suicidal, but he was ready. Roberta told me that he had so much time to prepare for his own death that he did everything he could to make it easy on the family. He sold his "toys": the RV, the boat, and the trailers; he reroofed the house, had new siding put on it, and paid off the mortgage. As Roberta and I sat in the Iron Horse, a bar and grill on Higgins Street in downtown Missoula, she told me how her father announced to the family that he was quitting chemotherapy treatment and entering hospice.

He had called all four children—Roberta is the youngest—and asked them to come home for Thanksgiving. But they weren't to bring the grandchildren, Robert insisted. He didn't want them to remember him as he was, wasted away and dying. The news was hard on Roberta, who had volunteered for hospice a few years before. She knew what was coming; hospice meant that there was no more hope he would miraculously beat his cancer.

"Let me tell you a story," Roberta said. "When I got there, I was out in the backyard. They have this huge cottonwood tree. And I saw a big chain up in the tree, so I asked my mother, What is that chain? And she said, your dad climbed up there because he was afraid that the tree branch would fall over and hit the neighbor's house. So one of the last things he did was chain the stupid branch up because he was protecting the neighbors from the tree. I'm sure that it took everything. Every last shred of power he had."

Roberta told me other stories about her dad. That he had talked about shooting himself, which scared Roberta. She thought of a former neighbor who was dying of cancer. He was in pain and depressed. When his dog died, he couldn't take it anymore. He took his shotgun into the backyard and shot himself in the head. "His wife had to clean it up," Roberta told me. Robert Baxter quickly ruled out that option; he didn't want his family to experience that kind of trauma.

When I asked Roberta to tell me what her father was like, a wide smile crossed her face. "He was funny," she said. "He was tough. He was gone a lot," driving long-haul trucks across the Northwest. "A chunk," she said, always a little chubby. And a curmudgeon. "Total Archie Bunker." She told me how much care and effort he put into the court case, how he kept it a secret from the children until Roberta asked him about stacks of paper on the dining room table one day. And she told me about how, after her father died, she and her two brothers and one sister all took turns crawling into bed with their mother. "She was in a big old king bed by herself. And of course my dad had died in that bed days before. We all did it. I mean we're talking fifty-year-old men slipping into bed with their mom, snuggling with her."

In July 2010, more than two years after her father died, new legislation was introduced in Montana to strike down the state supreme court's decision. Roberta wrote a guest column in the local paper, the *Missoulian*, titled "Fighting to Keep the Right to Die with Dignity." "His symptoms were so severe and his suffering so unrelenting," she wrote of her father, "that he yearned for death weeks before his life ended. From statements he made to me and other members of our family, it is clear my father would have availed himself of aid in dying if that choice had been legal in Montana and available to him. The fact it was not made his suffering and death much more painful and difficult than they otherwise could have been, and deprived him of the right to decide for himself how much suffering to endure before he died." She concluded, "I'm going to keep fighting to keep this choice in place, the one my dad should have had."

"There's something very heroic about Robert Baxter," I told Connell. I meant that it must have taken a particular determination to pursue a court case while he was terminally ill. But I was also thinking about the criticism he endured from opponents of aid in dying who claim the law is unnecessary. Some say patients are giving up, taking the easy way out instead of facing death. What they mean is that Baxter's pain and suffering were not important, or that they were expected and necessary. They mean that he should have accepted the authority of a medical system that had gone off the rails and the state laws that enforced it—and the machines and constant tests and treatments foisted on him. They said he was not in charge of his body, that decisions regarding life and death belonged to a higher power, one he didn't believe in. That he was defying nature by seeking lethal medicine. Baxter was never cowed by any of it. He was dying, suffering the ravages of his final months, and still he pushed on with the lawsuit. Baxter wanted access to a lethal prescription to end his own suffering, but he was committed to making that access legal for everyone, when he could have been at home, in the privacy of his family.

Other opponents of aid in dying say, why make a law? If someone wants to end his life, there are plenty of ways to do so. Guns, car exhaust piped through empty garages, ropes with clumsy knots slung over rafters, haphazard amounts of household poisons that often maim but don't kill the desperate. These are the options available to dying patients in pain, if they're still able to physically execute any of them. Others say that the alternative to a long and painful decline is hospice or palliative care, which allows a patient to be medicated to the point of comfort—and unconsciousness. Baxter saw no dignity in that option either. In his affidavit to the Montana court, Baxter explained why he did not want palliative sedation. The affidavit is a public document; Connell gave me a copy before I left his office. It is three pages long, sealed by a notary, and signed by Robert Baxter in large, curling letters. He wrote:

> I am appalled by this suggestion and the loss of personal auton-
> omy it involves. I understand that terminal or palliative sedation
> would involve administering intravenous medication to me for the
> purpose of rendering me unconscious, and then withholding fluids
> and nutrition until I die, a process that may take weeks. During this
> final period of my life I would remain unconscious, unaware of my
> situation or surroundings, unresponsive from a cognitive or voli-
> tional standpoint, and uninvolved in my own death. My ability to
> maintain personal hygiene would be lost and I would be dependent
> on others to clean my body. My family would be forced to stand
> a horrible vigil while my unconscious body was maintained in this
> condition, wasting away from starvation and dehydration, while
> they waited for me to die. I would want to do whatever I could to
> avoid subjecting my family to such a painful and pointless ordeal.

I knew that Robert Baxter had died at home before the supreme court case had been decided. I asked Connell what Baxter thought of the decision that propelled his case into the national spotlight and ultimately made Montana the third state in the country to legalize aid in dying. Turns out that Baxter never knew. He died the day the district court decision was made, before the case ever went on to the supreme court. Connell told me that when the district court called to let him know that the decision was ready, he called the Baxter home to tell them that it was favorable. Baxter's wife told Connell that she was sorry Bob was asleep but that he would be happy. "He died before he woke up. So he never learned about it," Connell said. Baxter never knew that Judge Dorothy McCarter had refused to stay the use of aid in dying while the case was on appeal. He never knew that his case went on to the state supreme court and that it was successful, that he had cleared the way for like-minded patients across the state to have another way out of a long, slow death.

In states where aid in dying has been the subject of intense public conversation, there are surprising end-of-life consequences for the overall population. Doctors' referrals for hospice (or palliative care, a medical discipline that rose out of hospice and focuses on alleviating pain) in Oregon increased by 20 percent after legalization. A 2013 poll by *National Journal* and the Regence Foundation found that Washington and Oregon residents were more knowledgeable about hospice and palliative care. In 1995, one year after Death with Dignity was legalized, Oregon issued its first Physician Orders for Life-Sustaining Treatment (POLST), a bright pink or orange single-page form in which patients can stipulate, in medical terms, what types of treatment they want when in distress. Because it's required that the form is taped to a patient's refrigerator, emergency workers know where to look. POLST is like an advanced directive that speaks a doctor's language. The forms are considered the best way available to inform care providers of patients' desired treatment. Doctors and emergency staff were suddenly able to respond to crisis situations not with "do everything" but according to what each patient wanted. Twenty-six US states have since adopted POLST or similar forms.

Oregon, Washington, Montana. All three states had one thing in common: the legal chops, the grassroots organizing, and the funding of the nation's largest aid-in-dying nonprofit, Compassion & Choices. C&C's lawyer, Kathryn Tucker, was Mark Connell's co-council in Montana. C&C's steady and practiced hands had ushered in both Oregon's and Washington's ballot initiatives. I attended the C&C annual conference in Chicago in June 2012. In fact, I presented at it. I'd struck up an online friendship with Carla Axtman, who was then C&C's online community coordinator. She had been helpful when I was arranging interviews across the country for research or articles, and I genuinely liked her; we'd spoken on the phone numerous times and I appreciated her feedback on what I was doing and who I was talking to. Yet, I always kept a wary eye on C&C's political objectives. I knew I wasn't an activist, at least not in the way that they thought I could be. More than once, I'd gotten a call from Carla or someone at the organization who challenged my use of the term "assisted suicide" in print. I balked at the oversight of my journalism. Theoretically, I was comfortable with the term; suicide has been contested, permitted, and even revered throughout human history. But politically, C&C was deeply invested in using "aid in dying." How the issue was worded made an undeniable difference in the support C&C could claim. As with the rental car clerk's reaction, "assisted suicide" is tainted by the stigma surrounding suicide. The terms that one uses—*death with dignity, aid in dying, assisted suicide, euthanasia*—often indicate the user's position on legalization. (I use the first three interchangeably because I view suicide as a tragedy that should be prevented, but also, depending on the circumstances, as a person's rational choice. Legal aid in dying in Europe is called euthanasia, despite the continent's World War II experience during the Holocaust.) The latter two terms, assisted suicide and euthanasia, when undefined, are often seen as immoral, the history of the terms as corrupt and inhumane. But when aid in dying is explained, most tend to favor legalization. As a June 2014 Gallup poll shows, a majority of the American public approves of aid in dying (70 percent, up from 50 percent in the 1970s) if it is worded as a doctor "being allowed to end a patient's life by some painless means if the patient and his or her family requests it." When asked if they support "doctor-assisted suicide," only 51 percent approve.

I'd met Carla in person at the C&C "Symposium on End-of-Life Advocacy" in Washington, DC, in 2009. Big-toothed, gregarious, and tireless, she exuded conviction in her organization's cause. Carla asked if I'd do a brief presentation in Chicago on how to sign up and use Twitter, a then-new social media tool that C&C saw as potentially helpful for advocates. In the spirit of "the more information the better" and as thanks to Carla, I said yes. Attendees—most white, most over fifty—had taken over the Hyatt Regency O'Hare Hotel, a monolithic, poured-concrete structure in the no-man's-land between Chicago's airport and downtown. The city was hot as blue blazes that week; stepping outside was like having all the air sucked out of you. A trip to diners, cafés, anything other than the hotel and surrounding banal business parks, required a car. I resigned myself to the air-conditioned comfort of my room.

I was cranky and tired for most of the three-day event, "Heights of Compassion, Bridges to Choice," a title that sounded a little treacly to me. By then I was accustomed to the language and issues that the organization pursued while tacking through the tricky political and legal landscape toward legalization. Compassion & Choices, in some form or another, has been around since the 1980s when Derek Humphry founded the Hemlock Society in Santa Monica. He also authored *Final Exit*, the book I gave my father when he began to talk about killing himself to escape his terminal cancer. Humphry is a controversial figure, but it's hard to tell fact from fiction in the stories most told about him. In a video made before her death, Humphry's ex-wife, Ann, accused him of "unwelcome pressures" to end her life. Humphry's do-it-yourself style, his embrace of the terms *euthanasia* and *suicide*, his lack of polish, came to be seen as a liability to the movement. What is sure is that he was a difficult and cantankerous character, not cut out to usher "aid in dying" onto the national stage and through the necessary political and legal hurdles. When Humphry left the organization in 1992, it was renamed Compassion in Dying. It merged with End of Life Choices in 2003, and the names were combined to form Compassion & Choices.

Many of the panels and presentations in Chicago sounded like a rallying cry for the troops, something I knew was absolutely necessary to an advocacy organization. Yet, I wanted to talk about the deeper issues underlying the curated message. Dear Abby—aka Abigail Van Buren, aka Jeanne Phillips—gave the opening address Thursday night. She was delightful and rousing. But the panel that caught my attention was presented on the last day, "Bioethics & End-of-Life Choice." It was the bioethics, the larger ethical considerations of aid in dying, that interested me. The copresenters were Thaddeus Pope, director of the Health Law Institute at Hamline University, who I knew from his "Medical Futility Blog," a site that examines the legal issues surrounding futile care, and Sue Porter, a sprightly woman who was on the board of C&C. I recognized Sue from her appearance in the documentary *How to Die in Oregon*, a film that had won the Sundance Grand Jury prize when it was released the year before. Sue lived in Oregon and had long been a counselor to dying patients on end-of-life services. In 1994, when Oregon legalized aid in dying, she also began helping dying patients use the Death with Dignity law. "What are the many considerations terminally ill people face when deciding to end their lives with a lethal prescription?" the panel synopsis asks.

Plenty of my hospice patients had told me they wanted to die. Sue's clear, straight talk about how to legalize such a bill in other states, and practical description of what patients in Oregon faced, was refreshing. In an opening scene of *How to Die in Oregon*, Sue's hands are shown dumping the white powder from pill after pill into a small, clear bowl, then mixing it with water from a sink. The spoon clinks on the glass. Below large windows in the next room, a man—white, about sixty-five or so (it's hard to tell, he's dying)—sits on a bed with his hands in his lap. His family members, of all ages, stand around him.

Sue leans in, her hands on her own knees, to look him in the eye. She's prim, in a gray sweater and necklace; her hair, nails, and makeup are perfect. She's calm. She says, "Before you take the medication, I'm going to ask you those two questions again. Do you know you have the right to change your mind?" Sue nods her head with each clearly articulated word.

"My mind's not changing," he says immediately, emphatically.

"And what will this medication do?" she asks.

"It will kill me and make me happy," he says.

Sue drops her head. I understood at once that she knew dying.

In the spring of 2013, I was teaching a journalism class at Drew University in New Jersey. I called it The End Is Near: Writing About Death, Dying and Destruction in Contemporary America. We read mostly long-form journalism that addressed suicide, war, murder, military post-traumatic stress disorder, and plane crashes. In one of the last classes, I asked Sue to join me for a screening of *How to Die in Oregon*. She was in New York to see friends and participate in a bike ride through the city's boroughs. She came into class with a box of tissues. *How to Die* examines the legalization of aid in dying in Oregon through the story of a terminally ill woman named Cody. Young and in her fifties, with the kind of beauty a camera loves, Cody struggles with her pain. We watch as she cycles through anger, hurt, and resignation. When she decides to take the lethal drugs, the camera trains on her bedroom window from the outside, but we hear her last words to her family. Despite seeing the film multiple times, I cried my eyes out in class. So did Sue. Cody's death is heart wrenching. But the students weren't as affected as she or I had expected. I wondered if, even after months of reading about death and dying, after a mere eighteen years of life, they were still grappling to understand what it's like to die. Sure some of them had lost grandparents, but for the most part, they didn't have the store of emotion, from either facing their own mortality or the absence of a loved one, for the movie to tap into.

During the train ride to and from Madison, New Jersey, Sue and I chatted about Compassion & Choices and new developments in the aid-in-dying movement. Sue was about to publish an article, titled

"Unintended Consequences: Obstruction of Patient Choice," that examined religious influence on health care, particularly on the informed
consent of patients in facilities that were managed by the Catholic
Church, which opposes aid in dying, even in states where it is legal.
"As Catholic hospitals merge with financially imperiled medical centers or acquire independent medical practices, they are instituting religious policies which prohibit doctors from any participation with
DWD," wrote Sue, referring to Death with Dignity. She was identifying a problem that had been spreading across the country, one
that reproductive rights advocates have been decrying for some time:
Catholic institutions prohibit their staff and doctors from discussing
medical treatments like abortion and aid in dying. What was legal was
not necessary accessible to patients in those institutions.

The discussion of whose conscience is most important—that of
the Vatican, hospital doctors, staff and administrators, or patients—is
now a common one to those who have been watching the Obama administration and the US Supreme Court struggle with cases involving
Hobby Lobby and Little Sisters of the Poor. The for-profit craft-store
chain and the nonprofit religious order both challenged the contraception mandate in the Affordable Care Act. The mandate would have
allowed millions of women to receive insurance coverage for contraception. Sue saw such challenges now directly affecting patients' access
to aid in dying because they established a hierarchy of conscience.
Corporations and religious institutions could interject their own beliefs into the privacy of the patient-doctor relationship.

Yet, the aid-in-dying movement continues to gain momentum,
perhaps, some would say, because patients fear the loss of control
exemplified in these cases. They feel that law and medicine—and now
their employers—have all got a hand in their health decisions, when
really what patients want is privacy and control. In May 2013, Vermont
became the first state to legalize aid in dying via the legislature. In the
January 2014 court decision, Judge Nan G. Nash ruled in the second

district court outside of Albuquerque, New Mexico, that "this court cannot envision a right more fundamental, more private or more integral to the liberty, safety and happiness of a New Mexican than the right of a competent, terminally ill patient to choose aid in dying." The case is now on appeal to the New Mexico Supreme Court. The next month, the *New York Times* featured a front-page article, "'Aid in Dying' Movement Takes Hold in Some States." I talked with Sue the day after it was published. She saw it as a positive sign that the paper used "aid in dying" instead of "assisted suicide." I was happy to finally see national reporting on the issue, reporting that didn't gravitate toward spectacle or disregard what patients were experiencing. Rather, it examined the loss and pain of desperate, dying patients.

On August 15, 2012, eight months after my trip to Montana, I flew to Washington State. By the time I met Robb Miller in his modest office on the second floor of a brick building in Seattle, I had seen him speak at several Compassion & Choices conferences. He's a small man, lean and athletic, always immaculately dressed. He has a ruddy complexion and short brown hair. Miller became executive director of Compassion & Choices of Washington in 2000 and spearheaded Initiative 1000, which made aid in dying legal there. The protracted deaths of two people propelled him into his advocacy: that of his father who was diagnosed with terminal cancer in 1994, and that of his longtime partner who was diagnosed with AIDS in 1995.

There is a reason why AIDS changed the end-of-life landscape forever. AIDS patients were young and their bodies were strong; their deaths were long and grueling, accompanied by internal bleeding, tumors, starvation, and a weakened immune system unable to fight otherwise curable illnesses like tuberculosis and pneumonia. The mysterious disease allowed many to project fear and hatred onto the gay community. A Public Religion Research Institute poll shows that, in 1992, 36 percent of Americans thought AIDS was God's punishment for immoral sexual behavior. In 2013, 14 percent did. Ian Dowbiggin, a professor of history at the University of Prince Edward Island, writes in *A Concise History of Euthanasia*, "As AIDS cut its lethal swath through the world's homosexual communities in the 1980s and 1990s, it helped to energize what had come to be called the right-to-die movement." Families and caregivers couldn't just watch their loved ones suffer so excruciatingly. Some patients, knowing what horror was coming, looked for lethal drugs illegally.

Next to the photo of Robert Baxter that I keep taped by my desk is a photo taken in 1990 by Therese Frare, then a student at Ohio University and a volunteer at Pater Noster House, an AIDS hospice in Columbus. The photo is black-and-white and shows the deathbed of David Kirby. His emaciation is breathtaking. He stares into the middle distance, eyes lost and blank but open. The skin of his face is stretched tautly over his cheekbones, his mouth is open, his jaw has already slackened. His hands are twisted and curled inward on his chest. Kirby's father, Bill, his face in anguish, touches his forehead to his son's as he cups his thick hand around David's hollow face. David's sister, Susan, and her daughter hold each other and watch. In many ways, the image is reminiscent of deathbed photos from a time gone by, when people died at home with their family, young and old, gathered to witness last breaths. The photo was published in the November 1990 issue of *Life* magazine and was picked up by countless newspapers, TV stations, and magazines across the country, thus humanizing the tragedy that families were experiencing because of AIDS. Twenty-five years later, *Life* posted the photo online, calling it "the photo that changed the face of AIDS." It's now been seen by more than a billion people.

Miller watched the epidemic from his partner's bedside. "I realized that hospice couldn't manage all of my partner's suffering. He was agitated, he was in pain, he had dementia in the last months of his life. I mean I don't need to give you the laundry list of suffering," Miller told me, never mentioning his partner's name. "I was promised one thing, and something else entirely happened. Hospice was a hollow promise. He died eighteen months after he was diagnosed, and he had an egregious death." Miller told me that he felt like they were abandoned by hospice. "They didn't stop providing care, but they did abandon us in terms of our wanting information about aid in dying or how to end his suffering. That's really what made me an activist for choice in dying."

It was a relief for me to hear Miller say this. For years, I'd carried around the image of my father writhing on his bed. Our betrayal of his last wish to die at home. Hospice's inability to give us drugs strong enough to keep him calm. While my father might never have pursued aid in dying had it been legal in Pennsylvania, he was in pain. He did not die a peaceful death. Some of that suffering could have been according to his wish, but I had to wonder, how much of it could we have done away with if hospice had a more inclusive understanding of end-of-life options. The founder of modern hospice, the British doctor Cicely Saunders, was a staunch and vocal opponent of what she called "euthanasia." She felt that pain and suffering could always be addressed, and while she credited both sides with advocating for the end of patients' suffering, she felt that, because of her Christian faith, because of her own projected idea of a good death, that aid in dying was immoral. Miller was the first person I had found who was able to clearly articulate why sometimes hospice is not enough.

Miller told me that he was a strong supporter of hospice—around 90 percent of the patients he advocated for were enrolled in hospice care—but found that it wasn't the right solution for everyone. Even if a patient's physical pain and symptoms could be managed, existential suffering—caused by dependence on others, loss of abilities—could still make life unbearable. Miller told me, "Opponents of aid in dying seize on the dependence on other people and they say, 'What's the shame in that?' or 'What's wrong with that?' Well, there's nothing wrong with it, but if you're a person who's been independent all of your life and the idea of not being able to take care of your most fundamental physical needs is abhorrent to you, then that's a problem for you. That's a form of suffering. Being that dependent on people."

I had asked Mark Connell, who spent much of his professional life representing personal injury cases, what the difference was between pain and suffering. The first was physical, he told me. The second was everything else—the sadness, the loss of control, the time in bed, the fear of what was to come, the dependence on family for basic needs— and that, too, was painful.

"Opponents often misrepresent hospice and palliative care as the alternative to aid in dying. They have a rather romantic idea of how people should die," Miller told me. "They believe in the idea of personal growth occurring at the end of life, that it prepares someone to die." Hospice workers wanted patients to talk about how they were feeling, to say their last goodbyes, to love and forgive family and friends, to seek love and forgiveness. I knew what he was talking about. As a hospice volunteer, I often felt as if my charge was not to just hold hands, but also to lead patients down a particular path that hospice considered the way to a good death. "The idea permeates hospice and palliative care, that if that period of personal growth is short-circuited by aid in dying," Miller said, "the patient is denied this spiritual growth and journey. Reviewing your life and all of those things. It's arrogant."

Through his work as a steering committee member with the Washington End of Life Consensus Coalition, sponsored by the Washington State Medical Association, Miller has gotten to know the medical and hospice entities in the state. While the WSMA did not support Initiative 1000—in fact, a poll at the time showing the support of a majority of its members pulled the rug out from under its opposition—Miller and Compassion & Choices of Washington now work with WSMA on other end-of-life issues, like access to hospice and palliative care and communication with patients about end of life. As a member of the POLST task force, Miller played a role in helping to bring POLST forms to the state. He also works with the state hospice association. It too was opposed to legalization of aid in dying but didn't campaign against it. A majority of the hospice facilities in its membership are Catholic affiliated. The president of the board is also director of a Catholic hospice.

Miller's advocacy, his life's work, is to give patients the autonomy to decide what medical treatments, including aid in dying, they want and to deny the ones they don't. Without moral or legal judgment. His work was profound to me; he wanted everyone to have the right to say how much pain—whether physical or emotional—we could stand.

CHAPTER FIVE

Hunger and Thirst

The Village at Alameda is an assisted-living home on Horizon Boulevard on the northern edge of Albuquerque, New Mexico. Balloon Fiesta Park, with walking paths and a museum, is across the street. The Village's beige stucco walls and turquoise trim are exactly what you'd expect of an elder care facility in the Southwest: neat, well-kept, slightly bland in the harsh sunlight. Armond and Dorothy Rudolph moved to The Village when they were in their eighties, as their health began to decline. Armond had a permanent catheter (a tube that drained urine from his bladder), and Dorothy was almost completely immobile. Years before, they had talked to their family about how they wanted to die, not like Dorothy's mother who suffered from years of cancer and poor health. They didn't want to spend their last years unconscious, unable to communicate, in pain. When they began showing signs of early dementia, they knew it was time to enact their long-laid plans. In August 2011, they stopped eating and drinking. Three days later, when The Village learned of what the Rudolphs were doing, willfully ending their lives, staff called 911 to report a suicide attempt and evicted the couple. The Village feared the legal ramifications and bad publicity that the couple's deaths might bring.

Neil Rudolph, Armond and Dorothy's son, flew to Albuquerque from Colorado to help his parents find a rental home where they could spend their last days. Armond was ninety-two, Dorothy was ninety; they had been married sixty-nine years. With their family around them and hospice caregivers visiting, Armond died ten days after their fast began. Dorothy died the next day. "They did find the dignified and peaceful death they both sought, but it's also a cautionary tale," Neil told reporters. While voluntarily stopping eating and drinking (VSED) is legal in all states, even the best-laid plans to carry out a terminal fast can be upended.

I saw Neil speak a few months later at a Compassion & Choices event. He was working with the organization, a relationship his parents initiated years before, to promote VSED, a legal way for seniors to avoid long, slow deaths they did not want. He was a no-nonsense talker, maybe a reluctant activist like Roberta King, but one with the conviction that his parents should have been able to do what they wanted without interference. The objective of C&C's campaign, "Peace at Life's End. Anywhere," is to make seniors aware of their rights and to acknowledge that even using legal means of ending one's life can often be difficult. In a 2011 article by Mikaela Conley of ABC News, Neil said: "The Village at Alameda failed to respect my parents' autonomy, imposing tremendous stress upon them when they should have been supported, not thwarted. The Village is not unlike thousands of assisted-living facilities in the country. Nearly one million Americans live in these facilities, yet most don't know how their end-of-life rights could be infringed upon as my parents' were. Their eviction shocked me." It seemed to the Rudolphs that The Village was unnecessarily trying to cause them pain. They never imagined that their place of residence could tell them to eat or get out.

VSED has grown in popularity since Neil took up his parents' cause. By July 2014, the husband of NPR talk-show host Diane Rehm had been residing in an assisted-living facility for two years. He had

Parkinson's disease and was losing mental and physical abilities almost daily. "He just kept getting weaker," Diane Rehm told NBC News. "We called in the doctor and John said to him: 'I am ready today.' He said, 'I can no longer use my legs, I can no longer use my arms, I can no longer feed myself.' And knowing Parkinson's is going to get worse rather than better, he said, 'I [want] to die.'" He asked the doctor for help, but there was nothing he could do. With his wife's reluctant approval, John Rehm stopped eating and drinking, his only legal option. He knew what the later stages of Parkinson's looked like and he wanted no part of them. "I would like to, in every state across the country, in every city, in every county, I would very much like to see a justification, an allowance, for aid in dying," Diane Rehm told NBC reporter Maggie Fox in June 2014. John Rehm died nine days after giving up food and water. Because aid in dying is largely inaccessible in most of the United States, VSED allows patients to legally bring about their deaths when their lives are, in their own estimation, no longer worth living. Seniors and the ill who stop eating and drinking aren't afraid of death; they're afraid of what comes before it.

We wrongly believe that we have the freedom to do what we want with our bodies, that our medical choices are our own. Our sense of freedom and independence, particularly in the United States, often blinds us to the ways in which our medical choices are limited. Like the Rudolphs, we can make careful plans, we can decide when enough pain and suffering is enough, we can fill out the advanced directives, the living wills, we can have the talk with our families, and still our choices can be delayed, disrupted, or completely denied. Freedom of choice, personal autonomy, and informed consent are clearly not enough to protect us from futile care or treatments we don't want. For various reasons and in countless ways, the decisions we make about what is done to our bodies are qualified by forces often seemingly outside our control.

Identifying these forces is key to understanding why Americans don't die the way they want to and to creating a more just and humane way of dying. Roughly mapped, there are three interdependent institutions that have some form of jurisdiction over how we die: the medical industry, religion, and the law. Each of these regimes is a highly complex system with its own multitude of cultures and subcultures, histories, and varying proximity to our bodies. What I have so far called *medicine* or *the medical industry*, for instance, is made up of doctors, nurses, bioethicists, and health-care providers, but also medical schools, associations, insurance providers, device manufacturers, hospital directors, and pharmaceutical companies. Medicine also has an ethics, or moral principles, that govern both practice and theory. All these moving parts are separate but connected, couched within a history that is, at least regarding *modern* medicine, sixty to seventy years old. Too, there are myriad power structures within modern medicine, good and bad. A research team has the power to create new drugs that may slow the effects of Alzheimer's. A bioethicist may develop a way to think about access to scarce medicines. But, too, a pharmaceutical company may challenge the production of a generic drug that rivals its own more expensive product. Some of these powers are hard, with direct access or influence on us, like a hospital director's decision to institute a hand-washing policy for employees, or soft, with influential sway over decision making, like a new report that shows interns perform better when they work shorter shifts. Some are intentional, like a company's decision to lower a drug's price, or unintentional, like a shortage of geriatric nurses in the Southwest.

Like modern medicine, religion has its own history, subcultures, components (priests, pastors, laypersons, employees of religious organizations, church charities, theologians) and power structures. Denominational theologies vary greatly, and within them, there is dissent and change. Nontheological ideologies—*abortion is un-Christian* or *Catholic hospitals provide more charity*, for instance—dynamically imbue our understanding of behavior and moral values, whether true or false. St. Patrick's Hospital, across the street from the office of Mark Connell, the lawyer who presented the case to legalize aid in dying before the Montana Supreme Court, may theoretically be subject to the governance of the local Catholic bishop, but that doesn't mean that all who work there oppose tubal ligation. The influence of Catholic theology on, say, a pharmacist who works in a Catholic hospital and is asked to fill a birth control prescription, depends on his own religious conscience, a patient's willingness to report being turned away, the oversight of the pharmacist's boss, his ability to find a job elsewhere, or the laws in his state that decide if he can deny prescriptions.

The legal system is shorthand for not only cops on the street but lawyers; judges in district, state, and federal chambers; jails and prisons (wardens, security guards, inmates, contractors); advocacy groups; bail bondsmen; and the set of laws that each of these nodes is charged with upholding. But, too, it comprises the cultures inherent in each of these groups. The discipline of power (as opposed to the good works power can do) is more overt in the legal system because it is meant to react to social values regarding behavior and because it comprises case jurisprudence and state and federal laws that proscribe behavior. Laws, established by court case rulings and lawmakers—under pressure from society, their consciences, or other forces—are meant to punish particular behaviors and to dissuade others from behaving in particular ways.

What, then, prevented John Rehm from receiving a lethal prescription of morphine or Seconal or Pentobarbital from his doctor? "There was nothing he could do," Diane Rehm said about her husband's doctor. Medical ethics, as interpreted by the doctor, may not have permitted him to make the prescription. Or he may have been affiliated with a hospital that opposes aid in dying and could therefore have lost his job for complying with John's request. The doctor may have had (religious) opposition to aid in dying. The Rehms lived in Maryland, a state where it remains illegal. John's doctor may have feared prosecution.

Yet a Goucher poll from February 2015 found that 60 percent of Maryland residents support legalization of aid in dying there. When a bill was introduced in March 2015, the *Washington Post* reported: "Even if the controversial measure makes it through the General Assembly, Gov. Larry Hogan (R), who is a Catholic, said before he was elected that he would oppose attempts to legalize aid in dying. 'I believe a physician's role is to save lives, not terminate them,' Hogan told the *Catholic Standard*, an archdiocesan newspaper, in October." The entire quote, recorded in full in the *Catholic Standard*, but only in part in the *Post* article, reads, "I believe in the sanctity of human life, and I believe a physician's role is to save lives, not terminate them."

The moral values of American culture have profoundly shaped medicine and law, and their influence on personal choice. In their book *Love the Sin: Sexual Regulation and the Limits of Religious Tolerance*, Janet Jakobsen and Ann Pellegrini write that the story we tell ourselves about the separation of religion from public life is deceptive. Particular religious ideas hold vast sway over what actions and behaviors we deem as acceptable, despite our great pride in separation of church and state:

> Underreported in the usual way of telling this story of modernity are all the ways in which religious ideas about the body have continued to be enforced by the newly secularized state. This, then, is the "after-life" of religion in modernity: secularization has not so much meant the retreat of religion from the public sphere as its reinvention. This reinvention is accomplished through a conflation of religion and morality, in which morality is assumed to be the essence of religion and, conversely, moral proclamation can be a means of invoking religion without directly naming it. In other

words, under cover of an official secularism, particular religious claims about "the good life," the way things are or should be, can still remain operative.

John Rehm knew that his doctor was not able or prepared to give him a lethal dose of drugs. He knew what his coming days with Parkinson's would be like. He also knew that there was still one thing he could do, stop eating and drinking. His moral code permitted him to make that decision. The Rudolphs also ultimately found the knowledge and support to stop eating and drinking. But others have not been able to choose when to stop eating.

In the spring of 2012, I was researching a series of contentious court cases that led to the 2005 death of a patient who was in a persistent vegetative state (PVS). Patients with PVS may open their eyes, yawn, breathe, even follow a regular sleep schedule, but they are unaware of their environment. They cannot speak or follow commands; their brain functions are limited to those that continue basic bodily functions. PVS patients have no cognition, but to someone who is filled with hope, to someone who is unfamiliar with the diagnosis but intimately familiar with his or her loved one, a PVS patient can seem to show signs of life. The patient, Terri Schiavo, had been in a persistent vegetative state for fifteen years when a final court ruling allowed her feeding tube, which had kept her "alive" all those years, to be removed. The media fervor made the case hard to ignore; it was the third of three spectacular cases that involved young white women kept on machines. (Karen Ann Quinlan in 1985 and Nancy Cruzan in 1990 were the other two.) According to medical ethics, patients have the right to discontinue—or not accept—any medical treatment they don't want. The principles of autonomy and informed consent intertwine to protect patient choice. But they're both complicated when a patient is not conscious or has not left explicit instructions that apply to her eventual medical situation.

In all three cases, the rulings to allow removal of "life support," a term that is currently in flux and often replaced with "physiological support," were based on a combination of patient privacy and informed consent. Family members proved that the women would not have wanted to live *like that*, as biological bodies—living, yes—but without sentience. The courts honored patient-doctor privacy based on that proof. What the media frenzy asked the public was something different: would you want to be kept alive in this way? The public resoundingly said no. Opponents and supporters alike asked: what is alive? The question deeply divided their two camps. One saw "alive" as having some form of consciousness; the other saw it as a beating heart, not a working brain. While the public discussed quality of life, the courts discussed privacy and autonomy. The Cruzan case established a precedent regarding feeding tubes; it considered them medical care, not comfort care, as opponents of removal had sought. If artificial nutrition and hydration, feeding tubes that are often inserted surgically into the stomach to decrease the risk of infection during long-term use, were considered comfort care, society (by the means of the state and the hospital) would be obligated to provide it. But the courts said feeding tubes were medical treatments and therefore something that individuals could deny.

The Cruzan case was a milestone for medical ethics, a theoretical and practical body of guidelines that exists as a guide for doctors and lawyers. But it didn't prevent the Schiavo case from being pushed around the courts only a few years later. And what about the thousands of other PVS patients in the United States, their bodily functions sustained by feeding tubes (and sometimes ventilators)? Estimates of their numbers vary widely, ranging from ten to fifty to a hundred thousand. Looking at the use of feeding tubes against this backdrop, I asked myself where else a patient could be fed *against her will*.

Only a few months after the death of Schiavo in March 2005, US news media reported that prisoners at Guantánamo Bay, a military prison in Cuba, were on a hunger strike. These prisoners, who protested both their incarceration and the conditions of the Guantánamo facility, were force-fed, a practice that is highly controversial across the globe and considered by most medical bodies to be torture in prison settings. Yet, the military found legal justification for the feedings in nonmilitary prisons in the United States and established it in their standard operating procedures for Guantánamo. I searched for a case of force-feeding on US soil and quickly found it: Bill Coleman in Connecticut.

On October 23, 2008, Bill Coleman was taken by prison medical staff and guards from his solitary cell to an examination room. He was strapped to a table and told that he was going to be fed. He was scared; he tried to stay calm. He told them he didn't want to be fed. Edward Blanchette, the prison medical director, told him that it wasn't up to him. The warden of Garner Correctional Institution, Scott Semple, had received a warrant from a district judge to force-feed Coleman on the grounds that Coleman's health was in jeopardy. He had stopped eating over a year earlier, on September 17, 2007, to protest what he considered a wrongful conviction. He had been found guilty of raping his wife. The only way that he had to protest, to exercise his First Amendment right to free speech, was to stop eating. To put his body in jeopardy. Doing so, to Coleman, was preferable to living as a prisoner, guilty of a crime he said he didn't commit. He didn't want to die; he wanted to live to see his two sons. But he felt he had no other way to challenge his conviction. Hunger striking was his last option for bringing attention to his plight. Now, sitting on the examination table, Coleman was shocked. In the United States, force-feeding has a long and contested history and is today reserved for the physically and mentally ill. A British citizen, Coleman thought that it was an outdated and inhumane treatment no longer practiced in the West. Staff proceeded to strap him down at four points and turn off the video camera.

Blanchette pushed a rubber tube up Coleman's right nostril, but the tube kinked. Blanchette pushed harder. When Coleman winced and twitched in pain, staff thought he was resisting and strapped a webbed restraint across his chest. One assistant held his head. Coleman gagged, Blanchette pushed. Finally the doctor realized that the tube had kinked; he removed it and inserted a second tube up Coleman's nose, down his throat, and into his stomach. Then Blanchette poured a can of Ensure, a nutrient drink, into the tube. Coleman gagged, he puked, his nose bled. Snot, saliva, vomit, and blood filled the cuffs of his sweatshirt as they led him back to his cell.

Over the next few years, staff force-fed Coleman more than a dozen times. The first experience was enough to compel him to drink for a while. Water, milk. But each time he stopped taking liquids, the staff walked him to the same examination room. He had lost over half of his body weight; he now weighed 106 pounds. He had a constant throbbing in his head and his blood pressure was too high; his mouth tasted of starvation, and his right nostril could no longer be used for feedings; he was so lethargic that walking was difficult. Still he refused to eat. No one knew how much damage had been done to his organs from malnutrition. He'd lost several teeth. In newspaper photos, taken during court appearances, he looks wan, weak, and exhausted. Still he didn't eat.

By the time I got in touch with Coleman, he had been on a hunger strike for more than five years. He had no more legal options for appeal. His lawyer, David McGuire, at the American Civil Liberties Union (ACLU) of Connecticut, gave me Coleman's address. I wrote a letter to Coleman asking if I could visit. I wrote a letter to Warden Semple with the same request. "It is the collective consensus that permitting your interview to take place would only further exacerbate inmate Coleman's condition, and we do not wish to contribute to his detriment," Semple promptly replied.

His detriment. The words chilled me. Semple's paternal "protection" of Coleman's interests defied Coleman's stated interests. Semple knew best, or he thought he did. And he had the power to enforce Bill's actions—and mine. Bill and I continued to exchange letters. I have stacks of them, dozens. In them, Bill is articulate, frantic, and exhausted in turns. The letters include descriptions of his daily life, documents from his trials—highlighted, starred, underlined—photocopied prison regulations, descriptions of his force-feedings, and vows to continue his strike. On each envelope, he has scribbled the date over the back flap so delays in mailing and opening by prison staff can be detected. He hints at things that he wants to tell me but, for privacy, made me call his lawyer to find out.

Then he put me on his phone list, using a prison phone service, Securus, which allows outsiders to put money into an account that enables prisoners to call them. A recording frequently interrupted our talk: "This call is being monitored." Coleman and I spoke every Tuesday and Thursday for the next twelve months. Calls were limited to fifteen minutes, so we spoke frantically, planning questions and comments in advance. I knew that he wanted me to take up his criminal case, but it was his other conviction, to not eat, that consumed me. His desperation, his denial of the one indulgence he had in prison, food—and for nearly six years—haunted me. Every sandwich I took a bite of, every fancy dinner I shared with friends, every potato chip I put to my lips, I thought of Coleman. "I want them to reexamine my case or to honor my living will and let me die," he told me.

There are two places in the United States where persons can be force-fed, where their autonomy is suspended by institutions, where persons are not free to choose what does or does not enter their body: a Catholic hospital and a prison. The case of Schiavo was complicated; while she was unconscious, the courts ultimately determined that she would not have wanted to be kept alive on a feeding tube. Across the country, thousands of other patients—whose families did not know their desires or didn't have the resources to stop continued intubation—are kept on physiological support. Their bodies are bathed, their soiled diapers are changed, they are rolled from side to side to prevent bedsores (if they are lucky), all by professionals in facilities. Like Schiavo, they are unaware of their surroundings, of their care, of the lives they led before. They are a new category of human life, one that few agree is, indeed, life.

Bill's case was similar to Schiavo's in one way: he was legally force-fed by an institution that considered his autonomy, his most private desire to not eat, to be secondary to its own concerns. Schiavo's wish was articulated by her husband, her legal medical proxy. Bill said loudly and clearly to everyone who met him that he did not want to be force-fed. In a 2005 paper in the *Stanford Law Review*, "Testing Cruzan: Prisoners and the Constitutional Question of Self-Starvation," lawyer Mara Silver examines US jurisprudence regarding autonomy for prisoners. Despite clear rulings in the cases of *Cruzan* and *Glucksberg* (a US Supreme Court case that ruled aid in dying was not constitutional, but reiterated *Cruzan* by stating that patients have a right to accept or deny any medical treatment), Silver writes, "Still, only a few state courts have refused to condone the procedure. Every federal court to address the issue has sanctioned the force-feeding of a prisoner." She concludes that this is because the rights of prisoners are considered less important than prison safety or security. Yet, wardens, who often have relationships with district justices from whom they seek force-feeding orders, have never proven that hunger strikes disrupt prison settings. Another reason claimed by wardens and supported by courts is the state's obligation to protect life by preventing suicide, an argument that becomes murky, particularly when a prisoner is on death row. The power and order of the prison legitimizes its actions; force-feeding is then characterized as humane and what's best for the prisoner. Punishment for a crime requires no action by the offender other than "doing the time," Silver writes. Starving oneself to death deprives the state of that time.

What, I asked, could we learn from comparing the use of feeding tubes in hospitals and in prisons? Movements for patient autonomy and informed consent developed in Westernized countries during the 1960s and 70s. Women's and civil rights activism countered medicine's paternalism. In 1972, the Tuskegee syphilis experiments, in which patients, most often poor black sharecroppers, had been observed but not treated for syphilis, were reported in the media. Women's lack of informed consent—at a time when a patient could go into the hospital for a biopsy and wake up from anesthesia with a full mastectomy—alarmed the public. Medical ethics was forced to acknowledge such injustices. But no such movement championed autonomy for prisoners.

Both institutions had religious origins. Priests and nuns set up early hospitals to care for the impoverished. Prisons were considered "a more humane form of punishment, a more Christian alternative" to Europe's "casual brutality of corporal punishment," writes Winnifred Fallers Sullivan in *Prison Religion: Faith-Based Reform and the Constitution*.

The modern state, she notes, "is also perhaps at its most religious when it exerts total control over its citizens and attempts to coercively remake them into new human beings. Religious and political authority and sovereignty in prison are homologous with each other in several ways: state/church, judge/god, crime/sin, prisoner/penitent." Both demand that the patient/prisoner improve, rehabilitate, and behave according to the demands of their institution. Today, about 20 percent of US hospital beds are managed by institutions with a religious affiliation. Even those that aren't religiously affiliated employ and serve those with various religious identities. Almost every hospital provides chaplaincy services. It's therefore rightly impossible to remove religion from the hospital setting; yet to acknowledge that morals and values vary greatly requires subtlety and a historical understanding of how American morals developed. In *After the Wrath of God: AIDS, Sexuality, and American Religion*, Anthony Petro writes that the term morality "doubles as both a religious and secular concept, often becoming the site of transition between the two. This is particularly true for moral claims about health." In the hospital setting, where the mission is to provide quality medical care as well as compassion and dignity, the slippage between secular and religious concepts of moral behavior is pronounced.

Arthur Caplan, head of the Division of Bioethics at New York University's Langone Medical Center, condemned Coleman's force-feeding to the media, saying it recalled the United Kingdom's contested history with force-feeding and the hunger-strike death of Bobby Sands and other Irish Republicans when Margaret Thatcher refused to give in to their demands. Caplan attended one of Coleman's hearings to testify on his behalf.

When I asked Caplan to describe Coleman for me, he said, "He was smart, certainly read all the relevant documents and medical association codes of ethics, all the literature on Terri Schiavo. He knew his stuff." That stuff was a body of jurisprudence in the United States that had been settled in the courts for years but had never been applied to prisoners. At the time I met with Caplan, Coleman was off liquids again. He had told me that the medical staff was feeding him a little bit and then letting him go for days. Coleman called it the "torture gap." "Cruel," Caplan said. "They're letting him slide. If you're gonna feed him, then feed him. If you're gonna sort of dangle him out there . . . it's cruel."

I met with Jacob Appel, a bioethicist and psychologist at Mount Sinai Hospital in New York, a few days after speaking with Caplan. Appel had written an article, "Beyond Guantanamo: Torture Thrives in Connecticut," about Coleman's case, and he was about to publish an academic article titled "Rethinking Force Feeding: Legal and Ethical Aspects of Physician Participation in the Termination of Hunger Strikes in American Prisons," which examined doctors' participation in force-feedings. In it, Appel writes that US courts continue to wrongly frame the debate as "a conflict between the life threatening choice of the individual strikers and the life preserving actions of the providers." Patient autonomy and bodily integrity are the wrong "vantage point," he argues. The best way to consider hunger strikers, he concludes, is within the broad and long history of hunger striking as "a form of political or social protest that only secondarily harms the protester, rather than the sort of suicidal action that has historically invited state and medical intervention." Essentially, hunger striking is free speech. As our conversation was ending, Appel said, "I would add, for what it's worth, once in my life I put a feeding tube in someone who didn't want it. Ethically, it wasn't a transgression—we were honoring his [earlier stated] wishes—but practically it was one of the most unpleasant things I've done in my life. I would never do it again, even if somebody wanted me to."

Medical ethicists like Caplan and Appel, doctors, and medical associations, in the United States and abroad, resoundingly consider nasogastric feedings—a tube inserted through the nose—to be torture when used on hunger strikers. In 2006, a group of more than 250 international doctors wrote an open letter in the *Lancet*, a British medical journal, decrying the force-feedings at Guantánamo. "Fundamental to doctors' responsibilities in attending a hunger striker is the recognition that prisoners have a right to refuse treatment," they wrote. The doctors called on the American Medical Association to sanction professionals who participated in the feedings. They condemned the military's screening of health-care workers before employment at Guantánamo to ensure that they had no ethical qualms with "assisted" feeding.

In January 2014, I drove to Connecticut to attend Coleman's hearing. His sentence had ended, but because he refused to sign the sexual offender list, he was given a warrant for five more years inside before ever leaving prison walls. He refused to sign because he said he didn't want to leave a guilty man; he refused to sign because he said he wasn't a sexual offender. I drove the five hours from Brooklyn to northern Connecticut in a torrent of rain. I was nervous. This would be my first time meeting Bill after months of regular communication. At the courthouse, between cases, a bailiff walked over to me, looked long and hard at my notebook and pen, and asked who I was there to see. I told him and he left the room. When he returned, he told me Coleman was "in the house," but that his case had been postponed. "As you can see, they are up to something," Coleman wrote to me the next week. His paranoia was infectious.

I never did get to meet Bill. He was deported at the end of June 2014. From a US prison to a UK hospital. He was staying with his sister, Nandy, the last we chatted on Facebook. In one of his profile photos, he's still pale, but his cheeks are slightly fuller. He's holding up a frothy glass of Guinness beer and smiling. I may never know if Bill is innocent or guilty. What I do know is that he served more than eight years in a Connecticut prison for raping his wife. And for most of the years he was there, he was force-fed by court order, a procedure that most of the world considers torture, whether the prisoner is guilty or innocent.

Terri Schiavo's death was particularly poignant for me. It consumed the media in the spring of 2005, as my father's health continued to decline. His options for stopping his non-Hodgkin's lymphoma had run out, and he told us that when we were home for our family's annual Easter gathering, he wanted to discuss his will. We celebrated the holiday, which occurred at the end of March, early that year, with ham loaf and Amish crackers, the traditional fare of our Mennonite family. And we doted on my ninety-five-year-old grandfather whom we'd sprung from the Lancaster Mennonite Home for the day. After waving goodbye to our aunts, uncles, and cousins, after clearing the tables and washing the dishes, Dad sat us down to discuss his will. He pulled the bound pages from a manila envelope. On the TV behind us, reporters interviewed protesters about their views on the removal of Schiavo's feeding tube as Dad told us that he wanted to be cremated, what his exact financial assets were, what would happen to the house we were in. Conservative senators and representatives made impassioned pleas for Schiavo's life as we sobbed, embracing each other and our grief. Our grandfather died two days later. Our family gathered again for his funeral. I watched my father as he sat next to me in the church pew during the memorial service. I knew that my turn was imminent.

Schiavo had collapsed in the kitchen of her home early one February morning in 1990. She had stopped breathing for more than four minutes, a period of time that doctors roughly consider the window within which patients can recover. Her husband had found her on the floor and called 911. When paramedics arrived, they resuscitated her heart beat and breathing and rushed her to a nearby hospital, where she was eventually given a feeding tube. For years, Terri's husband and her family, the Schindlers, attended her, hoping that therapy would restore her consciousness. But ultimately, Michael Schiavo accepted that his wife would not recover. Her family, Roman Catholics, did not. They became estranged when Michael sought to legally have Terri's feeding tube removed.

What unfolded after their rift is the stuff of legal, political, medical, and personal nightmares. Michael, his wife's legal guardian, received permission from a district judge in 2001 to remove Terri's feeding tube after providing witnesses and evidence that she would have wanted it. The tube was removed, but two days later, the Schindlers appealed the decision, saying that "Terri was a devout Roman Catholic who would not wish to violate the Church's teachings on euthanasia by refusing nutrition and hydration." The feeding tube was reinserted.

Again in 2003, Michael received court permission to have his wife's feeding tube removed. While the decision was on appeal, the Schindlers recruited Randall Terry, an antiabortion activist who had founded Operation Rescue, an organization known for staging protests and garnering media attention, to take up their cause. If the courts were not able to help them, they were willing to appeal to the broader public. Terry arranged vigils and protests outside the hospice where Terri Schiavo was a patient and put pressure on Florida governor Jeb Bush, a "pro-life" Republican and brother of the sitting president. Jeb Bush called a special legislative session the night of Sunday, October 19, 2003, and "Terri's Law," which overrode the courts and ordered the tube again be reinstated, was passed unanimously the following afternoon. Two hours later, the hospice was served with an order to reinstate the tube. Terri Schiavo's longtime doctor chose to resign rather than do so; another doctor at the facility performed the reinsertion.

But in 2004, the Florida Supreme Court overturned Terri's Law, ruling it unconstitutional. Governor Bush tried to appeal, but the US Supreme Court refused to hear the case. A new date was set for final removal by Florida District Judge George Greer: March 18 at 1 p.m. With no remaining options, the Schindlers met with the governor and other important officials. They enlisted the support of key antiabortion legislators, and House Majority Leader Tom DeLay headed an effort, according to William Colby in *Unplugged: Reclaiming our Right to Die in America*, to "pass a bill that would move the Schiavo case to federal courts," an effort meant to bypass Greer's chamber. Although most legislators had already headed home for the Easter break, those who remained decided in the early morning hours of Friday, March 18, to issue subpoenas "to trigger federal protection for Terri Schiavo." But one week later, writes Colby, Judge Greer called a hearing to tell federal legislators they had no jurisdiction in the case. "My order will stand," he told them.

An hour later, Terri Schiavo's feeding tube was again removed. Legislators called a "rare Saturday night session of the US Senate that was attended by only three senators, Senate Majority Leader Bill Frist, Mel Martinez of Florida, and John Warner from Virginia. Senator Frist said, 'Under the legislation we will soon consider, Terri Schiavo will have another chance,'" Colby writes. The federal law, titled "For the relief of the parents of Theresa Marie Schiavo," was brought before emergency sessions in both the House and Senate the following day, Palm Sunday. The Senate passed the bill, which became known as the Palm Sunday Compromise, unanimously, but in the House, the bill was blocked by eight Democrats who challenged it on weekend rules, requiring house leaders to wait until after midnight to pass it. President George W. Bush, informed of the bill's progress, curtailed his vacation and returned to Washington that day to sign it.

In the US House on Sunday night, DeLay stood to say, according to a CNN transcript of the session, "A young woman in Florida is being dehydrated and starved to death. For fifty-eight long hours her mouth has been parched and her hunger pains have been throbbing. If we do not act she will die of thirst. However helpless, Mr. Speaker, she is alive. She is still one of us. And this cannot stand. Terri Schiavo has survived her passion weekend and she has not been forsaken. No more words, Mr. Speaker. She's waiting. The members are here. The hour has come. Mr. Speaker, call the vote." The bill was passed at 12:41 a.m., and President Bush signed it into law at 1:11 a.m. But repeatedly, federal and Florida district judges refused to recognize the bill. New appeals were submitted and turned down. New bills, hastily written and frantically debated, failed to pass in Florida. Governor Bush threatened to use the Department of Children and Families to take custody of Schiavo by order. David Gibbs, the Schindler's lawyer and president of the Christian Law Association, called Michael Schiavo a "murderer." More motions were submitted and denied. Protesters called hospice workers "Nazis," "cowards," and "murderers."

Judge Greer wore a bullet-proof vest. His wife received a delivery of dead flowers; a card tucked into them read "no food, no water." At the Schindlers' request, the Reverend Jesse Jackson flew to Florida. Father Frank Pavone, national director of Priests for Life and president of the National Pro-Life Religious Council, accompanied Terri's siblings, Bobby and Suzanne, on their last visit to their sister's room. Terri Schiavo died on March 31, thirteen days after her feeding tube was removed.

To the Catholic Church, the Quinlan and Cruzan cases were tragedies, but Schiavo's death proved a pattern, one it needed to take action to stop. The recent legalization of aid in dying in Oregon, a practice that the church considered, like removal of Schiavo's tube, to be "euthanasia," compounded their need to address end-of-life issues. As the second-largest provider of health care in the United States (Veteran's Affairs is the first), church leaders realized that their authority was being challenged by the US justice system. Terri's parents, Robert and Mary, and siblings, Bobby and Suzanne, felt that Terri was not terminal, that with proper care she could have lived a long and healthy life. They insisted that she had been conscious and able to recognize them. Bobby Schindler has since said that his sister was killed by the state.

An autopsy performed on Terri Schiavo after her death definitively proved that she was incapable of feeling pain; in the years after her debilitating injury, her brain had atrophied to the point where only part of her brain stem remained.

The Terri Schiavo Life & Hope Network was founded by the Schindlers in the wake of Terri's death to represent those in similar situations and prevent the removal of respirators and feeding tubes from unconscious patients. The network raises funds from its listserv and mailing-list members, and connects patients' families to health-care facilities that share their view of removal from physiological support—that it should not be done until the heart has stopped beating, even if that heart is artificially assisted. Over the years, the network has played a role in a handful of high-profile cases that have contested general medical ethics.

An example of the organization's efforts was highlighted in an August 2014 fund-raising newsletter that was mailed to my house. The network sought funding to intercede in the case of a young woman (whose name was not publicly disclosed; Bobby Schindler recounts the case in an April 2014 interview with Matt C. Abbott at the Christian political website *RenewAmerica*) who went into cardiac arrest after an asthma attack and was diagnosed as brain dead, a term with a technical meaning indicating that all areas of the brain have ceased to function. The woman's parents asked that her ventilator be removed, but her young fiancé contacted the Life & Hope Network because he was certain that she was improving. Still, the ventilator was removed. She continued to breath, a feeding tube in place. The mailer, written by Bobby Schindler, director of the Life & Hope Network, shows the organization's political objectives:

> Another example of how Euthanasia is being practiced every day. It is cases like this that accentuate why Terri's Life & Hope Network exists—and why your support is so critical. The sad truth is that during almost 10 years of existence, we are seeing a growing number of cases where hospitals are more concerned with their best interest, rather than the best interest of the patient. In particular, is the reality that health care rationing will undoubtedly increase with Obamacare now running our health care system.

The moral conviction of the Life & Hope Network is that the state is complicit in a culture of death—through the passage of the Affordable Care Act, called Obamacare, via hospitals and courts that allow patients to be removed from physiological support and laws that support patients' decisions, and through support of cultural coercion that demeans these "lives"—and that it must be stopped. American morality regarding "the most vulnerable," according to the network, has fallen, corrupted by politics that have moved the United States away from its traditional moral character and founding principles.

CHAPTER SIX

A Small but Significant Minority

"I pledge allegiance to the flag of the United States of America, and to the republic for which it stands, one nation, under God, indivisible, with liberty and justice for all, born and unborn." So began the Pennsylvania Pro-Life Federation's annual meeting, held in the Hilton Scranton & Conference Center in October 2009. That last bit—*born and unborn*—shouldn't have caught me off guard, but it did. I was a paying attendee at the conference; I'd come to observe a group of Americans, predominantly Evangelical and Catholic, who challenged, with sincerity and conviction, prevailing notions of citizenship, patriotism, individual rights, privacy, and life. This group was deeply concerned about the future of their movement and ideology, even as their sense of persecution by broader society was a badge, a salvation, and proof that they were right. The introductions were chock full of challenges to criticism, taunts of wayward legislators, lawyers, and, of course, women.

Scranton is, like many former manufacturing cities in Pennsylvania, a hard-luck town. As I drove through quiet streets that morning, the city wore a bucolic fall-leaf mantle over its shabby core. Scranton's population, from a high of 143,000 in 1930, has been in decline since the mid-1970s. The unemployment rate hovers at around 8 or 9 percent. Today, with a population of seventy-five thousand and a growing number of new Hispanic, Asian, and African American residents, it is easy to identify the nostalgia in the city (and state's) politics. Titled "Lighting the Way for Life in the Electric City," the federation's conference harked back to Scranton's nickname, bestowed in the late 1800s when electric lights were installed along its neat streets and the nation's first electric streetcars shuttled beneath them. Extolling a glorious period—when "traditional" families cared for one another, gender roles were clearly delineated by a father's single-family income, the influx of new citizens was racially homogenous, and moral behavior was supported and policed by local churches—is nothing new for culturally conservative groups who oppose same-sex marriage, abortion, and euthanasia. The message of longing for a better time, of saving a culture in decline, particularly resonates in places like Scranton. Proof that the country is on the wrong track is etched across the city's landscape and history.

"Pennsylvania is 'pro-life' country," A. J. Munchak, county commissioner and "pro-life, Polish politician from Pennsylvania," declared from the podium. He welcomed us by chastising his fellow local politicians for declining to speak that day. "I never use the word fetus," Munchak said. "I use 'babies.'" The crowd of about three hundred let out a collective "awwww" and applauded. Munchak was followed by Michael Ciccocioppo, the CEO of the Pennsylvania Pro-Life Federation and the oldest of fifteen children. "We" were under assault by a culture of death that sought to slaughter the nation's most vulnerable citizens, he told us. As if to emphasize the point, he reminded us to wear our badges at all times. The federation was on the lookout for outsiders who could wander in and disrupt the day's schedule with protest at any time.

My conference badge entitled me to warm, even fawning, greetings as I moved from the hotel entrance into the scrum of displays and information booths throughout the hotel. Outside the ballroom, I had passed through crowds of seniors picking up literature on how to write op-eds for their local newspapers; photocopies of winning essays by antiabortion students; posters and flyers emblazoned with crime scene–like bloody photos of aborted fetuses; and tracts on the corrupting dangers of condoms, premarital sex (indeed, any kind of sex not meant for procreation), and euthanasia. In the center of the lobby was a giant papier-mâché cartoon baby, yellow, with a curling umbilical cord snaking from his belly (not to a mother but to a blunt end), named Umbert the Unborn. Umbert, I learned, was a popular cartoon drawn by Gary Cangemi. "The world's most loveable baby hasn't been born yet," Cangemi's website says. Umbert's five-foot-tall figure had been liberated from the purple circle "womb," a stylized stand-in for his mother, which he typically inhabits in the cartoon's frames. As if the Hilton lobby was itself a womb where he was safe. T-shirts and bumper stickers were on sale. "I support a woman's right to be born" and "Declare the womb a federally protected wetland." In this crowd, a woman's body was a national resource and should be under federal jurisdiction.

On one table, I caught a glimpse of a russet potato that was shaped like a fetus, scrubbed and lovingly placed on a bed of shiny blue cloth. A sign, I suppose, or a warning, to whoever had dug it up. By the ballroom entrance, I stopped to look at an oil painting of Terri Schiavo. *The Bride*, as in the bride of Christ, depicts her in a billowing white wedding dress, a saintly smile of peace on her young, virginal face. She gracefully holds a bronze crucifix in her hands. She has not yet been corrupted, indeed murdered, by her husband who, according to this group, is an adulterer and a killer. Lace reaches from her wrists to her neck. Twenty-five by thirty-six inches, *The Bride* was painted by Eric Menzhuber, an artist who studied theology and art in St. Paul,

Minnesota. The painting was commissioned by the Franciscan Brothers of Peace for the Schindler family after Terri's death. "The bouquet of flowers was replaced with a crucifix as a symbol of the new life and new joy she has in Heaven," writes Menzhuber on his website.

The Pennsylvania Pro-Life Federation's influence in the state—where urban centers and vast rural swaths, a spectrum of red and blue politics, hovers within deep purple—is hard to gauge. The organization boasts fifty county chapters (there are sixty-seven counties in the state), but membership numbers are hard to find. What the federation does very well is train its supporters, already entrenched in local church and elder communities, how to engage politically, call senators and state representatives, write letters, start blogs, use Facebook, and make phone calls. Many of the conference attendees knew each other, sat with their neighbors, and gossiped and shared photos of their grandchildren. They didn't see themselves as activists but community members, responsible for each other and the future of their beloved country. The federation's outreach and political activism is highly organized and aided by training seminars, flyers, representatives, official contact lists, guides for churches on how to support political candidates without jeopardizing tax-exempt status, and phone trees designed to keep volunteers accountable.

Ciccocioppo, tall, immaculately well groomed, and expensively dressed, is a masterful public speaker. In a tailored pinstriped suit, he's a cross between a wise authoritarian and a sensible banker. He has deftly woven singular news stories into the vibrant fabric of American patriotism, exceptionalism, conservative politics, and moral conviction to proclaim the tragic and destructive march of the "culture of death," a relentless crisis of national and individual character his organization aims to stanch, even as these new horrors justify the organization's frenetic work. In 2013, Kermit Gosnell, a doctor who performed abortions in Pennsylvania, was convicted for murdering three infants who were still alive after abortion procedures. On May 13, 2013, a statement released by Ciccocioppo was posted by Steven Ertelt at *National Right to Life News*: "For the sake of all Gosnell's victims, let us never forget the rampant disregard for life that was allowed to continue for decades in our state. We hope that in the future politics will not stand in the way of protecting the health and safety of women and newborns." He praised Pennsylvania governor Tom Corbett for new legislation that would "ensure that abortion facilities would be subject to the same standards as outpatient surgery centers." The law was contentious to many reproductive rights advocates who saw it as an excuse to place further restrictions on largely ethical care providers and women's access to them. It wrongly treated Gosnell's behavior as commonplace and equated typically safe abortion procedures with the invasiveness and risk of surgery.

"This is really the most that can be done under the tragic US Supreme Court decision *Roe v. Wade*, which brought us abortion on demand and the unspeakable tragedy of Gosnell. It's time to take a second look at *Roe*—in memory of Gosnell's victims," the statement read. Although reproductive rights advocates also decried Gosnell's practices, many like Ciccocioppo were able to characterize Gosnell as the murderous face of legal abortion.

When a Philadelphia nurse, Barbara Mancini, was arrested on charges of assisting her father's suicide, Ciccocioppo again narrated the case as a symptom of social decline, aided by nefarious outside forces that endangered everyone. Mancini's father, Joe Yourshaw, was ninety-three and enrolled in hospice at his home. His dying was long, slow, and painful. He asked his daughter to hand him a bottle of morphine. She did, and when a hospice nurse arrived, Mancini told her what she'd done. The nurse reported her for criminal conduct and Mancini was arrested. Compassion & Choices collected funds to fight the charge against Mancini. "The only reason they're targeting Pennsylvania is that they believe we might be vulnerable," Ciccocioppo told reporter Robert J. Vickers of the *Patriot-News*. "What they really want is for the attorney general [Kathleen Kane] to do what she did with the marriage law." Kane had declined to defend the state's ban on same-sex marriage. "They're thinking that if they can get her to do the same thing on assisted suicide, that gets them closer to full-blown euthanasia here and then the nation," Ciccocioppo said. Mancini's case was later dismissed by a Pennsylvania county judge.

To many not versed in the Evangelical narrative that throws all "unsavory" behaviors into the same ungodly, un-American pot, Ciccocioppo's segue from same-sex marriage to aid in dying to abortion may be confounding. Yet the project of placing those who don't abide by a particular set of values—what many Evangelicals nostalgically and falsely call "traditional"—is long-standing. In his book *After the Wrath of God: AIDS, Sexuality, and American Religion,* Anthony Petro shows that Evangelicals have long challenged access to state and federal resources (and freedom from imposing laws) for those outside its moral boundaries. "Government agencies have the authority to bestow or withhold the status of legal citizenship or to bestow it partially, as is often the case for those at the margins of society," he writes.

By conflating their own version of moral behavior with public health policy, law, and government obligation, Ciccocioppo was only employing a rhetoric formulated in the 1970s and '80s: one that deems the United States a godly nation and characterizes those who do not follow the same God and his principles as unlawful, un-American, even traitors to the country. Anything outside those moral parameters becomes unnatural, deviant, and pathological. Those who behave in ways that this group does not condone are a danger to the vulnerable among us (elders, fetuses, and—in the case of the lesbian, gay, bisexual, transgender, and queer [LGBTQ] community—children). It's what Petro calls "moral citizenship," an ideology that permitted everyone in the Hilton to change the Pledge of Allegiance, what gave them the authority to push for laws that limited rights for pregnant women, same-sex couples, and aid-in-dying activists. These groups—and others who did not ascribe to a "pro-life," "family values" understanding of the world—were outside the rights and laws of what Ciccocioppo and others deemed real America.

This narrative, that the most vulnerable among us are under attack by a fallen culture, is well known by the federation's members. While organizations have successfully knitted together abortion, same-sex marriage, and euthanasia under a "pro-life" umbrella, in large part because of fundamentalist theological principles, advocates for individual rights remain entrenched in their silo-like camps, unwilling or unable to depict their cause as one part of a broader objective. Feminists, and advocates for reproductive, LGBTQ, disability, and aid-in-dying rights all have their own territories to defend; finding their shared place within a broader ideological objective of patients' rights or conscience rights seems impossible. I was perhaps the only one in the Hilton Scranton ballroom struck by the "born and unborn" amendment to the Pledge of Allegiance. It gave me a shock to think that our old national "expression of fealty to the flag and the republic" needed to be changed, that it had to cut out some, those who disagreed with the folks in the Hilton. The change was a statement of separatism; the pledge was no longer enough for all of us. Ciccocioppo solemnly led us through the updated promise, like a minister leading a prayer.

After the 1973 *Roe v. Wade* decision, Catholic and Evangelical leaders formed an alliance that had previously been unthinkable. Part backlash to the liberalizing politics of the 1960s and early 70s, part enemy-of-my-enemy-is-my-friend, part trepidation at declining church enrollment and restructuring of the nuclear family, Catholics and Evangelicals found that their cooperation on so-called traditional values was a holy alliance. "This political and cultural realignment even helped melt divisions among Protestants, Catholics, and Jews, as religious identity came to matter less than one's moral and political positions regarding a host of key issues, including abortion, premarital sex, birth control, divorce, and homosexuality," writes Petro in *After the Wrath of God*. It intertwined grassroots church networks, priests who were willing and able to pressure legislators, international influence (for example, in US health policy abroad, that excluded condoms or abortion access), media empires (from Trinity Broadcasting Network to Jim Bakker and Oral Roberts), and American religious fervor. Since the 1970s, the Christian Right has ebbed and flowed, with various organizational forces rising to prominence and falling apart. From Jerry Falwell's Moral Majority, founded in 1979, to Pat Robertson's Christian Coalition, founded in 1989, their "successes at political mobilization—pushing apolitical religious conservatives to become voters, voters to become activists, and activists to become candidates—have become woven into the fabric of our national political life, particularly within the GOP," wrote journalist and scholar Frederick Clarkson, a senior fellow at Political Research Associates, on its website in 2013.

Rather than measure this group's achievements by the number of politicians who have risen to power, Clarkson writes, "Its greatest success, in fact, has been somewhat under the radar: creating an institutional network that fosters young conservatives and encourages them to translate conservative ideas into public policy." In 2009, prominent conservative Catholic and Protestant leaders signed the Manhattan Declaration, a manifesto declaring, "We are Christians who have joined together across historic lines of ecclesial differences to affirm our right—and, more importantly, *to embrace our obligation*—to speak and act in defense of these truths. We pledge to each other, and to our fellow believers, that no power on earth, be it cultural or political, will intimidate us into silence or acquiescence." (The entire text can be found online at manhattandeclaration.org.) In the declaration's formulation, legalized abortion is a keystone on which other issues like same-sex marriage, contraception, stem cell research, and euthanasia rest; the challenge to stop such corruptions can be understood through the study of the shifting definition of *religious liberty* in the United States.

According to Clarkson, these groups are invested in the "idea that those who favor reproductive choice and marriage equality are non-religious or anti-religious, and thus are prepared to trample the religious liberty of everyone." Religious liberty is now being used as a defense of a religious ideology's existing authority, at the expense of others' diversifying worldviews and rights; it's become an accusation that those who don't agree with a particular frame are simply wrong, fallen, depraved, or misguided.

The early foundational idea of religious liberty—in theory, if not in practice—was meant to protect individual conscience, to prevent authoritative powers of any sort from dictating the religious beliefs of citizens. But as Clarkson writes,

> The signers of the [Manhattan] Declaration cast themselves as patriots challenging "tyranny" in the tradition of the American Revolution and as warriors for social justice. While laying claim to the mantle of the Revolution is not new or unique to this group, the Declaration has ratcheted up the seriousness with which Christian Right leaders are treating the nature of the confrontation. "We will fully and ungrudgingly render to Caesar what is Caesar's," they conclude. "But under no circumstances will we render to Caesar what is God's."

By reinterpreting religious liberty (or stubbornly adhering to existing and/or idealistic forms), the Manhattan Declaration and its signatories claim their moral values to be rightly privileged above all others. In an increasingly diverse country where a multitude of moralities—religious and otherwise—exist, "pro-life" organizations are brazenly working to shape laws, systems of power, and national conversations to their own beliefs.

Countless Protestant denominations across the country support individual rights and medical autonomy; countless members of the declaration's signing denominations also ascribe to rights outside their leaders' dictates. Yet the religious left has proven relatively incapable of countering the religious right's heft, funding, and political clout.

In light of the passage of same-sex marriage legislation in many states, "pro-life" groups' inability to overturn *Roe v. Wade*, public approval of aid in dying and its passage in several states, and regular polls showing that Americans are rapidly leaving religious denominations, we may be lulled into thinking that the particular kind of moralizing religion that once shaped our culture is past its prime. Yet our laws, particularly those regarding public health, are shot through with moral expectations that have yet to catch up with the diversity—religious and otherwise—of the nation.

Ciccocioppo turned the gray-haired audience in the Hilton ballroom over to Teresa Tomeo, a tough-talking former "secular" TV reporter. Tomeo's *Catholic Connection* radio show is syndicated to two hundred Catholic stations across the country. She considers herself an expert on how the media corrupts young women (her books include *Extreme Makeover: Women Transformed by Christ, Not Conformed to the Culture*, and *Noise: How Our Media Saturated Culture Dominates Lives and Dismantles Families*). Tomeo is a small woman with short dark hair; she's serious and energetic. "Reclaiming" was the theme of her talk at the Hilton, a presentation that felt much like a testimonial, the Evangelical ritual of sharing with one's new Christian community how he or she came to be born again. She recounted her successful secular career—the money, the praise, the pride—and her rebirth as a committed Catholic, "passionate about sharing her faith and educating others on the truth," a whistleblower on the perverting powers of media. She was reclaiming feminism from selfish, wayward women and infusing it with God's commandments.

David Prentice, a senior fellow for life sciences at the Family Research Council (a Washington, DC–based conservative organization whose mission is "to advance faith, family and freedom in public policy and the culture from a Christian worldview"), presented the audience with PowerPoint proof that stem cell research was a "holocaust." Instead of the cure for cancer, all those embryos were really the next Einstein, the next Bach, the next Martin Luther King Jr. These potential geniuses, as yet only a gleam in a scientist's test tube, were being slaughtered. Applause filled the ballroom. A few years later, I interviewed Prentice for an article about a rancorous stem cell scandal. The Vatican had invested millions of dollars into research on adult stem cells, called very small embryonic-like cells (VSELs), which were proclaimed as an alternative to the destruction of embryonic stem cells. The work of the scientist conducting the research, Mariusz Ratajczak, was later debunked by leading secular scientists. At the time of the interview, Prentice presented me with his own testimonial, albeit one tactfully couched in science. He had been a researcher at Indiana State University when he realized that embryonic stem cells were not the answer. They didn't deliver. "Real people are back on their feet or still alive because of adult stem cells," he told me, citing contested, uncorroborated studies. Mainstream science didn't agree, he said, because of "a money thing, or a prestige thing, who's recognized by their peers as an expert." Science was a clique, hell-bent on keeping out alternative voices, Christian voices. The media was its handmaiden, refusing to tell the whole story about alternatives to embryo destruction. "There is a place for ethics in public policy," he said, meaning his brand of Christian ethics.

Within this paradigm of a secular world usurping the place of ethical Christian morals and truth, Bobby Schindler, Terri Schiavo's brother, has established himself as a "pro-life" rock star. What drew me to Scranton, to the federation's annual conference, was the chance to hear Schindler deliver the keynote address. In 2000, five years before

Terri died, the Schindler family established the nonprofit Terri Schindler Schiavo Foundation. According to a 2005 article in the *St. Petersburg Times* by reporters Stephen Nohlgren and Tom Zucco, documents submitted to the state reported that the purpose of the organization was to "help prevent her death, underwrite medical and neurological exams related to rehabilitation and care, increase public awareness of guardianship, marital infidelity and end-of-life laws and to lobby for greater parental rights under guardianship law." In short, the foundation sought to upend existing legal jurisprudence and established medical ethics. The "marital infidelity" focus arose when Michael Schiavo, Terri's husband, began a relationship with another woman years after Terri's collapse, but before her death. "What Terri's husband and 'guardian,' Michael Schiavo, is trying to accomplish by having the feeding tube removed is nothing more than a really late-term abortion of somebody else's daughter. And, like so many abortions, it would appear that the reasons have nothing to do with anything but selfish personal wants," wrote Doug Powers at WND, a conservative website, on March 21, 2005, a few days before Terri died.

After Terri's death, the Schindlers renamed the organization Terri Schiavo Life & Hope Network. The new mission of the organization, as stated on its website, became "to develop a national network of resources and support for the medically-dependent, persons with disabilities and the incapacitated who are in or potentially facing life-threatening situations." That network was to consist of a roster of like-minded doctors, lawyers, nurses, and facilities that could come to the aid of those who contacted the network. Suzanne, Terri's sister, was treasurer; Mary, Terri's mother, was secretary; Bobby was treasurer; and Robert (Bob) Schindler, Terri's father, was the president. When Bob Schindler died in 2009, only a few months before I made my way to Scranton, Bobby took over as head of the organization. He was Terri's devoted brother, in perpetual mourning, his father's reluctant but tireless successor, who had witnessed slaughter and had taken up the cause of the "severely disabled." A lone (unmarried) crusader who listened for desperate voices in the wilderness.

I returned to my table early from lunch to prepare for Bobby's keynote. I saw him nearby, talking to two women who listened rapturously, leaning in to be closer to him. They were dressed alike in long skirts, pastel jackets, and sensible shoes. When he walked away, they bounced on their toes, thrilled to have spoken with him. As Bobby approached the stage, surrounded by orange, yellow, and burgundy chrysanthemums, a nun handed him a small wrapped gift. The audience applauded thunderously. He placed the gift on the podium and stared at it until the room grew quiet. Bobby looked tired and sad. The brown suit he wore was too big for him. Fabric bunched around his ankles and wrists. He is a small handsome man with large facial features, dark hair and eyes, and a heavy brow. Without notes, Bobby recounted the timeline that encompassed his sister's last few years, the court battles, the doctors' testimonials on their behalf, the horror of courts who ultimately decided that Terri's feeding tube could be removed, and her "torturous death." "Terri's fight"—the foundation's web address is terrisfight.org—was also Bobby's fight; in the course of those years, Bobby told us, he had rediscovered his faith. Her death was his testimonial, his rebirth as a loyal servant of God, and he was forever thankful to his sister for bringing him back to the faith of his childhood. He told the audience that when his father died, he knew it was because the work of trying to save Terri from murder had broken him. "We just wanted a chance to care for my sister until her natural death," he said. "We loved her unconditionally, and we knew that she loved us back."

I felt sadness for the family; I appreciated their grief and their commitment, but the kind of love Bobby described sounded a little creepy to me. The Schindlers projected their own desires onto the unconscious body of their daughter and sister. Terri no longer existed, but in the Schindlers' minds, Terri was a fighter, committed to

the doctrine of her birth church, loyal to the same dogma they as-
cribed to. If her desires mattered at all, they believed she agreed with
them and, by extension, with the Catholic Church. Terri, by the time
of her death, was years past any conscious thought, any engagement
with what we call life or the world. The medical advancements that
had carried Terri from her kitchen floor to her hospital bed—the resuscitation, the ventilator, and the one that kept her in that bed for
more than a decade, the feeding tube—were no less advanced, no more
"natural" than other technologies they denied, like contraception and
abortion. The "natural" in "from conception to natural death" now
meant anything at all. Or nothing but a categorization of science's
developments based on body function. And the "hope" in the Terri
Schiavo Life & Hope Network meant hope beyond hope. It meant a
miracle, and the Schindlers believed that God was aware of their pleas
and able to deliver that miracle, until the state ended that chance.
While hope—which looked a lot like denial to outsiders—sustained
them, a feeding tube was the only thing "sustaining" Terri. At what
cost? I don't necessarily mean the financials. The Schindlers' radical
denial of Terri's state cost them the chance to face their loved one's
death, to grieve, to acknowledge that the one single thing humans
reliably do is die. I came to Scranton to understand Bobby's campaign
to usurp the rights of the dying; I left heartbroken by his endless,
bottomless grief.

The family has since contested that Terri was in a persistent vegetative state, despite a postmortem autopsy that confirmed the diagnosis,
preferring to see her as mentally disabled, a member of a vast community of Americans who are invisible to the rest of the country because
they are not whole, productive, fully functioning. They point out that
Terri was not terminal, that she could have lived a long life with a
feeding tube. And they reiterate the Catholic Church's classification
of a feeding tube as comfort care, not a medical treatment that can
be removed according to legal jurisprudence. Her husband, according

to law, was her legal guardian, and again and again the courts determined that to remove or not remove the tube was Michael Schiavo's decision. On March 18, 2005, less than two weeks before Terri's death, bioethicist Arthur Caplan wrote on NBCNews.com, "The time has come to let Terri die. Not because everyone who is brain damaged should be allowed to die. Not because her quality of life is too poor for anyone to think it meaningful to go on. Not even because she costs a lot of money to continue to care for. Simply because her husband who loves her and has stuck by her for more than fifteen years says she would not want to live the way she is living." Why would Terri want to die, the Schindlers asked, when they loved her unconditionally? When God did?

Tamesha Means wanted the doctors and nurses at Mercy Health Partners, a Catholic hospital in Muskegon, Michigan, to tell her why she was in debilitating pain. Means was eighteen weeks pregnant when her water broke. She dragged herself to Mercy Health Partners, the only hospital in her area. The staff sent her home twice over the next two days. On her third visit, as she was waiting to be discharged yet again, fevered with infection, she began to miscarry her fetus. Only then did doctors attend her. Means was lucky. The infection could have killed her, but she's since recovered.

The staff at Mercy, a Catholic hospital, had refused to treat Means during her earlier visits because doing so meant aborting the fetus, and aborting any fetus, including a terminal one, was against hospital rules. Those rules are provided by the United States Conference of Catholic Bishops (USCCB), not medical ethics or advisory bodies. Because of the rules, Catholic hospitals are prevented from performing any procedure that could result in the termination of a pregnancy. In a first-of-its-kind lawsuit, Means and the ACLU brought a lawsuit, not against Mercy hospital or its staff, but against the Catholic organization that dictates medical practice at Catholic-run hospitals nationwide, the USCCB. According to the USCCB website, there are 629 Catholic hospitals in the country, serving one out of every six patients: that's nineteen million emergency room visits and more than one hundred million outpatient visits each year. Catholic hospitals operate, like all hospitals, according to standard medical procedure, except when that procedure falls outside the Ethical and Religious Directives for Catholic Health Care Services (ERDs), seventy-two guidelines that are approved by the USCCB.

Oversight of hospital compliance was once very casual—local bishops were charged with directing the hospitals in their diocese—but several factors have pitted patients, doctors, staff, and the bishops in a contest for authority and autonomy over the past decade. Increasing mergers between Catholic and secular hospitals, due to economic changes in the field, have rankled local communities when reproductive services are discontinued. The Catholic Church's pronounced role in health-care legislation, including its efforts to avoid the contraception mandate in the Affordable Care Act, which would provide full health insurance coverage for employees of Catholic entities, has focused attention on Catholic facilities. Some doctors have lamented the days when ERD prohibitions were quietly ignored in their hospitals. But attention from both opponents of the ERDs and bishops has now changed the climate drastically. Reproductive rights advocates have increasingly challenged hospitals' denial of patient-doctor privacy regarding abortion and contraception, pointing out that while Catholic hospitals maintain their right to institutional conscience, they deny those rights to patients in their communities who aren't Catholic or are Catholic but don't agree with the ERDs. The Tamesha Means case, in other words, was a case waiting to happen. But it's likely that similar cases won't be brought against the USCCB again soon. According to the ACLU website, the case was dismissed by a federal district court on June 30, 2015, because "resolution of the case would involve reviewing religious doctrine."

Catholic hospitals are rightly known for their quality. The church has been involved in health-care provision since the beginning of modern medicine. In addition to hospitals, which employ half a million full-time and a quarter-million part-time workers, the church also oversees fifty-six health-care systems (HMOs) and thousands of facilities for children, elders, the disabled, and the ill. The refusal to provide some standard services is compounded by the church's enforcement of policy that prevents hospital staff from even informing patients of their full medical options or from referring them to facilities where they can receive desired care, which is why it's impossible to discuss health care in America today without considering the influence that the Catholic Church wields over the industry and the country's pluralistic population.

While most of the recent focus on Catholic health care has concerned reproductive services, the church quietly changed the ERDs in 2009 to address the use of artificial nutrition and hydration, specifically, the use of feeding tubes in patients in persistent vegetative states, like Terri Schiavo. In a question-and-answer document published by the Catholic Health Association on November 2009 on its website, changes to ERD #58 are explained: "In March 2004 Pope John Paul II addressed this issue and in August 2007 the Congregation for the Doctrine of the Faith issued a clarifying document on the issue. Therefore the Introduction to Part Five and Directive #58 have been revised in light of these statements." The pope's address was given the same month Terri Schiavo died. While the change allows tubes (medically assisted nutrition and hydration, or MANH) to be removed if a patient is terminal or if the tube is an excessive burden, the bishops "insist that the belief that a patient is never likely to regain consciousness is not in itself a sufficient reason for withdrawing MANH." The document is presumably written for medical staff as a guide to the new change. The tone is calm and reassuring. To the question, "Does the new Directive #58 mean that Catholic health care facilities will not honor a patient's advance directive?" the answer is a flat no, yet it goes on to explain: "There may be the occasional situation, such as some patients in a persistent vegetative state, when what the patient is requesting through his or her advance directive is not consistent with the moral teaching of the Church. In these few cases, the Catholic health care facility would not be able to comply." But this is nothing new. Directive #28 already notes that "the free and informed health care decision of the person or the person's surrogate is to be followed so long as it does not contradict Catholic principles." And Directive #59 echoes this: "The free and informed judgment made by a competent adult patient concerning the use or withdrawal of life-sustaining procedures should always be respected and normally complied with, unless it is contrary to Catholic moral teaching."

This is the scenario that keeps me up at night. Let's say I get hit by a bus on the streets of Manhattan. A bystander calls 911 and I am rushed to the nearest hospital, which happens to be Catholic. On the way, the paramedics are able to restart my heart, they are able to restart my lungs, but I was without oxygen for more than four minutes. At the hospital, a few days after I'm admitted, I'm given a feeding tube (all of which would happen at any hospital in the country). After a few weeks, let's say I'm diagnosed as being in a PVS. My brain stem still has some functionality, I can maybe open my eyes, I move, I sleep, and I open my mouth. But significant parts of my brain are gone, never to return. My sister drives up to the city, a copy of my advanced directive in her hand. As my medical proxy, she should, according to standard medical ethics, be able to have me removed from that feeding tube, now surgically embedded in my stomach. But if the hospital staff agree that the tube is not an undue burden (I'm so far resistant to infection) and I'm not terminal (I'm strong; my body could be kept "alive" by the feeding tube for years to come), my sister would not be able to remove the tube.

Tell this scenario to anyone—and I have—and you'll likely be re-minded that your sister can move you to another hospital. That's the premise of a free health-care market, right? Choice? But in order to move me, first my sister would have to know that Catholic hospitals are different from other hospitals; she would have to know that I can ethically be removed from a feeding tube; she would have to have the clarity, within her grief, to understand this (despite what the doctors do and don't tell her); and she would have to arrange for my move. The hospital would have to release me (knowing my sister's intent). And if it won't, my sister would have to raise the funds and find a lawyer to challenge the hospital on my behalf in a court of law. The chances are that she would win.

But let's say that my estranged mother hears of my condition. She rushes from Atlanta to New York, distraught, fearful that her oldest child is about to be "killed." She wants time to say goodbye; she wants the hospital to do everything. If she challenges my sister's attempts to remove my feeding tube, she would most likely lose. I have a medical proxy, an advanced directive. My wishes in such a case are clear. But what if I don't have these documents or if my sister doesn't know what I would want? Court cases, appeals, media, amicus briefs filed on be-half of my mother could leave me lying in a Catholic hospital, only a feeding tube between my body and something beyond. For years. Terri Schiavo was on a feeding tube for fifteen years.

There are more reasons to be concerned about Catholic health care than just the sadness of brain-damaged patients kept alive indef-initely on feeding tubes or the women who are unable to determine the course of their family planning. The entire public conversation about our social role in protecting rights and patient privacy is shaped by the power that the Catholic Church has over how care is given to bodies, our collective body. During the contentious fights over the passage of the Affordable Care Act, former vice presidential candi-date Sarah Palin joined a vocal number of groups to remove from the bill payment to doctors for discussing end-of-life issues with patients. "Death panels" became opponents' shorthand for secret panels that would make decisions about who should live and who should die. But the term was also extended to any type of conversation doctors could have with their terminal patients about their medical wishes for dying. The issue became politically lethal, and the administration dropped it from the health-care bill. (In June 5, 2015, more than five years after the Affordable Care Act was signed into law, two senators, Virginia Democrat Mark Warner and Georgia Republican Johnny Isakson, introduced legislation that would allow Medicare to reimburse doctors and other providers for end-of-life consultations.) Online, I've seen campaigns to dissuade seniors from filling out "do not resuscitate" orders, lest their doctors rush them to an early end. In states where aid in dying is now legal, Catholic hospitals never mention it. The hard power of the church, which retains its ability to decide the types of care millions of patients receive daily—even to decide what medical options patients can be informed of—has combined with the soft power of public influence and coercion. These deliberate efforts work in conjunction with our collective fear of talking about death, with our lack of knowledge about how it comes, and with our institution-alization of the dying. Independent choice is always limited, withheld from some along the lines of race or class or religion. But the role that the Catholic Church and its allies play in how health care is delivered and legislated further limits everyone's claim to choice.

The Cathedral Basilica of Saints Peter and Paul is at the corner of Ben Franklin Parkway and North Eighteenth streets in downtown Philadelphia. The massive domed and columned structure, completed in the 1860s, is built of matte brown stone. The cathedral faces the Franklin Institute, across Logan Square, with the public library and juvenile courts to the north and the Academy of Natural Sciences of Drexel University to the south. More than two hundred years earlier, not far from where I sat, revolutionaries including Benjamin Franklin set up shop and hammered out a new country with laws, rights, and freedoms; their legacy was the Declaration of Independence and the Constitution. I sat on a bench in Logan Square checking e-mail on my iPhone, waiting amid sunshine and spring flowers for my friend Anthea Butler, an associate professor of religious studies and Africana studies at the University of Pennsylvania. I'd asked her to go with me to the National Memorial Mass for Terri's Day at the cathedral and the Life & Hope Network's annual award gala that followed. Anthea was writing a book about Sarah Palin, and I thought she would be interested to hear the former Alaska governor, former vice presidential hopeful, and Tea Party star deliver the gala's keynote address.

Anthea pulled up to the cathedral's steps in a taxi and together we shuffled inside, surrounded by other attendees, to a side chapel. The yellow walls held framed Stations of the Cross, the depictions of Christ's walk to his crucifixion that Catholics and other Christians contemplate during Lent to remember his pain and suffering. Easter had fallen on the eighth anniversary of Terri Schiavo's death, March 31, 2014, so the memorial and gala were postponed until April 4. About 140 people, predominantly white and over fifty, filed into the pews around us. Dress ranged from fur collars and taffeta to a nun's full habit. The Catholic Mass—reverent, graceful—called to mind college days when I left my faltering Mennonite-inflected faith to complete catechism at the stained glass Catholic church down the hill from the university's Old Main. I turned to "extend the sign of peace" to the middle-aged man behind me. "Peace be with you," he said. His dark hair was parted in the middle and smoothed along each side of his forehead. "And also with you," I replied. Just then, several wheelchairs were pushed to the chapel door from outside. Bobby Schindler jumped up to help wheel them into the space before the pews in front.

Anthea was a perfect companion. Between us, we could identify many of the bishops and religious leaders assembled. Frank Pavone, with his pale face, glasses, and dark hair combed from left to right, in need of a trim, was present. Pavone is an outspoken and tireless Texas priest who is national director of Priests for Life and "one of the most prominent pro-life leaders in the world," according to his biography at the Priests for Life website. It also notes, "He was asked by Mother Teresa to speak in India on life issues, and has addressed the pro-life caucus of the United States House of Representatives. The Vatican appointed him to the Pontifical Council for the Family, which coordinates the pro-life activities of the Catholic Church. He also serves as a member of the Vatican's Pontifical Academy for Life. He was present at the bedside of Terri Schiavo as she was dying and was an outspoken advocate for her life." Pavone gave the first reading at Mass that day: "The stone rejected by the builders has become the cornerstone" (Psalm 118:22 and Acts 4:11) and "Jesus said to his disciples: Come and eat. And he took bread and gave it to them, hallelujah" (John 21:12–13). The second verse recounts the third time that Christ appears to his disciples after his crucifixion. The first was an analogy for Terri Schiavo's legacy in the church, her afterlife as a moral reminder to the "pro-life" movement.

Archbishop Charles Chaput was also there, the ninth archbishop of Philadelphia, appointed in 2011, the second Native American to be ordained in the United States. Chaput's tribe name means "the wind that rustles the leaves of the tree." One could say he takes this rustling seriously. *New York Times* reporter Laurie Goodstein wrote in 2011, "He is among a minority of Roman Catholic bishops who have spoken in favor of denying communion to Catholic politicians who support abortion rights. He helped defeat legislation that would have legalized civil unions for gay couples in Colorado. And he condemned the University of Notre Dame, a Catholic institution, for granting President Obama an honorary degree in 2009 because of his stance on abortion." Chaput has instructed Catholics to think of church allegiance, particularly regarding abortion and "bioethical and natural law doctrine" as more important than any other. "We're Catholics before we're Democrats. We're Catholics before we're Republicans. We're even Catholics before we're Americans, because we know that God has a demand on us prior to any government demand on us. And this has been the story of the martyrs through the centuries," Chaput told Catholic News Service's Jon Street, just before the presidential election. Being "good citizens means giving God his rights prior to the government making its claims upon us," he said. In the chapel, Chaput told the attentive crowd, "Ordinary lives are never the same after resurrection. Keep working." He was referring to the efforts of the Life & Hope Network and others to end the removal of feeding tubes from patients like Schiavo. "The Lord will surprise us."

After Mass, Anthea and I stepped out into the spring evening, shaking our heads. It wasn't so much that we were surprised by the service—it was predictable and consistent with Catholic action over the past few decades—but that we were taxed. The power, authority, and resources of the men we had just watched, the rhetoric they used to denounce Schiavo's death, the committed and sincere effort they were making to withhold the rights of all citizens, Catholics and non-Catholics, through whatever means possible . . . it all made me shudder. Anthea whisked me off to a local bar for a few necessary shots of whiskey before we faced our next trial, the awards gala.

In the upstairs lobby of the Philadelphia Marriott, we pushed through a throng of excited attendees. Many were dressed in formal attire—ball gowns and tuxedos. Young servers moved through the crowd with trays of hors d'oeuvres. Along a railing stood a row of easels with frames balanced on them. As we moved closer, we realized that the pictures were drawings and paintings that Terri Schiavo had made as a child, rudimentary animals and landscapes by an untrained, juvenile hand. They were painful to look at. What would she have thought of all this beatification? This overwrought emotion and lack of privacy, indeed this use of her private life to solicit financial and emotional support for laws that her husband swore—in a court of law, before various judges—she didn't believe in?

The gala emcee, Deborah Flora, actress, producer, radio talk show host and second runner-up to Miss America, welcomed us. *The Bride*, the large oil painting of Terri Schiavo in her wedding dress that I first saw at the Pennsylvania Pro-Life Federation in Scranton, sat on an easel next to the podium. I picked up a prayer card on my way in. It had a reproduction of *The Bride* on the front and a "Prayer for the Cause of Theresa of the Forgotten" on the back. "Merciful Lord, you filled the heart of Terri Schindler Schiavo with a spirit of profound sacrifice for love of neighbor. She became a holocaust offered to your Heart for the end of the culture of death." We were led through the Pledge of Allegiance; this time, the amendment tacked onto the end was "preborn and born," not "born and unborn." I'd noticed "preborn" popping up as a new term on "pro-life" sites the past few years. Video presentations were given by actor Gary Sinise and TV and radio-show host Glenn Beck. The Life & Hope Network has been incredibly successful in attracting support from celebrities. Actor John Stamos, the Beach Boys, and country music stars Randy Travis and Collin Raye have all lent their names and talents to network fund-raisers.

By the time Sarah Palin took the stage, we'd cleaned our $150 plates. I took notes on Palin's talk in a little notebook. I'm a good note taker. But her sentence structure made it difficult to capture fully developed ideas; instead, my notes are snippets, buzzwords, and observations: "Life is so unpredictable," and "her spirit is alive and continues to teach us, continues to inspire us to fight for the right to life." "God will never give you something you can't handle." Watching Palin speak was, for me, like watching live theater: the anxiety, thrill, and fear that something could go wrong. About three-quarters of the way through Palin's talk—the audience was rapt or glazed over, I couldn't tell—a man in a wheelchair began to groan loudly, drawing the attention of about half the ballroom. Palin talked on, not acknowledging the interruption.

More snippets. "Rationing," and "sitting in the seat of judgment," and "for those who cannot speak for themselves." She spoke of her son's Down syndrome and her "decision" to bring him to term. "The disabled shine the brightest," she said. "They are freer to love and celebrate the smallest victories." Standing ovation. Anthea and I looked at each other and again shook our heads, Anthea's big Afro swaying.

Journalist and lawyer Wesley J. Smith also spoke that evening. A self-proclaimed bioethicist, Smith has written more than twelve books that cover everything from frugality (with Ralph Nader) to "human exceptionalism," to *The War on Humans*. In 2011, Smith wrote for his regular column on "human exceptionalism" for *National Review* a piece titled "Assisted Suicide Is the Euthanasia of Hope." It read, "If we are seduced into legalizing assisted suicide, we will cheat at least some people out of the universe's most precious and irreplaceable commodity: time." That night, at the podium, Smith called Robert Schindler, Terri's father, the "second victim" of the Schiavo tragedy. He told us the Schindlers exemplified the "power of life over the seduction of death," and he warned that bioethics was becoming a rejection of human dignity. "Dignity is a property inherent in a living human body," he said. He called Schiavo's death "the Passion of Terri," echoing the Passion of Christ, in which, according to the Bible, Christ endured trials, suffered, and died so that you and I might live.

The "Terri Schiavo Life & Hope Award" was given to Moe and Sana Maraachli, the parents of a Canadian child who was born with progressive and incurable Leigh syndrome. When the hospital refused to perform a tracheotomy on the child, considering it painful, invasive, and futile, the Life & Hope Network, with the help of Father Frank Pavone, pulled together resources to fly him and his parents to a Catholic hospital in Missouri where the tracheotomy was performed. Known in the media as Baby Joseph, he died at his home several months later. The Maraachlis looked sad, grateful, and nervous as they were brought on stage.

Thirteen-year-old Jahi McMath checked into Children's Hospital Oakland Research Institute for an extensive tonsillectomy to correct sleep apnea on December 9, 2013. Three days later, after an unexpected hemorrhage caused cardiac arrest, she was declared brain dead by the hospital's doctors. The girl's parents, Nailah and Martin Winkfield, refused to let the hospital remove her ventilator. In news photos, the husband and wife wear matching white T-shirts that say "Pray for Jahi" in blue letters. Their daughter's picture covers their chests. Eight days later, they petitioned the Superior Court in Alameda County to prevent the hospital from removing Jahi's ventilator. They claimed that California's Uniform Determination of Death Act violated their religion and privacy, and asked that doctor Paul A. Byrne, who does not accept brain death as legal death, be allowed to examine Jahi. Byrne's testimony was not accepted by the court, but that of two other doctors was. They confirmed the hospital's conclusion that Jahi was brain dead. The court ruled that Jahi's ventilator would be removed on January 30. Omari Sealey, Jahi's uncle, told the *San Jose Mercury News*, "There's still time for a miracle. Christmas is tomorrow. It would be great if she woke up." The family scrambled to find a facility they could transfer Jahi to.

As I watched the media reports surrounding the McMath case, I again thought of what Tom L. Beauchamp and Robert M. Veatch wrote in the introduction to *Ethical Issues in Death and Dying*. Opponents of the definition of death based on the brain, instead of the heart, see the choice to remove life support as a "moral, religious, or philosophical one, not one that can be made solely on the basis of scientific evidence. It appears that a small, but significant minority will continue to hold that an individual with a beating heart is still alive even if that heart is maintained mechanically and there is no brain function." A ventilator was enough to keep oxygen flowing through Jahi's strong, young body and to keep her heart beating. Her parents were the "small, but significant minority" the authors were referring to.

"Terri Schiavo group secretly leading transfer efforts," reported the *San Jose Mercury News* on the last day of 2013. Jahi's parents now had the means to transport her from Children's Hospital Oakland Research Institute (they quickly raised $50,000 through an online fund-raiser); they had several potential facilities to transport her to, including a brain-injury treatment center on Long Island, New York, dedicated to Terri Schiavo and founded by a former hairdresser. And they had a doctor willing to perform the tracheotomy and feeding tube insertion that Children's Hospital Oakland refused. The hospital, despite having issued a death certificate, ultimately agreed to release Jahi's body "to the custody of her mother." The Life & Hope Network admitted having assisted Jahi's parents for weeks before going public. Its statement read, as reported by Matthias Gafni for the *San Jose Mercury News*, "Jahi McMath has been labeled a 'deceased' person. Yet she retains all the functional attributes of a living person, despite her brain injury. This includes a beating heart, circulation and respiration, the ability to metabolize nutrition and more. Jahi is a living human being."

Brain dead patients don't always look dead. When the US government issued its 1981 statement adopting the definition of brain death, "Guidelines for the Determination of Death," it laid out its rulings in two all-caps points: A. AN INDIVIDUAL WITH IRREVERSIBLE CESSATION OF CIRCULATORY AND RESPIRATORY FUNCTIONS IS DEAD.; B. AN INDIVIDUAL WITH IRREVERSIBLE CESSATION OF ALL FUNCTIONS OF THE ENTIRE BRAIN, INCLUDING THE BRAIN STEM, IS DEAD. Under B., it notes, "Peripheral nervous system activity and spinal cord reflexes may persist after death." These reflexes can be confusing, haunting, and hope inducing. Paul A. Byrne, the doctor the Winkfields had wanted to present to the courts, is the former president of the Catholic Medical

Association and an editor of *Beyond Brain Death*. The Associated Press's Lisa Leff and Terry Collins reported that Byrne wrote in court documents that he observed Jahi "responding to her grandmother's voice and touch with a squirming movement. In my opinion, this signifies she is not dead. She should receive treatment as she is alive just like everyone else with severe head injury. If she gets treatment, she will have a chance to recover brain function." Byrne's formulation of life makes no distinction between *biological* life and *sentient* life. That brain function can be recovered is controversial; some isolated research (with animal brains or in lab settings) has shown that parts of the brain can show new growth but the death of the entire brain—or even most parts of the brain—means the final death of those neurons.

A Children's Hospital Oakland representative told ABC News on January 2, 2014, that Christopher Dolan, Jahi McMath's lawyer, "has created a fiction and it's a sad one. This young lady is deceased. There is unfortunately nothing that this hospital or any facility, any legitimate facility, can do for her." Video that accompanies the news story shows pictures of Jahi before her fatal operation. In one, she is in a swimming pool, wearing a blue-patterned bathing suit, blue water glittering in the sunlight around her. She is smiling from ear to ear. In another, she is dressed in white for a formal occasion, her dark hair is up in a bun, her full cheeks gleam, and small pearls ring her head like a crown. Another shows her in a lavender hospital gown before surgery, standing in a doorway.

Jahi was moved from Children's Hospital Oakland; neither the date of her move or the name of the facility was initially released. In February, Nailah Winkfield issued a public letter to supporters, "Thank you to all of the people who view my daughter as the sweet, innocent, 13-year-old girl that she is and not a dead body or a corpse, I deeply appreciate that. Hopefully my daughter can change some of the ways brain death is viewed in today's society. Honestly, I think she already has. For those who believe, please, keep praying for Jahi.

God can overcome all things and I believe that His will has yet to be fully revealed. I love Jahi and where there is love, there is hope." The tagline for the Life & Hope Network is "Where there's life, there's hope," a quote the Schindlers attribute to Terri Schiavo (it's a version of Ecclesiastes 9:4).

Nailah Winkfield said in a TV interview with NBC Philadelphia anchor Tracy Davidson on March 28, 2014, that Jahi was "blossoming into a teen" and does what every teenager does: "she sits cross-legged in bed, listens to Rihanna and Beyonce on her iPod, and gets a manicure and pedicure every Friday." On May 25, a new post on the family's Facebook page read: "Jahi is still asleep but physically stable, no pic lines, no catheters, no I.V, she maintains all her vitals on her own, no medicines needed. Jahi is given lots of vitamins and fish oil through her feeding tube. She moves around so much that pillows are put around her bed. She responds to pain, cold and touch. Jahi can turn her head from left to right and her ventilator is set to room air temperature so she is not getting any extra oxygen like she was before."

It's hard to know what's true and what's projected onto Jahi. The Schindlers, during Schiavo's various court cases, produced photos and videos that they hoped would demonstrate that Terri was improving. They dressed her up and did her hair and makeup, they framed photos so that it looked as though she was making eye contact with family members. I want to believe that Jahi is improving, that the team of medical experts was wrong. The thought of her returning to her family is comforting. Their daughter's death is a tragedy. I imagine that the hospital staff is doing what nurses do across the country for bodies that are lost to their keepers. They are turning her so she doesn't get bedsores; they are cleaning her adult diapers and bedclothes. They are bathing her in a basin. Maybe they're brushing her teeth and cutting her hair. They are taking her temperature to ensure that she's not developing infection from the tube that runs through a hole cut through the skin of her belly and into her stomach or from the tube that runs from a ventilator through a hole cut in her throat. On June 12, 2014, the *Contra Costa Times* reported that Jahi would receive an honorary degree at her school's eighth-grade graduation, but article commenters have contested that. In fact, to follow the comments on articles about Jahi is to enter a world rife with speculation, self-appointed experts, angry (and often racist) sentiment, and billowing prayer. It is a netherworld of emotion that, like so many corners of the Internet, is both confounding and disheartening. Some see the Winkfields as money-grubbing grifters; others see them as pawns in an ideological struggle spearheaded by the Life & Hope Network; others see them as tragic and loyal victims who only want what's best for their daughter. The second "Terri Schiavo Life & Hope Award," presented at the 2014 gala, went to the parents of Jahi McMath.

On January 16, 2014, only a few weeks after the Life & Hope Network announced its involvement in the case, Bobby Schindler wrote, "My sister Terri Schiavo was alive like Jahi McMath," in an article for the *Washington Times* that conflates persistent vegetative state and brain death diagnoses. That same month, he wrote an article for *Time* magazine titled "Remember the Humanity of Jahi McMath," that repeats this confusion. He writes, "In the trenches of medical futility warfare, cases like these are often overlooked. Our experience, similar to those of Jahi and her family, is that people with severe brain injuries are treated like second class citizens, often being denied the treatment, care, and love that their humanity demands." The difference between the two, however, matters greatly.

PVS patients, like Terri Schiavo, still have brain stem activity. They follow a regular sleep schedule, yawn, open their eyes, blink, and move their arms and legs. Brain death, according to every state in the country, is the accepted legal definition of death. Brain dead patients have no brain activity; even the brain stem has ceased to function. To make this determination, doctors, as in Jahi's case, scan a brain to determine that there is no activity. The Catholic Church accepts the definition of brain death, which is why so many balked when the Life & Hope Network took up Jahi's case. Many ameliorated their surprise with something like, "Well, the hospital caused her 'brain damage'; doctors can't be trusted." Others pointed to a handful of cases where patients "recovered" from brain death diagnoses (exhibiting movement or regaining lung functionality); these are considered misdiagnoses or insubstantial recoveries by the medical community.

Even if Jahi's physiological support continues for years to come (something that is highly unlikely unless the hospital's doctors were wrong), any new cases like hers will be rare. In March 2015, Jahi's parents filed a malpractice suit against the hospital; if she is proven alive, their settlement will cover the costs of her post–death certificate care. Since Jahi's case was first reported, there have been dozens of law and medical school conferences about the ramifications. Will it upset medicine's understanding of brain death? No, is the short and definite answer. Will it lead to more families contesting their loved one's death certificate? Only time will tell.

CHAPTER SEVEN

The Most Vulnerable

The first thing you notice about Bill is that he's in a wheelchair, much as the first thing you'd notice about a tall person is that he's tall. With a tall person, though, you accept it; he's tall, and that's how it is. With Bill and his chair, you immediately have questions. Why is he in the chair? What happened? It's a fancy chair, expensive, sleek, and outfitted with small, fast wheels and a thick cushion, as if it's made for racing, for speed and a long haul. It's not a part-time chair; it's not a temporary ride. When you meet Bill, you immediately know that he's been in this chair for a long time, that it's part of him. He moves in it like it's an extension of his limbs; he's graceful, he doesn't think about the metal and fabric and rubber. He *inhabits* it and interacts with it with familiarity and dexterity, like an adult eating with a spoon or a carpenter using a wood plane. But that doesn't mean that he's not aware of the chair. He's incredibly self-aware; and he's constantly reading his surroundings and the reaction of others to him. He knows how you feel about him and his chair before you do. When moving around a restaurant or a park or the city streets with Bill, you notice that his spatial and emotional understanding of his environment is like a sixth sense, a heightened attention. In some way, it's like he's on guard.

I know Bill because we had a fight that neither of us wanted to let go of. In the early spring of 2010, I was spending a lot of time thinking out loud on my blog about end-of-life issues, particularly about the movement to legalize aid in dying and its "pro-life" opponents. I had just started editing the *Revealer*, a publication at the Center for Religion and Media at New York University that focuses on how the media discusses religion. It was the intersection of religion and health care, particularly around the issue of aid in dying, that consumed me. I was closely watching the language and media coverage created by "pro-life" groups like the Terri Schiavo Life & Hope Network. I'd posted an excerpt from an article by Douglas Todd at the *Vancouver Sun*: "In this increasingly bitter debate, disabled activists claim legalizing assisted suicide would be an ethical 'slippery slope' that would lead to all disabled people, no matter the degree of their impairment, being devalued as human beings." The use of *slippery slope*, here in quotes, interested me. It's a "logic device" that is often debunked because it posits that one action—in this case, the legalization of aid in dying—will lead to another, like the euthanasia of others. I had also noticed that Bobby Schindler was billing himself as a "disability rights" activist, using the slippery slope argument to show that the "threat" to one minority group automatically meant a threat to all. Some religious and disability opponents were using similar language. I was not ready to write about the controversy surrounding some disabled groups' opposition to aid in dying—there are also disabled groups that support legalization—because I didn't understand it, I hadn't thought it out yet, and I hadn't read enough. I was afraid of making assumptions. I was certain that I didn't need to be disabled to support the rights of the disabled. But I knew that I didn't have a grasp of why some disabled groups so strongly opposed aid in dying. I wrote as much quite clearly.

Then, up popped Bad Cripple. On his blog, he called my writing "infuriating." "In my opinion Neumann states many interesting things but always [seems] to take a wrong turn in her analyses. She acknowledges the rights of disabled people and supports their efforts to gain equality. Yet when it comes to opposition to assisted suicide, as an advocate, she takes disability rights activists to task." The reductive summary pissed me off. I wasn't taking disability rights activists to task; of course I supported efforts to gain equality. I was simply saying that I couldn't see how legalizing aid in dying countered or curtailed the rights of the disabled. Trading the rights of some, like the dying, for others, like the disabled, didn't make sense to me. Legal aid in dying was for terminal patients, those with six months or less to live. A paraplegic person wasn't terminal; he was paraplegic.

Bad Cripple said I didn't understand the threat to the disabled because I wasn't disabled. Because I didn't have any skin in the game, I couldn't comment on it (or rather, couldn't counter his view). Yet I was expected to take his word for it, to intuitively get the connection. I wrote, "I sympathize with the fear and vulnerability the disabled community feels toward the medical industry, the state, and society. But conflating two separate issues is just bad advocacy. With a little (understandable) paranoia thrown in." I understood what Bad Cripple was saying about the injustice of a world that didn't recognize "abnormal" bodies, that failed to extend equal rights and all kinds of services to the disabled community. But to be eligible for aid in dying, one not only had to be terminal—a medical diagnosis—but had to initiate a conversation with her doctor, had to ask for lethal drugs herself. I shook my fist for patient autonomy! Every patient, disabled or terminal or whatever. No one but individual patients should make their medical decisions. A doctor's job was to inform patients of all their choices. The job of each of us was to make those decisions, with the help of as much knowledge as possible. How would someone who wasn't dying, who didn't want to end his life, feel threatened by a law that didn't apply to them? Bad Cripple wrote:

> I doubt Neumann goes through the same mental gymnastics or experience[s] the fear people with a disability do when they go to the doctor's office or hospital. Perhaps Neumann can appreciate the difference between the terminally ill and disabled but I assure you most people, doctors included, do not. How else do I explain comments made to me such as "I would rather be dead than use a wheelchair" or "Are you sure you wish to receive medical treatment" or "How long have you suffered paralysis?" A clear message is being sent and it is not positive. Indeed, it is deadly and with the right spin can be lethal in some circumstances. My existence is open to question, my life less valuable. This is not paranoia but rather a social fact. Somehow I doubt anyone has openly questioned the value of Nuemann's [sic] existence or asked her if she really wished to receive medical treatment. Frankly I do not want Nuemann's [sic] sympathy or anyone else's for that matter. What I want is support; support for my civil rights.

For three long, obsessing days, Bad Cripple, readers of his blog (most with disabilities), and I scrapped it out on his website. Jen, the last commenter, ended with this advice to me: "I'd encourage you to seek out that degree of awareness through whatever means works for you—reading memoirs by people with disabilities, talking to disabled people, critically considering your own internalized beliefs about disability. . . . Otherwise you risk sounding like you are saying what you believe is necessary to gain our support without quite getting it." Then, *bing*, I got an e-mail from Bill Peace, aka Bad Cripple. "If you would ever like to have lunch it would be a pleasure to meet."

The scene opens darkly, with a close-up of corpses in the back of a wooden wagon. Mud, muck, and groans. *Clang.* "Bring out your dead." The sick cough and scurry around when they hear it. *Clang.* "Bring out your dead." They try to hide in baskets, anywhere, out of the sight of the body collector. A man approaches the cart with a body thrown over his shoulder. "Here's one," he says.

"I'm not dead," says the old man/body.

"What?" says the body collector.

"Nothing," says the man.

"He says he's not dead," says the body collector. The three continue their banter. Finally, the man asks if the body collector can do anything. He pauses, then turns and hits the old man over the head—*clunk*—and throws him onto the cart. On top of the other bodies.

The scene is from the 1975 movie *Monty Python and the Holy Grail.* It's called the "Not Dead Yet" scene. And it's funny, hilariously so. Not just because it's so dark, because the near-dead are scurrying around in the mud to avoid being hauled away, from having their last miserable but living moments curtailed, but because the able, the healthy, are trying to *unload* them. To off-load them onto a wagon, onto the cold bureaucracy of the state. *It's against regulations. Here's your nine pence.* We laugh because the profound and dignified struggle to survive is disrupted, is discredited by convenience and the business of order: the obligations of the state to collect what is no longer useful; the (practical) cold-heartedness of the man who is trying to dispose of *his* old man (his father, grandfather, neighbor?) and is willing to prematurely part with nine pence for the service. There's a plague going on; there are other mouths to feed. Why wait for the body collector's next round when, well, he's here right now?

"The definitive characteristic of human dignity (reason) must always be employed to maintain and preserve it; and thus, the incalculable value of such dignity remains in service of a certain economy, of the production and conservation of itself," writes Scott Cutler

Shershow in *Deconstructing Dignity: A Critique of the Right-to-Die Movement.*
The old man tries to prove that he is still alive. He tries to reason with
the body collector, with his carrier—he's not dead, he's getting better,
he wants to go for a walk, he's happy—by proclaiming his physical
and emotional abilities. His dignity. Dignity makes dignity. That's its
job. "Laughter and comedy, by contrast, are opponents of dignity, and
prime instances of the kind of thing that reason must keep in check,"
Shershow writes. We laugh because what should be the most humane,
the most important task for the body collector, for the old man's son,
for all of us, is preserving the old man's dignity. They (we) are obligated to care for him. All the old man wants to do is laugh, go for a
walk, to do the things that the living do; he makes the case for more
time. Yet, it's time that curtails his dignity. The body collector has to
keep going; he has a job to do; the man whose shoulder he's thrown
over needs to get on with his own life.

In the spring of 1996, Diane Coleman, who, because of neuromuscular disabilities has been in a wheelchair since the age of eleven,
founded Not Dead Yet, a "national disability rights group," according
to the website's "about" page, that's devoted to "disability rights opposition to legalization of assisted suicide and euthanasia." Coleman
took the group's name from the scene in *Monty Python and the Holy Grail.*
"Not Dead Yet: The Resistance" reads the heading of the group's website. Not Dead Yet is written in a sinister black script; long, pointed
daggers protrude from the N, Y, and Ts. The O in Not is the symbol
for a person in a wheelchair. What the group members are resisting
is a premature clunk on the head. They're resisting being thrown onto
the body cart before it's time. They're protesting for more time, proclaiming their dignity. And their definition of disabled is very broad.

Every one of us will be disabled at some point in our lives, Not
Dead Yet points out. The group opposes aid in dying because, it says,
"people who are labeled 'terminal,' predicted to die within six months,
are—or will become—disabled." The six-month window, required by

the Death with Dignity law, is "unreliable." But any legalization, it claims, is an affront to all of us, particularly to the disability community. It is the further erosion of disability rights. Not Dead Yet is right that each of us will likely someday be disabled, either by disease, trauma, or old age. Terminal diagnoses *are* unreliable. I've had plenty of hospice patients live fewer than six months but also longer. Doctors make errors all the time; the body is an unpredictable thing. If the disabled were properly cared for, if they were valued by our society and our medical system, we would accept that disability is a fact of life, Not Dead Yet says. And the disabled (those who use, support, or want to use Death with Dignity where it's legal) would not want to end their dying. They would not be "suicidal."

Not Dead Yet also disputes medical futility—the concept that patients are being overtreated at the end of their lives. Our obligation is to do everything possible to prolong a person's days, even if that person no longer wants to go on living, it claims. Those who do not want to live are suicidal and should be treated for depression; they should be shown their value. The group has vocally protested films that depict mercy killing, like the 2004 *Million Dollar Baby*, directed by Clint Eastwood, in which the protagonist, a female boxer, is helped to end her life. And the 2012 *Amour*, directed by Michael Haneke, in which an ill, elderly woman is smothered by her husband with a pillow. These movies, Not Dead Yet asserts, glorify mercy killing and devalue the lives of those who are in need of care. With that care, Not Dead Yet says, the dying would reevaluate. They would treasure the last days, regardless of the pain.

The group also protested the removal of Terri Schiavo's feeding tube and has supported the Schindler family in their challenge to guardianship and medical surrogacy decisions to remove artificial "life"-prolonging treatments. Surrogates and family members may not always have their loved one's best interest in mind, Not Dead Yet says. Which raises the question, who else would? As a society, we default to the assumption that families are the source of best interest for individuals, even as we watch for signs of abuse or coercion. Yes, elder abuse and medical coercion are real, but their occurrence is the exception, not the norm. And yet, Not Dead Yet's answer to why families may agree to remove "aggressive" treatments? Families are murderous.

Patients, Not Dead Yet says, might not have their own best interest in mind either. The desire to end one's life is suicidal, and our primary effort should be prevention, not support of their self-destruction. The group has long challenged POLST forms that allow patients, in advance of unconsciousness or incapacity, to designate their medical desires. Diane Coleman has written that the enforced use of POLST forms by those who are expected to die within the next twelve months is dangerous. In a 2013 video presentation to the Institute of Medicine's Committee on Approaching Death (the text of which is posted on Not Dead Yet's website), Coleman stated that the

> criteria are much broader than the hospice definition of terminal [six months versus twelve months], and sweep in many disabled people, people with muscular dystrophy, multiple sclerosis, Parkinson's, and many other conditions, including me. Many of us are working, raising families, and living normal lives with some adaptations. Medical professionals specializing in disability understand this "paradox," but most practitioners do not.

Coleman's and Not Dead Yet's position is this: as much as I fear being hit by a bus and kept around for years, even decades, on a feeding tube, a body with no awareness of the world, no consciousness, Coleman fears a situation in which she experiences a medical catastrophe and *won't* be kept alive. How does she account for people like me who don't want to exist in some mentally or physically disabled state? I'm biased against disability, she asserts. Plenty of people "with tracheostomies and ventilators" are "able to work, go to school, and live in their communities." In other words, I would want "life support" if I weren't prejudiced, both innately and by society, against those who are on life support, who need machines or wheelchairs to keep going. I'm ignorant and uninformed of all the beauty that a disabled life has to offer.

Informed consent is a misnomer; in our lack of understanding—in our disdain—for disability, we cannot know what we would want in such dire situations. Only the disabled know that every minute, every scrap of time, is worth living, and our obligation as human beings is to demand every scrap of time for ourselves and others. Coleman's defense of every minute on the grounds that those with tracheostomies and ventilators are productive and interactive—*able to work, go to school, live in their communities*—is proved by the fact, as Coleman notes in the video address, that she's "employed two women with 'trach-vents' over my career and many others with serious, progressive, chronic conditions." I suspect that Coleman's appeals to normalcy or productivity don't fully represent her measure of human value, but she knows her audience: a society that values lives based on contribution, too often defined as physical, psychological, and financial independence.

We have no proof that POLST forms misrepresent patients' wishes, no examples that show lives maliciously cut short. The forms are filled out by a doctor in consultation with patients. But dead patients don't talk; we can't ask them, after all, what they *really* wanted. This lack of proof, to Not Dead Yet and Coleman, means that there aren't enough studies to prove that the disabled, the elderly, and the infirm are being taken advantage of by biased doctors. Doctors are predisposed to see only the challenges of extensive lifesaving measures, not the value of lives supported by them. We can definitely use more challenge to the traditional and entrenched paternalism of medical culture, I say, but is the assertion of yet another group like Not Dead Yet that it knows what's best for all of us any better? Coleman and other Not Dead Yet members claim to know us better than we know ourselves.

Not Dead Yet doesn't go for theological justification of its position, like the family of Terri Schiavo, the Schindlers, or Frank Pavone.
It doesn't need to. Its members have experience; they know that life
is sacred with or without God or any other defined moral source.
Stephen Drake, who does much of the writing on the website and is
listed as Not Dead Yet's research analyst and media contact, has an
anger that is real and personal. He'll take whatever research, op-eds,
and media serve his argument, and he'll rail against what doesn't with
a defiant anger that demonstrates the fear that he and fellow disabled travelers have of medical culture, media culture, and culture at
large. After the suicide death of actor Robin Williams, in a post titled
"Robin Williams and the Hypocrisy of Suicide Prevention Organizations," Drake wrote,

> I, for one, am extremely unimpressed and underwhelmed by the
> suicide prevention brigade. Even in this latest episode of a publi-
> cized suicide, I see nothing in their messaging to indicate that any
> of the organizations or their reps care at all if old, ill, and disabled
> people kill ourselves (unless, of course, we're Robin Williams).

In the post, he highlights the connection between legal aid in dying
in Oregon and the high suicide rate there (according to the Centers for
Disease Control, Oregon has the second-highest rate in the country
after Wyoming, where aid in dying isn't legal; nor is it legal in the other
top-ten suicide states).

Drake castigates suicide prevention organizations for being blind
to such a connection. Even the use of the phrase "aid in dying" infu-
riates Drake. It's a euphemism that he considers an indication of how
far down the road (or the slippery slope) American society has gone,
how normalized suicide is. He's right that aid in dying is a euphemism. But in his formulation of social ills that cause the premature
death of the devalued and the vulnerable, Drake leaves no room for a

rational conversation about pain and suffering, for the "humane" or "dignified" position that pain can be worse than life itself, particularly if that life is unconscious, unresponsive, or terminal. Not Dead Yet's position has a tone of egotism: look at us, imagine how much pain we have suffered, how much discrimination, the fight that we must make every day to survive, to run this website, to be happy. If we can do it, if we can *resist* a world that thinks us unworthy, unproductive, inhuman, then so can anyone. And its members take this position knowing—railing against—a society that compounds that difficulty by not supporting the disabled, by not even seeing them. It's impossible to watch Not Dead Yet's activism and not be humbled, to not admire its work, to not rethink how easy it is to hop out of bed in the morning. The members give you no choice but to reconsider how you move through the world with physical privilege. Yet theirs is an arrogance comparable to the dominant position of hospice culture: we know the best way to die. In the case of hospice, that way is calmly, with reflection, caring company, and a dose of spirituality thrown in. With Not Dead Yet, that way is kicking and screaming. *Do not go gentle.*

Bill Peace, in my first interaction with him, which came through a series of scathing and convoluted blog posts, made it immediately clear that he was not "going gentle." Drake read a post I had written and responded to it on his site. He wrote that I disregarded disability rights concerns because of "ignorance or a simple wish to use misinformation." Peace responded on his blog that I was intentionally endangering the lives of the disabled—or stupid. I was surprised by the double attack. But, I had to ask myself, was my ignorance of disability making me inadvertently dangerous? Like the Americans who explain away the overwhelmingly high percentage of blacks in prison as a result of higher crime rates among the black community? Was I perpetuating a system that institutionalized inequality? In the case of disability, that institution was medicine, not prisons, or if not medicine explicitly, activists who wanted to kill off the most vulnerable around us.

On April 6, 2010, I drove up to Port Chester, a tiny coastal hamlet on the Connecticut–New York border, about an hour and a half north of New York City. Bill Peace and I had decided to eat lunch outside at Ebb Tide Seafood. Bill felt I was a perfectly safe lunch date—I'd never thought of myself as a danger to the disabled until our spat online— but I was now self-conscious. I spent the drive up to Port Chester cataloging my disability bona fides. There was my Uncle Frank who was epileptic and had what today we call Down syndrome and had lived into his eighties. When I was a teenager, I babysat for a deaf child. My aunt Martha Jane had survived polio. My hospice patient, Mr. C, had Parkinson's. I'd had colleagues, lovers, and friends with ADD, dyslexia, and Asperger's syndrome. I'd spent a lot of time with elders, both as a hospice volunteer and, well, as a person with a family. Not once had I tried to take one of them out. My cataloging made me feel like a white person counting up her black friends to prove she's not racist. I was determined to show Bill that I thought him every bit my equal. And that I wasn't freaked out by disabilities or "abnormalities." Bill, I was pretty sure, was determined to prove to me that he could do anything I could do, and also show that the world didn't understand him, that the world saw just a chair when it saw him coming. How we—the culture at large, me, me and Bill together—were ever supposed to change that perception of disability, I didn't know. Blacks and other minorities were often in danger because of public perception and prejudice. Other categories, like gender, and the danger that comes with being female, say, on a dark street, late at night, in heels and a short skirt? Now that's a danger I knew well. I had skin in that advocacy game.

I arrived early in Port Chester. The Ebb Tide was boarded up when I got there, so I sat on the parking lot curb clutching my phone and watching for Bill's van to pull into the lot. Bill, I knew, was about fifty, but when I saw him behind the wheel of his van, he looked younger.

He was casual, in jeans and a long-sleeve T-shirt; his brown hair was long and pulled back in a ponytail, a few inches hanging down his back. It was just beginning to thin along his forehead. Bill parked and we decided to go over to another wheelchair-accessible restaurant he knew nearby. I watched him change wheels, from his van to his wheelchair. The Indian restaurant was quiet. We were among the first to arrive for the lunch buffet. The wait staff hustled to move a chair from our table to make a space for Bill. I picked up my plate and said, "Shall we?" Bill put his plate on his lap, and we moved down the row of steaming stainless hotplates on the buffet. We stuffed ourselves on Indian food and talked into the afternoon, as the lunch crowd came and went. Both of us were surprised to find that we agreed on most things, including the fact that the Internet was a great place to vent anger and make assumptions about others—assumptions that disappeared when you sat down in person. We got our nuance back by sitting face-to-face.

Bill told me that around the age of ten or eleven, he began to notice neuromuscular problems. His limbs didn't move when or where he intended them to. His supportive family helped him to get the best treatment possible at the time. It was the early 1970s and a new era of treating paralysis was burgeoning. Once diagnosed with hydromyelia, a disease that widens the spinal cord and allows fluid to accumulate, Bill and his family knew what was coming. He would wake up early mornings and think about his big toe. If he could still move it, the day would be okay. Bill writes that when he was about twelve, a nun in his Catholic school told him, "You no longer need to do homework because you are one of God's special children." His mother would have none of it. She was determined that her son would receive the same education as every other child; Bill was promptly enrolled in public school. "No matter how sick I was and regardless of my ability to walk, I was not one iota different from my siblings and peers. I was a Peace, and in our family, my mother told us, we hold our heads up high and straight." By the age of eighteen, Bill was fully paralyzed from the waist down. But his paralysis wasn't like a straight line you could trace with your finger, above still feeling and below not. He was still able to sense some things, like pressure, below his waist. One of the first things I noticed about Bill was that he had a different sense of physical privacy than most. Except for my hospice patients, I hadn't encountered a person who was so uninhibited when discussing his bodily functions and treatments. Caring for Bill's body had been the task of many people.

Bill got his bachelor's degree from Hofstra and his PhD in anthropology from Columbia, graduating in 1992. "What is a bad cripple? It is a person such as myself with an obvious disability who is well aware of their civil rights," he wrote. Bill's activism is a strange mix of tough-guy resistance and vulnerability. Online, he wrote, "I don't want Neumann's sympathy, or anyone else's for that matter." Bill is certain that society is out to get him; it's been proven to him repeatedly. To counter that, he's fostered and been taught to prove he is equal to anyone else. Young Bill was "brainwashed into an extreme sort of self-sufficiency and independence." But as he's moved on through life, marrying, having a child, divorcing, and ultimately taking up disability rights activism, he's become aware of what that brainwashing prevented him from realizing. In October 2010, he wrote on his blog:

> I have been completely independent since I was paralyzed. Indeed, I consider independence central to my identity. Thus I am like most Americans in placing great value on independence. Unlike most Americans however I realize how fleeting independence really is. I have given great thought to why we Americans value independence. For those of us who are paralyzed, temporarily or permanently have lost independence, and the terminally ill we realize what a crock independence is.

How internalized that is, I'm not sure. But who of us can say we are without prejudice . . . or hypocrisy? In conversation, Bill's defense of the disabled seemed to wane or become more nuanced when discussing mental disability. Certainly it did when discussing patients who were severely brain damaged, like Terri Schiavo. He could contest doctors removing his own life support, even Schiavo's, but he had no easy way to discuss where the line between living and dead was drawn. His approach to disability rights was to always, without exception, err on the side of life, regardless of what that meant to the patient or her family.

In the spring of 2014, Bill wrote a controversial piece for a "Bad Girls" issue of *Atrium*, an annual report published by the Medical Humanities & Bioethics Program at Northwestern University's Feinberg School of Medicine. Rachelle Barina and Devan Stahl, writing on Bioethics.net, summarize Bill's essay like this:

> "Head nurses" were women who gave young paralyzed men like himself blowjobs in the late 1970s. Peace describes "shapely young women" giving "world-class blowjobs" to men who were worried their "dicks" did not work and they could not "fuck." Peace describes his own despair and his anticipated encounter with a "head nurse." Peace nostalgically claims, "This woman was able to provide me a level of care and a connection that no longer exists." "She reaffirmed my manhood and masculinity in a way I will forever appreciate." "[T]he nurse injected a compassionate eroticism that made me a better man," and ultimately, ". . . gave me myself."

The entire issue was resoundingly denounced across various bioethics forums for its "Bad Girls" theme (*girls* infantilizes women in the medical industry; the phrase invites sexist stereotypes of "promiscuity and deviance," perhaps not the pioneering women in medical history the report sought), but Bill's piece was particularly offensive to those sensitive to gender disparity (including me). "While sex and sexuality can be a site of power for women, we live in a culture where all too often women's bodies are assumed to be objects available for use by men. Regardless of the position of power a woman occupies, she is vulnerable to violence and exploitation by men who believe it is a woman's duty to affirm their masculinity," write Barina and Stahl.

Bill's version of determination and (masculine) independence is undergirded with an unwavering fear of the medical system, a sense of vulnerability and invisibility that is the result of his experiences over the past thirty-six years he's been in a chair. A constant refrain is how defiant and disruptive he is, and how he challenges the expectation that, because he's in a wheelchair, he should be sweet and agreeable, happy to take what he can get. He rails against doctors, nurses, and the able-privileged; the holy well-wishers who offer him unsolicited prayers; the Christopher Reeves of the world who are disabled and search only for a cure, not acceptance of their new bodies; the teachers who ask him again and again if he is indeed his son's father; the organizers of conferences on disability who ask him to speak but host the event in inaccessible lecture halls; the manufacturers who can and do offer necessary products, like his high-tech bed or seat cushion, at exorbitant prices; the legislators who say placating things about the disabled but do nothing to change laws; even the "pro-life" activists who have claimed disability for their own purposes.

Our conversation that afternoon never waned, but eventually we both realized that lunchtime had long since passed. The sun was low over Port Chester; the light off the water turned every smooth surface around us into a blinding white. It was time for me to drive back to the city. I excused myself to go to the bathroom, and when I returned, I found Bill being chatted up by a couple who was seated at the table next to ours. They had handed him a prayer card, a little tract that had scripture printed on it in a cursive font. They had asked him how long he'd been "like that." They had told him they would

pray for him. I contained my giggle. Bill was not the prayer type—
not in a foxhole, and not in a wheelchair. Outside, as we made our
way to the parking lot, Bill told me that such encounters happen all
the time. On *Bad Cripple*, Bill once posted an account of a man who
tracked him through the grocery store and stopped him as he was
loading bags of produce into his van. "God struck you down because
you have evil in your heart. You committed a mortal sin," he said. I
told Bill that I thought we were all guilty of profiling those around us
(although the grocery stalker's profiling was particularly pernicious,
an Evangelical overachievement). I clutch my purse when walking past
a group of young black men after dark. I know better, but I've caught
myself doing it anyway. I scowl and flip off middle-aged men who
tell me to smile, who tell me I look good in my work clothes, who
tell me my husband is a lucky man, but only when I'm in public and
feel safe enough to avoid physical retaliation. Race, gender, disability,
sexuality: we all make assumptions based on how we see a person and,
when we should know better, say things that show those assumptions. How do we change profiling? How do we stop discriminatory
comments? How do we prevent the physical danger that accompanies
them? Bill and I both shrugged. We keep doing what we do; we keep
pointing it out.

Bill explained to me that some discriminatory acts were more dangerous than others, and I agreed, particularly systemic inequality, like
the discrimination that medicine and other institutions have (developed or not addressed) against the disabled. It's built into systems; it's
part of the culture. The good news is that cultures can change, with
the right labor, messaging, and awareness. The deinstitutionalization
of disabled children has led to greater awareness of special needs in
education, for instance. The Americans with Disabilities Act changed
some things, but not enough. With the legalization of aid in dying,
Bill said, people like him—or those with even greater disabilities—
were being told their lives weren't worth living; it was a backward step,

or a lethal forward one. "Clinicians identify what is physically wrong with the body. Illness in contrast is what a patient experiences when they are sick—and all disabled people are thought to be sick in some way," he wrote on *Bad Cripple* (without acknowledging that chronic illness is also often debilitating). Still, I believed him, but I wasn't convinced that Not Dead Yet's approach—condemning those who didn't agree—was the best culture-changing tack. It wanted to be the audacious Black Panthers of disability rights, but its roots were in lashing, inexact, cynical (and often illogical) humor. And I still wasn't sure that thwarting legitimate rights for others—suffering, desperate others—was a moral or worthy objective. On that visit, he told me he had just joined the board of Not Dead Yet.

A few months later, I went up to Port Chester again, and we had another good lunch. Our friendship ambled on over the months and years, either one of us checking in on the other. In August, Bill wrote to tell me that he wasn't doing very well. He had had an unsuccessful surgery—ironically, he told me, on the twentieth anniversary of the Americans with Disabilities Act—to address a "grossly infected stage four wound." He had been bathing and noticed an odd sensation on his hip. When he pushed on it, his hand went through the flesh and to the bone. The smell told him it was infected. Pressure sores are common worries for para- and quadriplegics, for elders who don't move a lot, or anyone who experiences prolonged pressure on an area with a bone. The pressure stops blood from flowing to soft tissue, and the tissue dies. Bill is really good at shifting his weight regularly; one of the first things you notice about him is his constant movement, lifting one side of his body off the chair, then the other. He's lived with the threat of pressure sores most of his life. But his experience was now proof of how dangerous they can be. For weeks he was hospitalized; he went through two surgeries. For months he was unable to sit up, only working up to being vertical through laborious rehabilitation and dogged stubbornness. "Do you have enough help around? Are you recovering?" I e-mailed. Three weeks later, he wrote to say that he needed more surgery. In December, he wrote on his blog:

> I have thought of little else aside from my wound in the last 24 hours. I feel as though I have somehow failed or my body has failed to heal. I have been a model of "patient compliance" and know I am not to blame. I do not sit up often, my sitting is in fact severely limited. I try to bend my hips as little as possible in fact. None of this has done much good. I am worried—deeply worried. Flap surgery [in which skin with its own blood supply is moved from one donor to another] I see as a measure of last resort. If it fails I am in deep trouble. I worry not about the routine things that go wrong with surgery—I accept that risk as beyond my control. My worries are what happens if flap surgery fails. At that point I am at the end of the road—meaning I will never sit normally again. It will be just me and these four walls.

In the July-August 2012 issue of the *Hastings Center Report*, Bill wrote an essay, "Comfort Care as Denial of Personhood," describing an experience he had during those long months of surgery after surgery. "It is 2 a.m. I am very sick. I am not sure how long I have been hospitalized. The last two or three days have been a blur, a parade of procedures and people," the essay begins. He goes on to explain that he had been "miserable, fevered and vomiting for several hours" when a doctor ("hospitalist") entered his room. "What transpired after the nurse exited the room has haunted me. Paralyzed me with fear." The doctor asked Bill if he "understood the gravity" of his condition, and Bill said yes. The doctor went on to explain what could happen; it could take six to twelve months to recover, if the wound healed at all. It was possible that he wouldn't be able to sit up again, sit in his chair again. His independent life could be over. The financial and emotional costs he would face, regardless, would be staggering.

He told Bill what potential damage the antibiotics he was on could do to his organs, particularly his kidneys. He told Bill that recovery wasn't guaranteed; many don't survive. "This litany of disaster is all too familiar to me and others with a disability. The scenario laid out happens with shocking regularity to paralyzed people." Bill writes in the Hastings essay:

> His next words were unforgettable. The choice to receive antibiotics was my decision and mine alone. He informed me I had the right to forgo any medication, including the lifesaving antibiotics. If I chose not to continue with the current therapy, I could be made very comfortable. I would feel no pain or discomfort at all. Although not explicitly stated, the message was loud and clear. I can help you die peacefully. Clearly death was preferable to nursing home care, unemployment, bankruptcy, and a lifetime in bed. I am not sure exactly what I said or how I said it, but I was emphatic—I wanted to continue treatment, including the antibiotics. I wanted to live.

To anyone—me—who has been writing about informed consent as a means to achieve medical rights for patients, the essay is shocking. In my mind, the doctor was doing his job; he was telling Bill what the future could hold and was giving Bill the chance to determine what exact medical treatments he wanted. But Bill saw it as a threat. He writes that disability memoirs often document discrimination, but few include experiences such as his. He considers the doctor's stark disclosure of what could happen to him as "the ultimate insult," particularly because he was so low and so ill. He compares the experience to assisted suicide: "In a visceral and potentially lethal way, that night made me realize I was not a human being but rather a tragic figure. Out of the kindness of the physician's heart, I was being given a chance to end my life." And he condemns the use of do not resuscitate (DNR) orders for patients like himself, who are desperate, perhaps even willing to die rather than endure the pain and suffering. He writes in the Hastings essay:

> I narrowly avoided the outcome that the physician described, but he was correct in much of what he told me. I was bedbound for nearly a year. Insurance covered few of my expenses. I took a financial bath. But the underlying emotion I felt during my long and arduous recovery was fear. My fear was based on the knowledge that my existence as a person with a disability was not valued. Many people—the physician I met that fateful night included—assume disability is a fate worse than death.

The Hastings Center published several responses to Bill's essay, including one by Anita Silvers, also an academic who has been in a wheelchair since childhood. She writes that although she's "not yet believed myself to be fighting for my life against professional health-care providers," she knows why Bill was so shaken by the encounter with the doctor: it's not because Bill is unaccustomed to discrimination, or because comfort care was mentioned as "one among several alternative courses from which the patient is free to choose." Rather, she thinks Bill's reaction was because of the "different perspectives" Bill and the doctor had on "the risks involved." Bill and Silvers are exceptional. They've lived most of their lives with disability and are familiar with the challenges, the pain, and the patience necessary to live their lives in chairs, to carry on in the face of discrimination, with the thoughtlessness of our laws; the biased values the rest of us hold dear, and the lack of ramps, parking, and job opportunities, resources and care, and on and on. Those who encounter disability later in life, from trauma, old age, or disease, simply don't have the same ability to say, I'm okay never walking again, as Bill proudly has.

Bill doesn't fear disability because, for thirty-six years, it's been his life. He's learned how to be independent, to tolerate pain, to fight. Bill contests measures of quality of life because he has a different scale. Being in a chair doesn't scare Bill (or Silvers), but it scares me . . . and maybe Bill's doctor. After years of hospitalizations and treatments, Bill surely has a higher pain threshold than I do. And after years of fighting for his health and mobility, Bill is definitely stronger and tougher than I am. We should all praise that scale, but we don't—and can't—all abide by it. "People like us," writes Silvers about herself and Bill, "are experienced at being functional under adverse health conditions and thus have developed not only knowledge, but also adaptive skills, capacity to maintain morale, and endurance that surpass those of the 'normal' patient. These are strengths that everyone, and not just health care professionals, should learn to appreciate."

Peter Strauss, ostensibly the progenitor of elder law in New York State, asked me to speak at a conference he was organizing at New York Law School on end-of-life issues. Strauss's conference, "Freedom of Choice at the End of Life: Protecting the Patient's Rights over Government, Health Care Providers, and Pressure Group Resistance," was a clear defense of greater rights for dying patients, including legalization of aid in dying. Strauss is on the board of Compassion & Choices. He asked me to present on a panel titled "Special People, Special Issues." At the time, I was researching Bill Coleman's case. He was still in a Connecticut cell on a hunger strike, being force-fed by the prison medical staff. My talk compared the use of feeding tubes in hospitals and in prisons. I followed the Reverend Martha Jacobs, a pastor at Briarcliff Congregational Church and a professor at Union Theological Seminary, who spoke about various religious views regarding end-of-life issues; and Alicia Ouellette, a professor at the Mt. Sinai School of Medicine program in bioethics. Ouellette's talk directly addressed the concerns of those in the disability community regarding legalization of aid in dying and removal of treatments at the end of life. She knew Bill Peace, and her talk referenced his writing.

With nuance, Ouellette examined the reason why so many in the disability community fear the health-care system, and she suggested a path forward:

> Advocates for choice in dying might better serve their cause by listening to—and learning from—people with disabilities about their experiences in the health-care system, and then advocating for systemic change. In order to break the impasse between advocates for choice in dying and disability advocates (an impasse that has played a role in stalling the adoption of choice-in-dying laws around the country), advocates for choice in dying would be well served by working to reshape the legal and health-care system more broadly to ensure that it respects people with disabilities while they are living.

It was a smart talk. Afterward, I walked out into the lobby of the law school to find the bathroom. In a row cutting across the center of the lobby were activists from Not Dead Yet who had come to protest the event. They were a profound presence: silent, some on ventilators, with signs in front of them as they sat in their wheelchairs. I took their flyer. NOTHING ABOUT US WITHOUT US: WE ARE DISABILITY RIGHTS ACTIVISTS WHO OBJECT TO A SYMPOSIUM THAT CLAIMS TO ADDRESS DISABILITY RIGHTS CONCERNS BUT INCLUDES NO PRESENTERS FROM THE DISABILITY RIGHTS MOVEMENT. They rightly challenged that no one speaking that day, no one on the (insensitively named) "Special People, Special Issues" panel, was from the disability community. "Ouellette [is] someone who relates slanted, distorted and outright 'straw man' versions of disability critiques" and "gets many things wrong about disability issues in her book." It was an unfair assessment of Ouellette's work. But the group's accusation was right; the person talking about the disability community's concerns did not identify as disabled.

I flipped the flyer over. "Ann Neumann, instead of giving a fair account of the concerns of disability rights advocates about these issues, inserts extreme slogans from the Religious Right—and then implies that *we* are jumping on *their* bandwagon because we are just poor, scared little cripples who can easily be 'recruited' by the right propaganda. She denies the agency of disabled people, asserting that those stands we take that she disagrees with *can't* be our own." It was a horrible, dishonest distortion of my position and work. I had backed my way into disability (as a reader and blogger) from religion, not the other way around. I walked to the bathroom and cried my eyes out. But I finally understood that Not Dead Yet took no prisoners. Professionalism, honesty, even the kind of integrity that I expected in the loose and fast world of journalism—these niceties are the privilege of people who don't every day feel their lives are being threatened by medical efficiencies, a blind press, and people like me. I knew Bill Peace well enough to know that survival for him meant projection of his fear and vulnerability onto anyone, everyone. He had no time for refinement, for dallying over terms like "brain dead" and "autonomy." His pain and the discrimination he lived with were his authority. Bill and the members of Not Dead Yet didn't need me or Peter Strauss or Alicia Ouellette to tell them that they were safe. They knew they weren't and we were all guilty.

In August 2013, a man named Timothy Bowers fell out of his deer stand, crushing his C3, C4, and C5 vertebrae, three of the seven in his neck. Bowers faced a future on a ventilator and in a wheelchair. He was thirty-two and a newlywed; he and his wife, Abbey, were expecting their first child. According to the wishes of his family, doctors brought Bowers out of a coma to ask him if he wanted to remain on life support. "Tim Bowers got to decide for himself whether he wanted to live or die," read *People* magazine. "The last thing he wanted was to be in a wheelchair," Abbey told the press. "To have all that stuff taken away would probably be devastating. He would never be able to give hugs, to hold his baby. We made sure he knew that, so he could make a decision. Even if he decided the other thing, the quality of life would've been very poor. His life expectancy would be very low." About seventy-five family members crowded into Bowers's room as he was dying. Doctors removed the breathing tube from his mouth, and he was able to communicate with them. "I just remember him saying so many times that he loved us all and that he lived a great life," Abbey said. "At one point, he was saying, 'I'm ready. I'm ready,'" said his sister, Jenny Schultz.

Bowers's death was personal for Bill Peace. But for the grace of his family and his fight, Bill would be dead like Bowers. In fact, every day Bill has no choice but to fight to stay alive. "I am disgusted. Ashamed really of American society. His death is a tragedy," Bill wrote on his blog, *Bad Cripple*. He blamed everyone: Hollywood, probably poised to make a movie out of Bowers's life; doctors, nurses, bioethicists, Bowers's family. "Bowers needlessly died. In fact when I first read the story my first thought was this man was murdered. Legally killed by his family and physicians. Bioethicists are providing the post mortem cheer squad. Patients [*sic*] rights reign supreme." Bill closes his post with what, to me, is a greater tragedy than Bowers's death: "In choosing death Bowers was a hero. In choosing life I am disparaged, disliked, and seen as an economic drain. My existence is deeply stigmatized. Dying is easy, it is the living that is a bitch."

Bill presented a paper to the Future of Disability studies group at Columbia University the month after Bowers died. (It was distributed to attendees but has not been published.) "Kevorkian's Body Count," a bit of a logical mess, argued that the "primary reason the debate surrounding end of life care and assisted suicide legislation is polarized is due to the legacy of Jack Kevorkian." Kevorkian was convicted of second-degree murder in the late 1990s for helping 125 people die. To some, Kevorkian was a deliverer; to others, a media master. To the aid-in-dying community, Kevorkian was a monstrosity and a setback for its efforts because he flouted the rules they hoped would make aid in dying palatable to legislators, the medical community, and society. To Bill and others in the disability movement, he was a cold killer, part and parcel of the "right to die" movement. Bill's paper chronicles his effort to contact the family members of those who Kevorkian helped die. Rather than see Kevorkian as a lone actor, a wild eccentric with a mission, Bill uses Kevorkian's outsized media profile to paint a broad picture of what he considers a "culture of death," a culture that aims to eliminate the depressed, disabled, and sick. He points to favorable media—movies, songs by rapper Ice T, "You think your life is tough? Call Kevorkian"—to show that Kevorkian "helped change the cultural perception of death and assisted suicide."

The paper roams around various subjects: choice, informed consent, patient-centered care. But it doesn't have a clear logical thread. It's an activist's screed. It points at subjects disapprovingly, mockingly, and then moves on to the next. Patients and families don't know what they need; Bill does. But he gets a lot right, too. "The way disability is framed is misleading. The overwhelmingly negative perception of severe disability reinforces a normative view about the quality of one's life." I knew he was right. But I also knew that I wasn't changing my living will any time soon.

I drove up to Bill's house in Katonah, New York, a few months later for dinner. It was a cold night and I arrived after dark. It's an open-plan house of red brick with lots of windows. I brought the wine and salad; Bill roasted Cornish hens; their crispy little bodies were nestled side-by-side and decorated with spices. We laughed, we argued, we caught up on what was happening in our lives. It was as if I knew two Bills: the one online and on paper who raged against the world, and the one who gave me a tour of his house and cooked dinner for me.

That night, after the dishes were done and we both began to yawn, Bill gave me a present—a gorgeous wooden box slightly larger than a cake box. The heavy wooden lid is beveled so that when you place it back on the box it makes a solid, echoing sound. Indigenous paintings, graphic, rounded faces of men or animals in red and black, cover its four cedar sides. A circular, petaled stamp on the bottom says "Upper Skagit Tribe." The tribe was one of many that populated the Puget Sound area until the mid-1800s when it was pushed onto a reservation, its religion and hunting restricted by law. In 1968, the tribe was retroactively paid $385,471.42 for its land. Today tribe members operate an enormous casino and a 103-room hotel and conference center near Everett, Washington. Bill had picked up the box on a trip there years before. He was cleaning out his house to prepare for a move to Syracuse where he was starting a new teaching job; he was preparing for a new phase in his career.

The aid in dying movement has entered a new phase as well. Some of the movement's leaders have taken to heart Alicia Ouellette's challenge to advocate for aid in dying from an allied position within disability rights. Kathryn Tucker, the longtime director of advocacy and legal affairs for Compassion & Choices who argued key cases before state and federal supreme courts (including *Baxter v. Montana*, the case that made aid in dying legal in the state), became executive director of the Disability Rights Legal Center (DRLC) in September 2014. Prior to the appointment, on September 13, 2014, Not Dead Yet's Diane Coleman wrote an open letter to the DRLC, posted on the Not Dead Yet site, that stated, "As organizations many of which have partnered with DRLC in the past, and which hope to have productive collaborations with you in the future, we would be very troubled if the hiring of Ms. Tucker were seen as a message to the disability community—or to society at large—that the DRLC has taken, or may take in the future, an opposing position to that of the established disability community on the legalization of assisted suicide, isolating itself from its natural allies." Two dozen disability and related groups signed the letter. Five months later, Tucker and DRLC brought a case against New York State for the right to aid in dying.

CHAPTER EIGHT

Dying Inside

I only met Mr. Moore once, but that was enough. He was sitting up in his hospital bed when I entered his room. I said hello as I approached him. He was ready for me, looking at my notebook and pen as if he wanted something from me. He had a manic energy, as if he was on the make. When he stretched out his hand to me in greeting, I shook it. I got the feeling that he hadn't shaken a woman's hand in a long time. The room was quiet and very clean. The sheets on Moore's bed were crisp and white. There was a cup of water on the bedside table. He was wearing pajamas, and his hair was clean (one of the ways, I've learned, that you can judge the quality of patient care), but in need of a trim. Outside the window, the late morning sun was still coming from the east, casting a shadow off the fence that made a hatched pattern on the neatly trimmed winter grass. Moore looked sick. He looked washed up, spun out, as if he was running on empty but running nonetheless.

Immediately, Moore launched into an account of his ailments and worth, appealing for a strange mixture of pity and respect from me. He'd had seven surgeries on his left knee. His new $95,000 car was gorgeous and, boy, I should see it. He had a bleeding tumor in his rectum. His best friend was a cop. He had worked as a veterinary assistant. He owned four homes in Florida and was about to build one more. His odd deference and effort to impress me were unnerving. I couldn't tell what was real and what was not. As we chatted and I took notes, his hospice volunteer, a Latino man named Mr. Ramirez who had short hair and a broad face, entered the room. Mostly, Ramirez said, they just talked during their time together. "Sometimes we watch TV." He pointed his chin at the television mounted on the wall at the end of the bed. They both told to me how great the room was, so much better than the one Moore had been in before. The hospice rooms were prized because they had TVs and radios. They were quiet and private.

When I asked Ramirez why he was a hospice volunteer, he said his time with Moore made him a better person and made him think about what's important in life. He said they talked about the things they would do differently if they could. The things they were going to do in the future, like ride around in Moore's new car. Or visit each of his beautiful homes in Florida. Ramirez was happy to be a hospice volunteer because it gave him something meaningful to do; spending time with Moore was an honor. I could feel the staff in the hallway outside the room, visible through the window in the door over my left shoulder, watching me, watching Moore, watching my notebook. When I felt the staff getting restless, I began my goodbyes. "Send me the article you're working on," Moore said. He asked if we could exchange addresses. I paused, uncomfortable with the request, then wrote down my office address for him. He recited his address to me, repeating the numbers to be sure I had written them correctly: Jonathan Moore, DIN [department identification number] 01F4775, Walsh Regional Medical Unit, Mohawk Correctional Facility, Rome, New York.

I drove the four and a half hours to Rome, New York, the night before I was scheduled to visit the prison hospice program at Mohawk.
Google Maps took me on highways to Albany, then northwest past
towns named Amsterdam, Little Falls, Herkimer, and Floyd. I arrived
after dark and stayed in room 147 of the Quality Inn on South James
Street, which runs southwest from the town of Rome, past Route 365,
and makes a sweeping easterly turn when it reaches the prison campus.
Carl Koenigsmann, deputy commissioner and chief medical officer
of the New York State Department of Corrections, had written in
an e-mail that I needed to get to the facility at 9:30 for our 10 a.m.
meeting. Security protocol would take a while. "You cannot bring
any electronic devices or photographic equipment into the facility,"
he wrote. "This includes pager, cell phone, BlackBerry, electronic pad,
laptop recorder etc." The desk clerk at the Quality Inn gave me directions to Mohawk the next morning. "You can't miss it," she said in a
raspy voice.

Mohawk had once been a residential home for the developmen-
tally disabled. It occupied the southernmost corner of the 150-acre
Mohawk-Oneida campus and was converted to a medium security
prison in 1988. Today, it houses about 1,400 inmates, 112 of whom
are inside the "skilled nursing facility," Walsh Regional Medical Unit,
which takes in prisoners from the central and western parts of New
York State. In addition to the various programs offered to inmates,
including substance abuse and sex offender treatment, the prison offers a horticulture course, "resulting in well-manicured grounds and a
wide variety of plants decorating classrooms and offices," according to
a Correctional Association report from 2010. But there were no plants
to be seen when I arrived on a cold winter day in 2013.

The parking lot at Mohawk was almost empty. I left my purse behind the driver's seat of my car and nervously entered the front doors.
I had never been inside a prison before. There's nothing like an entry
protocol—and an entourage—to make you feel self-conscious. It was

immediately obvious to me that my visit was more of a big deal than I anticipated. As I was scanned, carded, and logged in, a group of staff collected in the lobby. Paul Gonyea, the prison superintendent, and Koenigsmann escorted me into a narrow conference room as nurses and doctors from Walsh followed behind. The initial presentation included introductions and a video that highlighted Mohawk's various benefits to prisoners: rehabilitation and activity programs that gave prisoners structure and a sense of purpose. The video included a brief history of the facility and details about the campus, including staff and prisoner counts and programs such as general business, academic education, and transitional services that prepared prisoners for release. Mohawk also produces all the food for the region's prisons. "Offenders employed at the Food Production Center learn marketable skills which better prepare them for successful reintegration into society and the workforce," an online description of the program reads.

What the hospice program did was prevent patients from dying alone. Terminal patients, particularly those dying inside prison, need human contact, companionship, and a chance to talk about their lives, the nurses told me. The program also provided healthy prisoners who had good behavior records the chance to train as volunteers, to give back to their fellow inmates. The program provided a real "sense of satisfaction to our guys," the daytime hospice nurse told me. "They're proud of what they're doing. They're putting someone ahead of themselves. They've put themselves first until now." She was calm and pretty, wearing all black and a large, tasteful ring. The group told me that volunteer training took place once a year (and lasted one week), but that applications came in throughout the year. She called the patients in Walsh "my patients" with a kind of endearment that expressed her commitment to them and the program. Among them, eleven were dying of AIDS and seven had major illnesses, like cancer. Special accommodations were made for dying patients—like private rooms with TVs and radios and special meals—but the staff was prepared for the "traps" that such accommodations could bring: trading morphine for cigarettes, being alone with female staff. The program, I was told, accepted patients with six months or less to live, although some live longer. "They have the chance to get involved with their own feelings," one of the nurses said.

The conference room looked as if it could be in any corporate office, except for the miles of fence that framed the landscape outside the window. There was an aerial map of the campus on one wall, and leadership posters—the kind you see in earnest start-up offices—on another. Bookshelves and a media shelf filled the wall farthest from the door. The meeting had a business tone to it as well. I was here to be sold on the benefits of the hospice program, on the efforts that the staff made to treat patients and prisoners like they mattered, to prepare volunteers for a life of compassion after prison. I was surrounded by professionals who took their responsibilities very seriously, who were committed to the lives and welfare of the prisoners. If the general public pays attention to prisons at all, it thinks of them as a necessary evil, terrible places that house terrible people. I was presented to those at the table as someone who would publicize my experience at Mohawk. It made sense to me that they were emphasizing humane treatment, educational programs, and health care. Abuse charges against prison staff and leadership are common, such as a 2014 class-action lawsuit that charged Pelican Bay prison in California with overcrowding and overuse of solitary confinement, and the horrifying 2014 reports of beatings, sex with prisoners, and drug dealing by wardens at Rikers Island prison in New York. The Mohawk staff was keenly aware of how often facilities across the country were caught violating ethical behavior and so focused the presentation on safety, value, and ethics.

But there was another feeling of defensiveness at the table that interested me. Because of my time spent as a hospice volunteer—*Why would you want to take care of dying people?*—the tone these staff members used caught my attention. They were proud of the jobs they were doing; they felt they were contributing to the betterment of society. They found their work rewarding and fulfilling. And they wanted me to know, without a doubt, that they did. Sure, I was being sold, but the staff members and directors around me believed in what they were selling me. I was in awe of them even as I balked at the paternalistic role they played in helping these prisoners—caged, monitored, "employed," removed from the world—to "give back." The concept of rehabilitation may haunt any conversation about incarceration, but the extent to which anyone believes in it gets lost in the practices of policing, sentencing, and incarcerating. It's easy to suspect that this is in part because of the power dynamic involved. Prisoners are subjected to a particular role inside, one that punishes them for any kind of deviation. They are constantly subject to an unbending authority. When prisoners go into hospice, either as patients or as volunteers, the rhetoric that surrounds their roles is constantly infused with ideas of reform.

Walsh, it seemed, was replicating the hospice model, now decades old, inside its walls. And the old hospice directive that patients be helped to think reflectively and reckon with how they've lived their lives fits surprisingly well in prison. It dovetails with the belief that men were incarcerated because they had not taken responsibility for themselves, because they did not understand compassion, did not follow the rules, and did not make themselves productive and useful members of society. Hospice is a way for them to find forgiveness for their sins and to make peace with their world and themselves.

Since prisons were established in the United States, there have always been prisoners dying inside, but the recent rise in the age of the prison population and the need for prison administrators to find ways to care for the elderly, sick, and dying provided them with a new opportunity for rehabilitation: care for the dying. What better way to help a prisoner face his sins than turn his face toward death?

Health care in the "free world," the world outside prison, is in crisis. More than $2.7 trillion—over one-sixth of the US economy—is spent on health care each year. These soaring costs threaten our national economy, local governments, families, and seniors. More than $800 billion is spent on wasteful and inefficient care. Still, despite all this expense, in 2014, the Commonwealth Fund, a nonprofit foundation, ranked US health-care quality (based on safety, effectiveness, timeliness, and other characteristics) dead last among other industrialized nations. The study, *Mirror, Mirror on the Wall: How the Performance of the US Health Care System Measures Internationally*, by Karen Davis and colleagues, found that the United States overspends all other countries in the study by more than $3,000 per patient per year. In 2012, according to the latest data from the US Census Bureau, those sixty-five and older made up 15 percent of the US population; by 2030, the number of Americans over sixty-five will have doubled. There are still more than thirty million Americans without insurance. The state of our health care is a disaster, and it will only get worse over the next few decades.

If you really want to know what the health-care crisis means for the poor, the sick, and the elderly, go to prison. Every social challenge to accessing quality, effective health care is compounded in this population. Every inequity, discrimination, and injustice is pronounced in prison. There are 2.3 million adults in jail or prison in the United States. That's the largest number of incarcerated people in the world. Between 1995 and 2010, the number of prisoners over fifty-five quadrupled. By 2030, they will account for one-third of all incarcerated, estimates a 2014 report, *The High Cost of Low Risk: The Crisis of America's Aging Prison Population*, by the Osborne Association, a prison advocacy group based in New York. Behind prison walls, where every social malady is compounded, is the perfect place from which to consider the future of health-care access and end-of-life care in the United States.

According to the National Hospice and Palliative Care Organization's 2012 report, *End of Life Care in Corrections*, there were more than seventy-five hospice programs in US prisons in 2012. Fifty percent of them rely on inmates as volunteers. A 2011 paper by Katie Stone, Irena Papadopoulos, and Daniel Kelly in *Palliative Medicine* suggests that the benefit for inmate volunteers is that "they are able to offer patients a level of empathy that cannot be achieved by free people regardless of intention or training." Inmate volunteers know what it's like to be a prisoner and can better share experiences and understanding with incarcerated hospice patients. The paper suggests that volunteers "gain valuable psychological rehabilitation" through a "renewed sense of responsibility and care." But such programs, according to the study, have two primary challenges: pain and trust. Pain management in a facility where drug use is rampant—and, indeed, a major cause of incarceration—is problematic. Doctors and nurses can find it hard to believe a patient who tells them he's in pain. "A culture of suspicion emerged concerning the illicit drug trafficking of narcotics intended for pain relief," the *Palliative Medicine* report states. The "macho" prison culture also prevented many in pain from admitting what they felt. But a larger issue, one difficult to measure, exists: "prison healthcare staff may believe that prisoners deserve their suffering." In other words, pain is punishment. Staff members tend to default on the side of pain when prescribing narcotics to hospice patients. If anyone deserves to be in pain, the thinking goes, don't thieves, murderers, drug users, rapists? In church parlance and even in broader society, the belief that pain makes us better people is commonplace. In prison, suffering is part of the centuries-old plan.

It's also hard for prisoners to believe that staff members have their best interests in mind. Can you trust doctors who work for a system that controls every aspect of your life? A system that was established to punish, subjugate, discipline, restrain, subdue? Decisions to limit care (or not pursue every option) can make prisoners even more distrustful of their caregivers. Couple that with the requirement that, in 55 percent of prisons, patients must sign DNR orders before they can enter hospice, and a climate of deprivation, ill will, and doubt about the facility's objectives can grow. Patient safety is tempered with a paternal "we know what's good for you" attitude; prisoners who feel their lives are less valued think the system doesn't care about them or is invested in getting rid of them. Yet sending prisoners to external hospices, as is done in the United Kingdom, or releasing those who are too ill to violate laws, is also a problem. The saddest sentence of the *Palliative Medicine* report is: "For some the prison and its inhabitants are all that is familiar due to institutionalization."

The Walsh Regional Medical Unit is a prison within a prison, at the center of the sprawling Mohawk campus, with its own gates, fences, and guards. The winter air was cold as staff and I walked the quarter mile from the front entrance facility to Walsh. The campus was bare and otherworldly. Broad macadam walkways, gray in the cold, stretched this way and that to surrounding buildings. A silver above-ground pipeline bisected the campus. Brown grass ran for acres to the external fences. To enter Walsh, we walked through a cage of wire fencing shaped like a square tunnel at least forty feet long. The guards were expecting us. We signed in and passed through a metal detector; we were leaving medium security for maximum security.

Inside, Walsh feels clean and new, with a large cafeteria and seating area surrounded by wings and wards. The first patient I met was Howard Biggs. He had been diagnosed with stage-four stomach cancer six weeks earlier. Biggs was from Albany, one of eight children. When he asked where I was from, his face lit up at my answer. He had friends in Lancaster, Pennsylvania, and had spent time there. We talked about landmarks we both knew, about where to get the best Philly cheese steak. I asked him what he was in for. "For selling," he told me, "for parole violation, for resisting arrest, for curfew violation." He turned his head to the side when telling me, looking at me from the wrinkled corner of his eye. He was proud that he wasn't in for more than drugs—crack, specifically—but also ashamed of his incarceration. I wasn't staff. I wasn't another prisoner. I was a representative from *out there*, the rest of the world. He knew how society looked at people in prison. "We are all having to be governed by few when we should be governing ourselves," he said. His failures were his own. He didn't blame his education, job opportunities, addiction, or race. None of these things mattered. He was penned up, he was dying, and he was contrite. "My spirit has gotten brighter here," he said about the hospice ward. "Every day since I was diagnosed, the snow was coming down. But today the sun is out," he said, looking out the window. He told me he was afraid to go to sleep. "Yes, I belong to the state right now, I'm a ward of the state," he said with acceptance and resignation. There was no more "getting out." Biggs knew that the future was the bed he was in and that no longer being a ward of the state meant no longer being alive.

I returned to the huddle of staff people outside Biggs's room. We all remarked at how calm and comfortable he was. *Or*, I thought, *defeated.* "We treat patients here as we would outside prison, with the same quality of care," Koenigsmann said. "The challenge is that we can't lose compassion or cross a line," a nurse told me, her tone warm and professional. Inside these walls, she was also a ward of the state. Her medical training—her loyalty to the patient, a bedrock of medical ethics—was tempered by her job as an employee of the prison; her employment was conditioned first by the morality and ethics of state laws regarding incarceration. Her professional oath as a care provider was second. Her compassion, then, is predicated on her compliance with laws (and a prison culture) that adhere to a particular morality, institutionalized and enforced, a morality that allows little room for aberrant behavior, that stigmatizes and degrades and then asks for "good behavior."

Prisons and hospitals have much in common. They're places where we put people who are not right, who are not like us, who are sick, deviant, abnormal. A fear of death and ill health stigmatizes patients (and propels us to be ardent health consumers), just as a fear of crime stigmatizes prisoners. In both cases, those fears may be irrational and overblown, but they are primary factors in the *health* of both industries. The hospital requires patients to be compliant, to do as the doctor says, to adjust to its rules and expectations; patients do this, with their mental discipline, in order to heal their sick bodies. We put people in prison and discipline their bodies in order to heal their sick minds. In both institutions, we believe that good behavior heals, rehabilitates, and returns the patient-prisoner to a state of normalcy so that it's safe for him to reenter society. But this equation—good behavior equals return—is not guaranteed. We believe in the healing power of hospitals, often wrongly; we no longer, if we ever did, believe in the healing power of prisons. A prison hospital may have bright, clean walls, smiling nurses, and attentive doctors, but it is still the place where the harshest characteristics and expectations of both a prison and a hospital come to bear on those held within it.

Gonyea, the prison superintendent, joined us in the hallway. He described for me the particular medical challenges that the Walsh staff faced: high rates of communicable and chronic diseases like HIV, AIDS, and hepatitis; patients who experienced organ degradation from living on the street and from years of drug abuse and lack of medical care; mental illness, depression, anxiety; and the deteriorating effects of imprisonment. I asked Gonyea if condoms were supplied to prisoners to prevent HIV and other sexually transmitted diseases. No, he told me, condoms weren't distributed because sex was against the rules. "But people here have sex, right?" I asked. "They're not allowed to," he said. The nurses and staff in the group exchanged glances. Prisons have disproportionately high numbers of HIV and AIDS cases. Since 2003, the Prison Rape Elimination Act has required the Department of Justice to report the number of prison rapes each year. In 2012, the most recent data show that rapes occur at a rate of 4 percent, but health advocates have contested the low number, stating that reporting is not thorough and that prisoners are afraid or ashamed to report rape. Infection of any sort, even of the deadly sort, is a near certainty to many victims. A death sentence with your sentence. The rate of consensual sex in prison? Anyone's guess. Fifty-five percent of inmates with HIV haven't been identified by health services, estimates the Correctional Association of New York. There's little incentive to address sex-related disease, to address prison rape incidents. Pain is punishment, or rather, pain is what prisons use as punishment. You don't follow the rules? You pay.

There are other health challenges unique to prison populations. Prisoners age faster than those of us outside. "Incarceration not only compounds existing health issues and heightens the risk of further health problems," states the Osborne Association's 2014 paper, "but—most alarmingly—has a deteriorating effect on the bodies of incarcerated people." Incarceration may slow down a prisoner's perception of time, but it accelerates his body's. Incarceration takes more years out of a life than just those required by a sentence. Lack of proper mental and physical health care and abnormally high levels of stress and anxiety can make fifty-year-old prisoners' bodies seem ten to fifteen years older. Of prisoners over fifty, 40 to 60 percent have mental health challenges.

Prisons weren't designed for elders, either. They require that prisoners climb into bunks and haul themselves up stairs or across long distances. Meals must be eaten in twelve minutes. Daily routines are strictly timed and regimented; one error—due to dementia, disorientation, physical inability, or pain—and punishment is delivered. The physical discipline of prison, meant to rehabilitate the weak, evil, or selfish mind of a criminal, is a questionable approach to reform, at best. For an elderly population, it looks like abuse. But renovating America's prisons to meet the needs of an aging population isn't in the budget. Dealing with the needs of prison elders will take a variety of approaches, none of which look easy.

The costs of prison health care are, like the costs of public health care, rapidly increasing. The United States currently spends about $16 billion—more than the entire Department of Energy budget—on incarceration of prisoners over the age of fifty. While it costs about $34,000 a year to keep an able-bodied prisoner locked up, elders can cost as much as twice that amount.

Early parole and compassionate release are rare. Parole boards are appointed by state governors and are highly political. Everyone fears a prisoner's deadly re-offense. Yet elder crime and recidivism are low. Writes the Osborne Association, "Only seven percent of those aged fifty to sixty-four and four percent of those over sixty-five are returned to prison for new convictions." (The national average of prisoners who commit crimes within three years of release is 43.3 percent.) "Similarly," the report continues, "arrest rates among older adults decline to a mere two percent by age fifty and are close to zero percent by age sixty-five." Compassionate release laws exist in thirty-six states but are seldom used.

Health care in the United States is a business. This means that it is, in part, a method of deriving profit from ill, disabled, elderly, and terminal bodies that otherwise would not contribute to society. Whether non- or for-profit, health-care companies—from insurers to pharmaceutical manufacturers, from providers like hospitals to research organizations at universities—all financially sustain themselves on payment for care from individuals. That payment may come from private savings accounts, private insurers, or state and federal governments, but ultimately it comes out of private pockets (in the form of insurance payments, salaries, and/or taxes).

The business of US prisons is both analogous to health care's transformation of unproductive bodies into profit and a facet of that transformation: corporations increasingly use prisoners for deeply discounted, government-subsidized labor. Many major corporations, including Walmart, McDonald's, JC Penney, Kmart, and the US military, rely on prison labor either directly or indirectly, for manufacture of products: items as diverse as uniforms, utensils, jeans, dentures, and chicken patties. Some corporate contracts with prisons require minimum facility occupancy rates of 90 percent—and as high as 100 percent—or the government must reimburse the corporation for "lost labor." Even corporations that aren't directly manufacturing with prison labor (which is grossly underpaid—cents on the hour—and highly incentivized by government reimbursement) are deeply invested in the benefits of the world's largest enslaved workforce. Organizations like the American Legislative Exchange Council (ALEC), a private nonprofit that is corporate funded, work with legislators to craft incarceration laws that benefit "free enterprise."

Since its inception forty years ago, ALEC has been heavily involved in both health-care and prison lobbying on behalf of corporations. The organization works directly with senators and representatives (indeed, it was cofounded by legislators and corporate CEOs) to draft legislation that enforces longer and stricter sentencing and "three strikes"–like laws, which are a means of expanding or maintaining the high prison population while providing corporations with access to prison labor and contracts to build or maintain facilities. If you build a new prison, "they" will come. The rise of ALEC's power, when coupled with President Bill Clinton's Crime Act (passed in 1994), the increase in life sentences, class disparity, high unemployment rates, and a post-9/11 culture of fear that has militarized local police forces and increased public surveillance, has produced a bloated prison system, increasingly privatized, whose inhabitants are a revenue stream for multinational corporations. In the chilling landscape of modern incarceration, punitive laws enslave citizens inside a system that then offers up their bodies for corporate profit, subsidized and enforced by the federal government and taxpayer money. All in the name of rehabilitation.

Some states, like New York, have banned or halted new contracting of prison facilities and services to private corporations. But under the country's high-incarceration, free enterprise paradigm, the rhetoric of prisoner rehabilitation—"teaching prisoners to care about others," to be "productive members of their community," "to give back" to society—becomes justification for ill-paid labor, overpriced services (like Securis, a phone company that charges prisoners and families exorbitant prices), and lucrative health-care contracts.

The only US citizens with a constitutional right to health care are prisoners. The Eighth Amendment of the US Constitution guarantees that prisoners have access to medical, dental, and mental care. Because prisoners are not eligible for Medicare or Medicaid, state and federal funding pays for prisoner health services that are often contracted to local universities or for-profit companies. Corizon, a corporation with $1.4 billion in profits each year, operates in prisons in twenty-nine states and has been sued more than six hundred times for malpractice, according to the ACLU. Corizon has been delivering health care at New York's Rikers Island since 2001. The understanding that prisoners deserve whatever suffering they encounter is deeply entrenched, a public apathy that fails to acknowledge prisoner neglect—and unfettered corporate profit.

Cruel and unusual punishment. That's the Eighth Amendment phrase that requires prisons to provide health care to the incarcerated; it appears in the Bill of Rights, which was passed in 1791. But it is also the standard by which executions should be conducted. *Cruel and unusual* has a long history of jurisprudence regarding prisoner execution, includ-ing the 1972 Supreme Court case *Furman v. Georgia.* The 5–4 decision, written by Justice William J. Brennan, notes four criteria that determine whether an execution is cruel and unusual. Punishment cannot be "de-grading to human dignity," "inflicted in a wholly arbitrary fashion," "totally rejected throughout society," or "patently unnecessary." The confusing decision—none of the judges' statements agreed; because it was considered "arbitrary," the objection to execution seemed limited to the specific case—caused a moratorium on executions in the United States until 1976. With the case *Gregg v. Georgia,* supporters of capital punishment were able to legally work around the Furman decision by shifting the focus from method of execution to prisoner sentencing.

Of Brennan's four criteria for a cruel and unusual execution, lethal injection, the primary method by which prisoners have been killed since the 1980s, meets all but one: rejected by society. Americans have largely lost their taste for capital punishment except in the few states, mostly in the South, where a culture of execution continues to thrive. While thirty-two states still have laws on the books, most execute prisoners rarely, if at all. In the past seven years, six states have abolished the practice. Yet executions still occur at a rapid pace; the United States has the fifth-highest number of executions in the world after China, Iran, Iraq, and Saudi Arabia. Texas is responsible for the most in recent years, eighty-four between 2009 and 2013. Ohio (twenty-four), Alabama (eighteen), Oklahoma (seventeen), and Flor-ida (fifteen) round out the top-five executing states. Seventy-nine per-cent of executions in that five-year period occurred in Southern states. Increasingly, execution has become an arbitrary practice, dependent on a prisoner's region, race, class, and access to resources like lawyers.

Although the American Medical Association forbids doctors from participating in capital punishment, the association has no means of enforcing that standard; I've found no record of a doctor who has lost a medical license for doing so. North Carolina, for instance, has a law that prevents doctors from being penalized for participation. A 2003 Supreme Court case, *Singleton v. Arkansas*, ruled that prisoner Laverne Singleton be treated with drugs "that would render him sane enough to be executed," writes Mirko Daniel Garasic in a 2013 article in the journal *Medicine, Health Care and Philosophy*. Elsewhere, doctors are often required to pronounce executed prisoners dead and to care for death row patients so that they may be killed by the state and not "escape" their punishment through natural death. Since the advent of lethal injection, the role of doctors in prisoner execution has become a highly contested issue. Some, including opponents of the death penalty, insist that doctor participation helps prevent lethal injection from being cruel and unusual punishment; placing needles and calculating proper doses of drugs require medical knowledge. Because of the criticism of participating doctors, many states shield the identity of executioners, guaranteeing anonymity.

When introduced, the lethal injection procedure was seen as an advanced alternative to the snapped necks of hanging and the charred bodies of the electric chair. Oklahoma chief medical examiner, A. Jay Chapman, developed lethal injection in 1977 when two state legislators approached him to create a means of execution by drugs. "The law turned to medicine to rescue the death penalty," writes Deborah Denno, a professor at Fordham University School of Law, in "The Lethal Injection Quandary: How Medicine Has Dismantled the Death Penalty." "At each step in the political process, concerns about cost, speed, aesthetics, and legislative marketability trumped any medical interest that the procedure would ensure a humane execution," Denno writes. Chapman, without consulting doctors or studies that existed at the time, came up with a three-drug cocktail: a barbiturate to make the prisoner unconscious, a paralytic, and potassium chloride to stop the heart. It was easy, cheap, clean, and seemingly nonviolent. Other states rapidly adopted the method. But from the beginning, and despite its clinical facade, the humane nature of lethal injection has been questionable. The first use of lethal injection took place in Texas in 1982. Executioners had trouble finding Charles Brooks Jr.'s vein; he was painfully poked with needles until one was found. The Death Penalty Information Center has listed on its site more than thirty problematic executions since then, one for every year that lethal injection has been used.

A scandal over how prisons obtain the drugs used for execution has refocused attention on lethal injection in the past few years. Wardens, with executions on their docket, found themselves running low on one of the three drugs in 2011. Hospira, the US manufacturer of the trademarked barbiturate sodium thiopental (sodium pentothal), had stopped making it. Prisons were forced to find another source. California and Arizona were able to buy the drug from England, but the country then prohibited export of sodium thiopental because of its opposition to capital punishment. Without a source for the drug, prisons across the country went into a panic, resorting to a host of illegal and desperate means to get their hands on sodium thiopental or a similar barbiturate. Some states switched to pentobarbital, but it too proved difficult to find. Maurice Chammah, writing in the *Texas Monthly* in June 2014, noted that a desperate corrections officer from Missouri, Dave Dormire, "testified according to court documents, that he paid $11,000 for pentobarbital to a pharmacy that he found in the Yellow Pages ('I take them cash,' he said in his sworn statement)." In 2010, Oklahoma needed sodium thiopental; prison officials asked Texas if it had any. It didn't. In 2011, Texas asked Oklahoma how it could get its hands on pentobarbital. It didn't know. As Chammah revealed, the search for available barbiturates became a macabre, inhumane joke. His article quoted e-mails from Oklahoma prison officials, later uncovered in court:

"Looks like they waited until the last minute and now need help from those they refused to help earlier," Oklahoma assistant attorney general Stephen J. Krise wrote to a colleague. "So, I propose we help if TX promises to take a dive in the OU-TX game for the next 4 years." Another official from Oklahoma dubbed his colleagues "Team Pentobarbital" and said he would request, at one of these football games, "an on-field presentation of a commemorative plaque at halftime recognizing Oklahoma's on-going contributions to propping up the Texas system of capital punishment."

When a British activist outed the name of the only Federal Drug Administration (FDA)–approved manufacturer of nonveterinary pentobarbital, the Dutch company Lundbeck wrote to sixteen US states asking that they not use the drug for lethal injection. Lundbeck began requiring that buyers sign agreements saying their purchase was not intended for human executions. In March 2014, Gregg Zoroya wrote in *USA Today*:

> Prison guards meet in the desert to hand off chemicals for executions. A corrections boss loaded with cash travels to a pharmacy in another state to buy lethal sedatives. States across the country refuse to identify the drugs they use to put the condemned to death. Oklahoma officials agonized in court papers Monday about a shortage of lethal drugs necessary for an execution Thursday. They said they are scrambling to find more. "This has been nothing short of a Herculean effort," Assistant Attorney General Seth Branham said. "Sadly, this effort has (so far) been unsuccessful." This is the curious state of capital punishment in America.

States began to change their execution protocol in January 2009. Either they found secret sources for the required drugs—compounding pharmacies, for instance—or they switched to using only one drug. Ohio was the first to use a single drug for execution (of Kenneth Biros in 2009). Arizona, Idaho, Texas, and South Dakota followed in 2012, and Georgia, in 2013.

When pentobarbital rolled across my computer screen, in news items brought up by a Google alert, I called Sue Porter, the Death with Dignity counselor in Oregon. I knew that pentobarbital was being used for aid in dying there, along with other barbiturates, including Seconal, Nembutal, and Secobarbital. Doctors in the states where aid in dying is legal prescribe lethal drugs to patients who have met the requirements of the law. In Oregon, Seconal was used for years, but the price of the drug skyrocketed in 2011. To save patients money, doctors switched to pentobarbital, Porter told me. Often the drugs were acquired from a trusted compounding pharmacy, in powder or pill form, and dissolved in the patient's preferred liquid, like orange juice or beer. What's the difference between the use of pentobarbital for aid in dying and execution? How can one cause a peaceful death and another not? With doctor involvement in the dosing process, first of all. And the difference between what it takes to end a healthy life and what it takes to end a terminal one. But for those of us watching the frantic controversy over how capital punishment is conducted in the United States, we must consider another harrowing factor: consent. Death comes differently to you when it's at the hand of your government, and comes after years, even decades, of notices, appeals, and waiting.

An October 23, 2014, Gallup poll, the results of which are posted on its website, shows that 60 percent of Americans support capital punishment, the lowest number in thirty years. That poll was taken while a series of botched lethal injections in 2014 came to public attention, undermining its clean, clinical public perception. In April 2014, when Oklahoma began its first double execution in almost eighty years, things went terribly wrong. Prisoner Clayton Lockett, once injected, thrashed on the table and continued to breathe for forty-five minutes. The governor stayed his execution, thinking that the first attempt was unsuccessful. As Lockett struggled against the drugs, prison staff closed the curtain between the execution chamber and the observation room. Lockett died after his execution was stayed. The second execution, of Charles Warner, initially scheduled for two hours after Lockett's, was delayed until November. I spoke to Warner's lawyer, Madeline Cohen, on the phone for an article I was writing at the time. She was asking the courts to require that procedures in Oklahoma no longer be kept secret; lack of transparency regarding the drugs or the procedure used was "cruel and unusual." "This is not about prisoners," Cohen told me. "It's about us. I get asked all the time why we should care if an execution is humane. We should care because it says a huge amount about who we are as a society. We are a society bounded by law. The death penalty is a deeply broken system. Taking a life in secret puts all of us in jeopardy." Warner was executed by the state of Oklahoma in January 2015.

The first letter I received from Moore, the Walsh hospice patient who asked for my address, arrived on April 1, 2013. After he and I had visited in his room, I returned to the circle of staff members outside his door. I thanked them for the chance to meet him and said that I looked forward to corresponding with him. "You can't write him letters. He won't receive them," the head nurse said. After corresponding for years with Bill Coleman, the Connecticut prisoner who was on a hunger strike and being force-fed by prison medical staff, I didn't understand why I couldn't exchange letters with Moore. Before I could ask questions, the group turned and headed down the corridor. In the three months after my visit, I had thought about Moore quite a bit. I wondered how and why the staff members selected the patients they allowed me to visit. But I assumed that if I couldn't write to him (and I wasn't enthusiastic about doing so anyway), he couldn't write to me either.

Then his letter, with "NEW YORK STATE DEPARTMENT OF CORRECTIONS AND COMMUNITY SUPERVISION INMATE CORRESPONDENCE

PROGRAM" printed on the back flap of the envelope, landed on my desk. The letter was written by hand in all caps on eight-and-a-half-by-fourteen-inch yellow lined paper. "I am sorry about taking up your busy time. But if you remember talking to me. You said you would like to write me." Moore went on to tell me that little had changed in Walsh for him. He was looking forward to being released in the coming fall and was very busy scrutinizing designs and selecting a construction company for the new home he was building. He said that he was still in the same room, but that the staff was trying to move him. "I have refused and filed paperwork to try and stop them." He said a doctor wrote a letter stating that Moore still required a private room, but "the security department and his boss" forced the doctor to change the letter. Moore said that because I was able to learn a lot about him during our visit, he wanted to know more about me. "How old are you? Are you married with children? What do you like to do for fun?" The rest of the letter was about his other house in Florida—"going to be sold on the 25th"—his love of hockey, and desire for new clothes. He couldn't wait to take his new car "for a spin." The last sentences were a plea for a letter from me. He closes with "God bless. Stay safe and healthy."

The letter confused me. Either Moore was not a terminal patient, as I had understood, or he was holding on to ideas of a future in order to cope with his death. The letter made me feel guilty. My life over the past several months had been a crowded mess of articles, social engagements, hospice visits, research, and full-time work. It had snapped by in a blink. Moore's sense of time was probably quite different. But also, I didn't want to write back. I didn't, at the time, ask myself why. He had made me uncomfortable from the moment I entered his room. But how much of that was Moore, the smarmy lies and the way he looked me up and down, and how much of that was the taint of his location, the prison? I carried his letter in my purse for about a week and then placed it on top of a pile of articles about prison hospice. It was quickly buried.

The second letter I received from Moore arrived in August, four months later. It looked like the first: the same envelope, the same paper, the same all-caps handwriting. "We have heard nothing," he wrote. Moore told me that his hospice aid, Ramirez, had quit "for some reason." The bragging about his assets continued. Moore said that he and his lawyer had settled on a lawsuit "on my cancer" for $7.8 million. He said his lawyer was right to encourage him to settle rather than "take the chance of maybe dying before the case is done in court." He'd sold three of the four Florida homes. His brother had died. His mother was taking everything very poorly. But he was looking forward to getting out in five months (although in his first letter he said he would be released in the fall). When he got out, he was going to come to the city to meet the New York Rangers. "I thought you didn't want to write me back. Well I hope you answer this letter? I also hope you are doing well?" the letter closed.

Compassion is a complicated thing. It's an emotion, both abstract and concrete, shown both in our broad support for groups or issues and in the care that we give those around us. *Compassion. sympathetic consciousness of others' distress together with a desire to alleviate it.* I can write for years about equality for minority groups, the disabled, the ill, the dying, the incarcerated. I can feel that compassion sincerely, but I also know that compassion in theory is not always compassion in practice. I know what it feels like, but it's not universal. I don't have it for everyone who is suffering. I don't have the capacity. Compassion in practice, when I do feel it, is fickle, too. I've cared about some hospice patients more than others. I've taken care of some loved ones more than others. And I've wrung my hands in guilt for the disparities. It's easier to care for people when you trust them, but also when you know you have power over them. When you know they need you.

It is easier when you get to decide how recipients feel about you; they are expected to be compliant, respectful, grateful. Trust or safety, then, can alter our levels of compassion. I felt guilty for not having more compassion for Moore, and I didn't know if it was because of him or because of where I met him. I didn't want him to be in pain. I didn't want him to be treated unfairly. But I didn't want anything to do with him, either. That, I realized, was the line that prison medical staff people had to draw. They may use prison rules or state laws or medical ethics to draw the line. And those laws and rules may make their work easier for them. But it was an institutionalized way of grappling with very complicated emotions like trust and safety and even personal chemistry. Their work is made possible by *an* ethics, not to be confused with a universal set of moral principles. The ethics of the prison medical staff members was unique to their place of work, a prison. We can and will, as a society, argue about what the laws should be, about what our conscience should let us do.

We've developed policing, legal, and incarceration systems that decide for us how to treat those who behave in ways that are unfit for society. For some who work in prisons, their job is to do the work, to treat the prisoner/patient, to get the paycheck, to tell themselves they're doing an important job. Their behavior is contained within a framework that they've accepted as just (or maybe just accepted). But what if it isn't just? Sabine Heinlein writes about incarceration in her book, *Among Murderers*: "If millions of Americans were affected with a dangerous virus that cost us billions of tax dollars, destroyed families and livelihoods, and left a large part of the population homeless and mentally ill, no one would question the government's attempt to find a long-lasting solution." Scholars, journalists, and legislators have speculated about what those long-lasting solutions should be for the criminal justice system, but progress has been slow. The broader public isn't clamoring for change. In the months after I met Moore and received his two letters, I wondered if my perception of him had something to do with why prisons are such a large part of American culture. I distrusted him and wanted little to do with him. I feel strongly that our criminal justice system is deeply flawed and ruinous to individual lives. That second part of compassion—*to alleviate others' distress*—moved me, but not enough to reply to his letters.

CHAPTER NINE

A Good Death

I was standing outside Anthology Film Archives in Lower Manhattan chatting with a friend who had just given a talk about China Girls, the women whose faces were once spliced into the first frames of a film so that projectionists could adjust for color and skin tone. As part of her talk, Genevieve Yue, a professor at the New School, had shown us a dozen such clips, women who were perhaps now old or even dead, but their young faces were forever caught on celluloid, their brief cinematic images—their afterlives—now a part of film history. I noticed that I had a phone message; it was from Marvin, the husband of my hospice patient Evelyn Livingston, who I've been seeing for over four years. I stood in the mild November air against a brick wall and listened to the message. Evelyn, he said, had never tasted a Twinkie. He wondered if I would bring some along the next day when I visited. I stopped at several delis on my way home to Brooklyn but couldn't find any of the infamous snack cakes, rumored to be so processed that they have an endless shelf life. But they were not on the shelves anymore. Invented in 1930, a spongy yellow cake filled with vanilla cream, Twinkies were as old as Evelyn. News that Hostess, the manufacturer of Twinkies, had filed for bankruptcy was all over the papers and TV. Evelyn had heard the news, I suspected, and understood that she was about to miss her last chance at knowing what one tasted like. On my way to the office the next morning, my birthday, I searched the shelves of every deli and grocery store around. Twinkies, I found, were gone. Like anyone with limited time, I searched Amazon and slapped down $25 for a box. Twinkies were gone, but they were now Internet collectibles. I had them shipped directly to Evelyn's house.

Evelyn was having her own afterlife, one practically unthinkable when she found herself in the hospital with a terminal diagnosis, desperate to get out and go home. She's a small woman, fine-featured and beautiful. But also fierce. She got herself into a wheelchair and made her way to the hospital entrance. "Get me out of here," she told any staff member who tried to steer her back to her room. Evelyn didn't have a hospital phobia; she was a medical doctor (and a psychiatrist, a doctor twice over). But she knew that she was dying and she sure as hell didn't want to die in a hospital. She had seen it all before: the florescent lights, the polite but removed nurses, the runaway infections that elders are prone to, the sad blank faces of dying patients removed from family, the comforts of home, from anything familiar. So, with a determination that belied her illness, she got herself home.

Doctors know much about the physical horrors that medicine can exact on frail bodies. They have seen the torture that tests and drugs and "extraordinary measures" can cause. In a 2014 study, "Do Unto Others," by Vyjeyanthi S. Periyakoil, Eric Neri, Ann Fong, and Helena Kraemer, two thousand doctors were asked what they would want if they were given a terminal diagnosis. Fifty-five percent said palliative care, 43 percent said hospice care, and 39 percent said do not resuscitate. And yet "extraordinary measures" are what most people get, when they could be at home, like Evelyn, living out what's left of their lives. Why is this so? Why would doctors avoid medicine's advancements in their last days, yet inflict it on their patients?

"Our current default is 'doing,' but in any serious illness there comes a tipping point where the high-intensity treatment becomes more of a burden than the disease itself," Periyakoil told Stanford's Tracie White about the study in 2014. "[But] we don't train doctors to talk [to patients about end of life] or reward them for talking. We train them to do and reward them for doing. The system needs to be changed." Evelyn took out the middle-man doctor and got herself home. She called in hospice care, which could provide her with a couple hours of care a day, morphine to keep her pain free, and oxygen to keep her cancerous lungs working. And then a funny thing happened. She continued to live. After she outlived her first six-month terminal diagnosis, the hospice doctor was required to recertify her. Yes, he concluded, Evelyn was still actively dying. Yes, she still qualified for hospice. But she was yet another example of how hospice can extend the lives of those who have given up curative treatment for the comforts of home.

"One of my staff members said, 'I think it's a really amazing thing when we have patients who stay for a long time because it demonstrates that whatever we're doing, it's prolonging their lives,'" Kathleen Pacurar, president and CEO of San Diego Hospice, told Randy Dotinga of *Kaiser Health News* in 2013 for an article titled "Slowly Dying Patients, An Audit and a Hospice's Undoing." Pacurar's organization and others across the country have come under scrutiny for essentially doing their jobs too well. Patients like Evelyn who exceed the six-month period have shined a federal spotlight on long hospice stays. The US Department of Health and Human Services, concerned with trimming Medicare and Medicaid budgets, has begun to target hospices like San Diego.

While hospice care is significantly cheaper than care in a hospital or facility, the rise of for-profit hospice programs at the same time that the media has focused on patients who outlive their six-month diagnoses creates a fear that hospice programs are acting fraudulently. A number of investigative reports, like "Hospice, Inc.," published by the *Huffington Post* in 2014, exacerbate the problem. These articles overlook a number of important factors: for-profit programs are seen as a violation of hospice's traditionally nonprofit model, a model viewed as altruistic and, because it deals with dying patients, corrupted by for-profit concerns. Yet we've accepted that so much of our health-care system is for profit. Medical diagnoses are not exact, and hospice care can extend a patient's life by keeping her comfortable, out of dangerous facilities, away from taxing treatments, and in her home, so when we examine end-of-life care, hospice is very much a cost-effective approach. Also, if we consider how patients spend their last years, we've failed to find a way to care for those who need regular care, want to stay at home, but are not terminal (at least not in the hospice window). We've neglected patients who have been nearing the end of their lives for decades, or we've put them in hospitals. Hospice care can and does often fill that gap. A handful of fraud cases have allowed reporters and oversight agencies to shut down any conversation about the overall good of hospice care for longer-stay patients and to curtail any discussion of how to better serve those who fall into that care gap.

Patients who can only get the medical services they need through hospice programs are being told that they now have to get by on their own, without medication, hospital beds, oxygen machines, and nurse or aide visits. In other words, the one thing that our medical system gets right for dying patients—hospice care—is being penalized for extending the lives of patients. Most patients have no alternative care options. Since 2010, studies have shown that hospice patients live longer, but such research hasn't prevented increased scrutiny by the government, which has blindly failed to see the problem in terms of how end-of-life care is structured, and which has failed to think creatively about what terminal patients want and need. Instead, such investigations highlight how tone-deaf financially focused oversight in medicine has become. Call it capitalism, stinginess, or apathy toward terminal patients. The end result is budget and rules policing, without a reevaluation of what could best work for the dying.

Now in her eighties, Evelyn is lucky; she's got money. Over the course of the four years since Evelyn left the hospital, she's been able to employ full-time home health aides to ensure that she eats, bathes, and takes her medication. They are with her for the twenty hours a day that hospice can't be. As her health has slowly but steadily declined, the aides have gone from providing "just in case" support—ensuring that Evelyn doesn't fall, for instance—to helping her perform basic tasks like using the toilet. Her aides, three women of color who work in shifts, are all paid $10 to $15 an hour. Day and night. In cash or check. For some of the toughest, dirtiest emotional and physical labor you can imagine.

Because of Evelyn's training as a doctor, because of her financial privilege, even because she has outlived her deadline again and again, many would say that she's having a good death. But, sometimes, I'm not so sure. Yes, she's spent time with her daughters and grandchildren, time with her husband. Yes, she sometimes still laughs. She keeps up with the news and is cared for by a skilled and caring staff. But she hasn't been physically comfortable in years. She's lost her great love of reading to blindness. She is no longer able to stand. She's waiting. And she increasingly has little more than her memories to keep her occupied. She thinks about the old times, about first meeting her husband; about her parents, long dead; about her years in medical school. Nostalgia is powerful and vivid around her divan. But nostalgia is powerful for all of us. Twinkies were reintroduced the year after Hostess went bankrupt because of public outrage.

Regrets are powerful, too. We regret never tasting a Twinkie, never telling our estranged daughter that we loved her, never writing the book we always knew we had in us. We regret never apologizing for that drunken bout of anger or not seeing our granddaughter's first birthday. Regrets can haunt a dying person. They can dislodge any comfort painkillers might provide, and they can torture the otherwise peaceful. When coupled with the fear of dying—the unknown is always scary—regret can agitate even the most privileged and cared-for person. Hope is our emotional counter to fear and regret. It can make us call that estranged daughter, and it can get us to the first birthday party. But hope is complicated.

Hope is an accepted, powerful, and trusted medicine that doctors find useful in sustaining patients. In the journal *Theoretical Medicine and Bioethics*, Jack Coulehan wrote in 2011, "Since hope helps to alleviate suffering, physicians have long believed that instilling hope is an important feature of medical treatment." Coulehan and many doctors are convinced that hope works to make lives better. Coulehan coins the term "deep hope" for a hope—"a universal balm"—that has no objective, that doesn't delude the one who hopes, but can be based on incremental emotional needs, like enjoying the day or going for a walk. It won't cure ailments, but according to Coulehan, it has a "more complex and resilient quality than physicians previously believed." Coulehan is advancing a centuries-old medical idea, but hope can cause problems, too. Very easily, hope makes us feel better about keeping ourselves and patients in the dark about grim futures. Hope can also mask our own fears. "Deep down, despite all I thought I stood for, I had hoped to avoid any serious discussion with Mr. Woodrick because I did not want to tell him the truth: I did not want to let him down," writes David DiBardino in an essay called "Hoping Within Reality." Mr. Woodrick was dying, and his days were fewer than DiBardino wanted to admit. In her brilliant and complex book *How We Hope: A Moral Psychology*, Adrienne Martin, professor of philosophy at University of Pennsylvania, challenges our assumptions that hope is always a virtue. In a 2014 interview with Robert Talisse for the online journal *New Books in Philosophy*, Martin said, "A popular view of hope is that it's basically a good thing." But she goes on to name the risks that can come with hope: bad decisions and disappointment, for instance. "These tend to be the only negative aspects the popular view of hope recognizes," she said. Martin's book is an exercise in identifying how that popular view is wrong . . . or deceptively hopeful:

> Once you start attending to the ways that hope engages imagination, it opens up the possibility for a lot of other ways hope can go wrong. Hoping for a certain outcome can make a person more passive if they allow their imagination to substitute for their agency. Hoping . . . can lead you to overvalue the outcome by representing it as having more good features. It can also lead you to neglect other projects in virtue of the way hope narrows your focus. I don't think hope is a magical well . . . of motivational energy.

Martin points to the popularity of self-help books and positive psychology as examples of hope that may look like the answer to a certain problem but can turn out to be irrational. Hope can become a maxim that limits our options, that can wrongly provide us with reasons to act in a certain way, and that can prevent us from planning for what to do if our hope doesn't pan out. She tells us that hope and faith are closely related and, in some ways, are the same thing:

> Faith is a kind of reliance on God's knowledge and hope is a kind of reliance on God's goodness. I don't think hope is necessarily a virtue. There are certain outcomes we can attach our hopes to that outstrip our conceptual resources. An obvious example would be salvation. Presumably we can't conceptualize what it would be like to be saved and when we pin our hopes on these kinds of inconceivable or unimaginable outcomes that's when we can consider hope to become a kind of faith. Hope becomes immune to disappointment in various ways.

Marshall, my hospice patient at Avenue House, hoped for salvation. He knew his cancer would not be cured. He hoped for a miracle, but that hope was tempered by the unimaginable. He had faith, however close to the end of his life he found it, that he was going to a better place, that his pain and suffering would end, and that somewhere in the afterlife he would be healed and cleansed of his sins.

Mr. Cortez, my hospice patient in the projects who had Parkinson's disease for decades, was beyond hope. He was happy because his mental faculties had freed him of the existential questions, the fear of the unknown, even knowledge of what was happening to him. If Mr. C had hope, it was of the moment: the joy of seeing his wife, of thinking about himself as a young man, of eating the things he liked, of listening to good music.

Amy, the wife of Jack, the man who had suffered a heart attack and was on the hospice ward, a ventilator huffing through a tube in his throat, was in shock. Her hope was not yet tempered by reality. She had no way to imagine life without her husband; she hadn't even realized that he was in a hospice ward, that he was dying. She hoped it was all a dream, she hoped for survival, his and her own. And in some ways, she hoped someone would step in and tell her what to do.

Robert Baxter hoped for the best and planned for the worst. When he joined with Compassion & Choices to make aid in dying legal in Montana, he simply didn't want to sit around, in discomfort and pain, waiting for death to come. He wanted to go at it head first.

Bill Coleman, the Connecticut prisoner on a hunger strike, didn't want to die. He didn't want to be force-fed either. But he hoped—a hope beyond hope, it turned out—that his protest would change the judicial system. He had used all his legal appeals and had exhausted all his options to change his sentence. He hoped his hunger strike would give him a new way to not leave prison a convicted criminal. In 2014, he was, without warning, deported to his native Liverpool, UK. He called to tell me that the first thing he ate after not eating for over six years was dry toast.

The families of Jahi McMath, the dead child whose body is being kept on a ventilator and a feeding tube, and Terri Schiavo, who was in a persistent vegetative state until the courts allowed her husband to remove her feeding tube, have a hope against hope. By asserting that their faith can work miracles, they work to legislate salvation. Their effort is to make laws that institutionalize their version of hope for all of us.

Bill Peace isn't dying, of course. He's a paraplegic with a lust for every day he can squeeze from the world. Few things scare him more than a doctor who wants to give him comfort care. He disdains those who wish to make us face the possibility of pain and suffering, because he sees them as part of life. Bill is hopeful, but realistically so, that we will all take the pain and tribulations of every day. Every last one. "That we will not go gentle into that good night" with everything we have. And he hopes for—fights for—the chance to do so.

My father—and I—hoped that he would go home to his bed and quietly die. He never imagined he would lose his ability to go to the bathroom on his own, to brush his own teeth, to speak and think clearly. He had planned for everything but the loss of what he would have called privacy and what many call dignity.

What does Evelyn hope for now, after so many years of waiting for death? It is sneaking up behind her, like a languorous fog. Ultimately, I think she's tired and bored. Who could blame her? She's lost her sight almost completely. She hasn't left the living room in years. She has the company of her aides and her husband—and me on Sunday nights for a few hours. She has the company of the hospice chaplain who visits her for an hour on Thursdays, although she likes him for his intellectual conversation, not any of the theological wares he's got to offer. Her hope for a comfortable death hasn't enabled her to resolve any lingering regrets. Evelyn works hard now, these last months, to keep regrets and bad thoughts at bay. She wants me to tell her what the world is like out there beyond her window, what I've been up to; she wants me to read her happy, chipper stories. Every now and then, she wants to try something she never has—like Twinkies.

A few months after September 11, 2001, I attended a lecture by philosopher Jacques Derrida at Columbia University. His later work often addressed mourning, and it was *The Work of Mourning*, published in July that year, that he was lecturing about. The book is a collection of Derrida's writing, spanning more than twenty years, each piece written on the occasion of a friend's death—Roland Barthes, Paul De Man, Louis Althusser, Edmond Jabés, Gilles Deleuze, Emmanuel Levinas, and others. Some of the most prominent and celebrated philosophers of the era. Gayatri Spivak, a Columbia professor known for pairing saris and combat boots, introduced Derrida. After her introduction, Spivak sat in a wooden chair at the far edge of the stage, right of the podium. Derrida was a small, compact man with a shock of white hair. As he spoke, Spivak's cropped head bowed, as if in prayer. As if she had nodded off.

At the time of the lecture, the first of the major deaths in my life— that of my grandmother at the age of ninety-two in 2003—had not yet occurred. My father's death was still four years away. I had no way to fathom the absence that Derrida discussed in *The Work of Mourning*. Like the Vietnam Memorial in Washington, DC, by Maya Lin; like the incipient September 11 memorial in New York by Michael Arad; like the names listed in neat rows in the obituaries on the back of the *New York Times*, here in my hands was Derrida's list of the dead, a book that chronicled loss by name. The loss of a lover, of jobs, of childhood even. Yes, I had known these, but the profound absence of a loved one was a largely alien emotion for me, one I only knew from music or poetry or art, cathartically.

"One must respond even when one does not have the heart or is at a loss, lacking the words; one must speak, even reckon, so as to combat all the forces that work to efface or conceal not just the names on the tombstones but the apostrophe of mourning," write Pascale-Anne Brault and Michael Naas in *The Work of Mourning*'s introduction. When someone we know dies, we have no choice but to respond. Yet, when we do so, we are exercising what I call the vanity of grief. We are necessarily talking about someone as if she were ours. We are telling her story, even as we tell our own. And this is something innate within us, as humans who have lost. We must tell of those we've lost. It is not a command, but an observation. In "The Deaths of Roland Barthes," the first chapter in *The Work of Mourning*, Derrida writes:

> I do not yet know, and in the end it really does not matter, if I will be able to make it clear why I must leave these thoughts for Roland Barthes fragmentary, or why I value them for their incompleteness. . . . These little stones, thoughtfully placed, only each time, on the edge of a name as the promise of return.

These "little stones," Derrida tells us, are "for him," the dead Barthes, even as he knows they will never reach Barthes. "So where do they go? To whom and for whom? Only for him in me? In you? In us?" The memories of Barthes are *in* Derrida, in others. Derrida knows now that Barthes no longer exists but in his memory. When we talk to or about the dead, we do so because we miss them, because we have things to tell them, because we are desperate not to forget them. And then time marches on and we watch another person die. Derrida died in October 2004.

"With each first death the whole world is lost, and yet with each we are called to reckon our losses. Each time we mourn, then, we add another name to the series of singular mournings and so commit what may be called a sort of 'posthumous infidelity' with regard to the others," write Brault and Naas. Every death we add to our list of deaths is both a first death and a unique death. We cheat each preceding death when we mourn a new one, yet they are in a string of mournings that constitutes one emotion: absence. How do we mourn? We remember, we say the names, we follow rituals that give form to each unique death. We mark each death. And we tell stories.

"Narrative can become a protest against mortality, against the ways in which our bodies sever the same bonds they've made: bonds of sex and love and kin and blood and care," wrote Leslie Jamison in a 2014 review of Marilyn Robinson's novel *Lila*. "There is sublimity in these details, but also a preemptive sense of mourning—our mortal attachments are only ever distractions from the eternal, precursors to inevitable loss."

I first met Evelyn Livingston on a hot summer evening, Wednesday, July 13, 2011. The New York heat was ruthless and stifling. My hospice coordinator had called to ask if I would meet a patient who wanted a volunteer who was a writer, someone to help her with her memoir, something she regretted never writing. The address—the Upper West Side—was about forty-five minutes from my office and at least an hour and fifteen minutes from my home in Brooklyn, if the subway cooperated. "I know it's far for you," the coordinator had said, "but we can't find anyone she likes. Just see if you get along." I finally said okay, thinking that it would be for only a few weeks, at the most a few months, about the amount of time I had spent with prior patients.

I left work a little early and exited the subway on the edge of Central Park. The heat in the green trees and grass smelled lush and fresh. The Livingstons' building, one of New York's iconic residential structures along the park, had been built between the two world wars. It was the last of four twin-towered residences designed by Emery Roth, who had begun construction in 1929. The Great Depression halted progress for a few years, but commitments from wealthy tenants like

Barney Pressman, the founder of Barney's clothing stores, pushed it to completion. Tall, manicured shrubs in enormous concrete pots flank the green awning of the front door. It's a gorgeous, glamorous building with art deco symmetry and design details, renovated in the past fifteen years to please its residents, the likes of which have included Michael J. Fox, Garrison Keillor, and Faye Dunaway. When the Livingstons moved there in the 1960s, a bevy of psychoanalysts lived on the upper floors. Jacqueline Kennedy Onassis had been spotted in the elevator at least once. The broad front desk inside the lobby is gray marble, shot through with white veins and adorned weekly with massive, fresh flower arrangements.

I was wearing an old 1940s dress I had picked up in Los Angeles more than a decade earlier; the sheer fabric was patterned with the black-and-white outlines of umbrellas, but, from a distance, it had the optical illusion of gauzy spider webs. It was a witty number, classically boxy with a scalloped neckline. It was a hit with Evelyn, whose eyesight had not yet slipped away. It appealed to her sense of how a proper woman should dress; she considered it a show of respect. Her husband, Marvin, had let me in and shown me to the front living room where Evelyn sat on her sprawling divan. She wore a collared man's shirt with the sleeves rolled up and wide linen pants that swallowed her thin body. Her gray hair was pinned up in a bun, slightly mussed by the linen-cased pillows around her. She had a patrician lilt to her voice, one bestowed by a well-to-do family, years of private school, and a lot of time abroad. I first sat in an overstuffed chair across the room from her, but eventually pulled up a tan leather footstool so I could sit at her feet. We got on famously, in part because she appreciated my deference and in part because, however many visitors she had, most of her days were solitary. She was lonely. In our time together, we toured her vast library, and we looked up the origins of words in the dictionary. She wanted to talk and I knew how to ask questions. I spent the first months interviewing Evelyn. We would sit in the sunny room, drinking whiskey and talking about her parents, her medical school training, her psychiatric work with Harlem kids.

Four months after I began weekly visits with Evelyn, her husband, Marvin, was hospitalized for a blockage in his colon. The first operation was unsuccessful. Evelyn was at home alone most of the day, and I worried that she wouldn't be able to manage the house by herself—order groceries, pay the staff, keep the bills. I began visiting twice a week for hours at a time. I took on some of the household responsibilities, learning what foods to order for delivery, paying the cleaning lady. Evelyn couldn't get to the bank, so I brought her cash. Meanwhile, I visited Marvin in the hospital. He was confused, fraught with anxiety, incredibly weak. What would happen to the two of them when he came home? How would they manage? "What about hospice for Marvin?" I timidly asked Evelyn. It would double the hours of help they had in the house each day. But the suggestion also ventured my own pessimism for his prognosis. Evelyn, sitting on the edge of her divan, a trio of perfectly ordered tables clustered to her left, reached for her glass of whiskey without looking at it. "I thought of that," she said. We were keeping vigil. Marvin had gone into surgery that morning, and as evening drew on, we waited for the surgeon to call. Even routine operations are dangerous for the elderly, however spry and healthy they may be. The instability of the body's systems as they age is hard to predict. When the phone finally rang, eight hours after surgery began, we both started. I could hear the surgeon's warm but tired voice as he told Evelyn that the second operation was successful, but Marvin now needed a colostomy bag. We both slumped into our seats with relief. Soon, we hoped, he would come home, but how the two of them would manage as he recovered was still a mystery.

Two days later, Evelyn asked if I would stay late to help her interview a woman who had applied to be a home aide. A heavy rain delayed her, and Evelyn and I sat waiting, discussing hours and rates.

Privy to the Livingstons' finances, their home, and their inner lives, I had long gone past the boundary of hospice professionalism. Their daughters lived in other states; I worried that I was doing the work of family, that I was inadvertently usurping the role of their children. "Boundaries are important," my hospice coordinator had told us during training. "Don't be afraid to say no." But how could I say no when the Livingstons' needs were so great?

I loved Martina from the start. She was a big Latina woman with cornrows and bright, floral print blouses. It took Evelyn a little longer to warm up to her, but necessity made us hire her on the spot. "Did you see those fingernails?" Evelyn said to me after we finalized Martina's start date and said goodbye, her class prejudices coming through. Soon Martina brought on Mariana—between the two of them, they were able to ensure that someone was in the house at all times—and the household stabilized. Marvin came home, and the women oversaw his recovery and Evelyn's demands. She isn't easy. She requires that they call her Dr. Livingston, and she blows a whistle when she needs something because her voice is too weak to call. She has a very distinct sense of class and service. Slowly, Marvin took back the chores and finances of the household. Their youngest daughter, Katherine, began visiting every few weeks.

I became part of a family. I was a witness to the signing of a new will, one that smoothed over a long estrangement between Evelyn and their oldest daughter, Beth; I vacationed with Katherine in Maine the following summer; I met distant relatives and foreign friends. I've celebrated three wedding anniversaries with them, drinking champagne and eating cake that Katherine baked and Martina decorated with white icing and little silver candies. Evelyn has helped me make career decisions; she's read—or I've read to her—everything I've written since we met. She's advised me on relationships, travel plans, and my own finances. After nearly four years together, we've become interdependent, resilient, and patient.

One Friday afternoon while Marvin was in the TV room, Evelyn asked me if I thought marijuana might help her. She was anxious and irritated, never comfortable. Her symptoms included difficulty breathing, aches and pains, and, of course, death's constant looming. I told her I thought weed was worth a try and promised to bring her some on my next visit. As a doctor, Evelyn knew only the trauma of drugs. She'd watched her Harlem patients get swept off the streets, their lives destroyed by prison sentences. In the emergency room, she'd seen the ravages of drug use up close. But she was old now and dying; her fears and moral boundaries had rearranged themselves, subservient to her discomfort. She was willing to try anything that might calm her down and make her days more tolerable.

The following week, I showed up with a little bag of weed tucked into my purse. It was easy to buy. It was good stuff, pungent and fuzzy. On the back of a book of poems I'd bought Evelyn for her birthday, *Louise Glück: Poems 1962–2012*, I broke the sticky weed into pieces and then expertly rolled it up into a small joint. I was embarrassed to let Evelyn see how good I was at it. Then I removed the oxygen tube from her nose, put the joint between her lips, and lit it for her.

"Not too much," I said. "Only a few puffs should be enough. It's not like tobacco." A lifelong smoker, Evelyn had only quit cigarettes when she went into the hospital. Now she was never without her little metal e-cigarette, extra batteries and cartridges on the shelf beside her.

"Magic," she said lazily after a few minutes. "I had no idea."

It became our habit each Friday, soon after I arrived, to retire to Evelyn's office so she could get stoned. The office was tucked behind the foyer, a tidy room with thick white carpeting and Danish Modern furniture. For years, she had received patients in that room, talking about their mental health, about their abusive families, about their drug use. Tall filing cabinets in the next room kept all of Evelyn's records. They were confidential, so she wanted to go through them and discard the ones that should never be read. She'd sit in a chair next to her desk and take a few puffs of marijuana while I read the files to her. A teen girl sexually assaulted by a teacher; a mentally disabled boy with anger problems; a young boy who had grown up in foster homes and had been arrested for theft. For decades, Evelyn had fostered relationships with children who had been handed impossible circumstances. She may have come from money, but she had spent her career in a world where poverty was fate. Reading and remembering this work was gratifying for her. It had meant something. As much as the weed, this reassessment of her life's work settled her restlessness.

Evelyn had escaped lung cancer until her late seventies. Now she and I were spending our Friday evenings together in her office. An illegal drug, marijuana, was making her last days tolerable, the same drug that, in many cases, had caused tragedy in the lives of her patients. The irony was not lost on either one of us.

Dr. Livingston is what everyone calls Evelyn. She is proud of her station, her profession, her heritage. She is proud. But from the first day, she's allowed me to call her by her first name. It's an intimacy that I acknowledge and cherish. From the beginning of our relationship, that first hot July day when I entered their home, calling her Evelyn has meant that I will see her through. I will call her by her name now, as she is living and dying, and I will call her by her name after her death, when she no longer exists but in my memory. Perhaps her desire to write her memoir was a challenge to impending mortality, her way of claiming her name in the face of death. And after. If her story can live on, so can she. Hers would be the immortality of story, an afterlife in words, like the afterlives of China Girls in celluloid. Over the years, though, Evelyn has lost her ability to focus. She hasn't the stamina to write anything that would capture her stretch of eighty years, from the Great Depression until now, our present that too will become history to those of us who live on. She was never seriously invested in writing her story herself, I think. She never understood the work of it, a lack of knowledge that only dawned on her as she and I talked about her life, as I interviewed her. She quickly realized that she didn't have the ability, or perhaps the desire, to revisit all that history in detail.

Slowly, silently, Evelyn passed that labor on to me. And perhaps her unsaid desire that I write about her is meaningful. She trusts that I will—that this book will—give her that afterlife. It's a beautiful trust to me, but one that I know would ultimately be unsatisfactory to her. Whoever likes to read what others have written about them? Books, words, the act of writing can aim to capture detail—the true story—but they will always fail. History is always inexact, incomplete. The most I can do is name her, as she lives and after she dies. Yet, of course, Evelyn Livingston is not her real name. It is the name I've given her in order to write about her. Write Brault and Naas in their introduction to Derrida's *The Work of Mourning*:

> To have a friend, to call him or her by name and to be called by him or her, is already to know that one of the two of you will go first, that one will be left to speak the name of the other in the other's absence. Again, this is not only the ineluctable law of human finitude but the law of the name. Mourning thus begins already with the name.

American author Ursula Le Guin, who is about the same age as Evelyn, has written dozens of books, seven of which are based in Earthsea, a fictional world made up of thousands of islands. Her seminal Earthsea trilogy (the first book of which was published the year I was born, 1968) introduces us to a world of adventure, magic, dragons, and cultural diversity. The books cover the life of the mage Sparrowhawk, who is born a goatherd and eventually becomes the archmage of all Earthsea. Magic in Earthsea is predicated on knowing the true names of all objects, animals, and people. In the last book, Sparrowhawk and his young companion, Arren, who will become the one king, set out to the far reaches of Earthsea to find out why the world is dying. Everything and everyone has been stripped of joy. The cause of the blackness, Sparrowhawk explains to Arren, is the desire to live forever. "The traitor, the self, the self that cries *I want to live, let the world rot so long as I can live!* The little traitor soul in us, in the dark, like the spider in a box. He talks to all of us."

> "I have learned to believe in death," Arren replies. "But I have not learned to rejoice over it, to welcome my death, or yours. If I love life shall I not hate the end of it?"
>
> "Life without end," the mage said. "Life without death. Immortality. Every soul desires it, and its health is the strength of its desire. But be careful Arren. You are one who might achieve your desire."
>
> "And then?"
>
> "And then—this. This blight upon the lands. The arts of man forgotten. The singer tongueless. The eye blind. And then? A false king ruling. Ruling forever. And over the same subjects forever. No births; no new lives. No children. Only what is mortal bears life, Arren. Only in death is there rebirth. The Balance is not stillness. It is a movement—an eternal becoming."

Sparrowhawk's lesson to Arren is that the great beauty of life is its ephemerality, its temporality. Like the beauty of the cut flowers in the lobby of Evelyn's building, life is precious because it is not eternal. New flowers will grow and bloom, then be cut and die. New lives will replace the lives that have gone before. The world, this moment, is real, yes, but it is also always new. *This too shall pass*, we tell those who are suffering. The adage is considered to have originated with the Sufi poets in medieval Persia. In another story, it is the inscription on a ring that, when he slips it on his finger, can make a happy man sad or a sad man happy. In Jewish folklore, a great king is humbled when told, "This too shall pass." His glory and great life of works will be, in only a few years' time, nothing but memory: *passed*, the past. *He has passed*, we say when someone dies. She or he is history.

It is the necessity of mortality—or rather the damages of seeking immortality—that bioethicist Ezekiel Emanuel wrote about in his article for the *Atlantic* in 2014, "Why I Hope to Die at 75." "Death is a loss," he writes, but "living too long is also a loss." He paints us a picture of what life after seventy-five most often looks like. There's no skydiving, no horseback riding, no great adventure like the pharmaceutical ads for seniors promise us. There's physical and mental decline, frailty, a loss of creativity. One of the flaws of Emanuel's article is his focus on a particular class of Americans, white, economically stable professionals. He doesn't address what end years are like for those unlike himself and so fails to acknowledge that many don't have the privilege of dreaming about skydiving. But what Emanuel describes is very much the kind of life that Evelyn has now. She has some joys, but she is absolutely removed from the world. Her body has sapped her mind of focus and creativity. So why do we invest so much time and energy in living as long as possible? Because death "deprives us of all the things we value," Emanuel writes. Like Sparrowhawk's lesson for Arren, immortality is a ruse, but it's a powerful one.

"Americans seem to be obsessed with exercising, doing mental puzzles, consuming various juice and protein concoctions, sticking to strict diets, and popping vitamins and supplements, all in a valiant effort to cheat death and prolong life as long as possible. This has become so pervasive that it now defines a cultural type: what I call the American immortal," writes Emanuel. We've been lured into thinking that we can cure aging itself, that we can put off death for even longer than we do now. Eighty is the new sixty! But there's a cost to all the denial that such hope reinforces. We are blinded from living now, we allow hope for more years to direct our decisions, we put off attending to regrets, we forget that all life is like a carton of milk: it comes with an expiration date.

Susan Jacoby, in her sly book *Never Say Die*, reminds us that our need to face mortality is an ancient lesson. Odysseus is living a life of lust and luxury on an island with Calypso, a gorgeous goddess who wishes him to be her immortal husband. Odysseus is enchanted and happy for a few years, but slowly awakes from the dream of immortality. He decides that he must go back to his wife Penelope, who has waited for his return to Ithaca for years. As a mortal, she represents for Odysseus a beautiful finitude. Zeus hears Odysseus's prayer and orders Calypso to set him free. "Odysseus's return to the travails of suffering humanity and his rejection of infinite pleasure among the immortals are seen as the morally superior choice not only by conservative bioethicists but by nearly all writers in the classical tradition," Jacoby writes. Returning to mortality, turning away from life everlasting, what Emanuel calls a fantasy, is moral because it reduces the stigma of death to its natural place. Accepting that we all will die increases the chance that we—and our culture—will better value those who are dying. It gives us the chance to improve care for the elderly, the sick, the disabled. And it gives us the opportunity to plan for our own deaths. The body is a strange thing; it doesn't always obey our well-laid plans. Doctors can only do so much. But putting aside our futile quest for longer and longer life-spans helps us to live in the real world. That is the world of tragedy and disease, the world of seasons, a world where we honor the dying by caring for them, then interweaving their names and memories into our finite lives.

There is no good death. That's what I told myself as I wandered my father's quiet house the first days and weeks after he died. What had it all been for? The worry and pain and wasting away. The puke bucket and the sleeplessness. But I also asked the nihilistic question: what was life for? All his years of nurturing a business and raising a family, building a home. Everywhere there was proof that he had been in the world: his clothing in the closet, his old boots by the door, the knife he always kept in his pocket now exposed on the dresser, his letters and bank accounts no longer private. All the things experienced, the lessons learned, the knowledge accrued. The stories of his childhood, the grip of the handsaw, formed to only his hand over years of use. All his rules for me, the edifice of expectation, the fear of a strict parent, the love of a wise father. For what? For the great gaping yawn that was now nothing but absence? It was my grief rattling me. Dad had not died the way he wanted. He was sixty, far too young. He died not at home but at a hospice facility in town. He had died kicking at me. Yet, that was the best we could give him. My sister and I had done everything we could. Still, as the weeks became months, as I began volunteering for hospice, as the images of his death slipped away, I wondered what a good death was. I searched for it, like the explorers of old searched for the fountain of youth. Like the gerontologists searching for answers to aging.

There is no good death, I now know. It always hurts, both the dying and the left behind. But there is a good enough death. It is possible to look it in the face, to know how it will come, to accept its inevitability. Knowing death makes facing it bearable. There are many kinds of good enough death, each specific to the person dying. As they wish, as best they can. And there is really one kind of bad death, characterized by the same bad facts: pain, denial, prolongation, loneliness.

By all accounts, Evelyn is having a good enough death. Every Sunday afternoon when I enter the living room and sit by her knee, I first ask how she is doing. "Crummy," she invariably answers. But it's a tolerable crummy. She is able to increase her morphine dosage when she is experiencing too much pain or discomfort. She could use more stimulation, more company, more people sitting with her as I do weekly and reading to her or telling her stories. She no longer puts her dentures in when I visit. Sometimes the sheet on the divan is stained with food, with feces, with blood. She also tires very quickly now. Sometimes her puffy face nods toward her chest as I read. Sometimes she drinks too much whiskey and falls into a restless sleep. But she always perks up when Marvin enters the room. He's skilled at engaging her in conversation about poets, people they've known, places they've been, old stories of family members long dead. Often Marvin and Evelyn and I talk about Ireland, a place I've never been but that they happily visited every summer for a dozen years. They would fly into Galway or Dublin and, in a tiny rented car, meander north over narrow, poorly marked roads to Donegal.

"We once stopped to see Yeats's grave," Marvin remarked one afternoon as the sun leaked out of Central Park. "Do you remember that?" he asked Evelyn.

"Sligo," she said, indicating the county where William Butler Yeats, the great Irish poet, was ultimately buried after his body was interred in France for a few years. I asked them to tell me about the grave.

"Very plain," Evelyn said. "Looked like the other graves in the yard." Her breathing was labored. Her feet and legs had become swollen in the past weeks, making them uncomfortable and achy. In addition to lung cancer, Evelyn has a long history of stable angina, caused by the heart's inadequate blood flow, that she controls with medication. I suspected that it was now getting the best of her, filling her feet and legs with fluid.

"What was on the stone?" asked Marvin, searching his memory. "A very famous quote."

"Something about 'horseman,'" she replied. I looked it up when I got home. It's an entreaty to think not about our time on earth or where we go after, but to consider our legacy and what we've given to the world.

"We'd driven by it for years before we finally stopped," Marvin continued.

"Ah, well," said Evelyn, "I never like Yeats anyway." She leaned back on her pillows as Marvin and I laughed. We had all tried to get Evelyn to tell us how she would like to be buried. When I first met her, she thought cremation was what she wanted. But, over time, she said that she might like to be buried. Where? In what kind of casket? She now seemed unable to think about it, to focus on such details. For months she obsessed over writing her obituary, but every time I sat to take her dictation, the words slipped away and she would take up another subject. All these arrangements will fall to Marvin and his daughters once she dies.

I never signed up for this, I tell myself sometimes. For more than four years of weekly visits, for the worry, for the grief that I know is coming. "In mourning we find ourselves at a loss, no longer our-selves, as if the singular shock of what we must bear had altered the very medium in which it was to be registered," write Brault and Naas. "Speaking is impossible," writes Derrida, "but so too would be silence or absence or a refusal to share one's sadness." I will mourn Evelyn. I will continue my visits to their home on the Upper West Side to see Marvin. He'll be alone, and widowers are particularly susceptible to quick physical decline. Then I will mourn Marvin.

Acknowledgments

To the families of the dead, the caretakers, nurses, chaplains, doctors, academics, bioethicists, and advocates, to those who generously allowed me into their homes and lives, I can only hope this book honors the warmth and community you've shown me. For the sake of privacy, I've obscured or changed the names of many, but I hope they know how much their access and support has meant to me—and to this project. To William Peace, Mark Connell, William Coleman, Carl Koenigsmann, David McGuire, Roberta King, Anthea Butler, Sue Porter, Madeline Cohen, and Robb Miller: thank you for allowing me to share your work and experiences and please forgive any liberties I may have inadvertently taken. Your insight and generosity are unmatched.

Arthur Caplan, Jacob Appel, Thaddeus Pope, Carla Axtman, Frances Kissling, Peter Strauss, David Leven, Caitlin Doughty, Colin Dickey, and George González have over the years and without hesitation answered my questions, however odd or complicated. Your expertise has humbled and encouraged me.

This book would still be a pile of notes on my floor if it weren't for my other family at my other home, the rich and fostering community at and around the Center for Religion and Media at New York University. Angela Zito, still the best mentor and thinker I know, has always had my back, even when I didn't deserve it. Adam Becker and

Elizabeth Castelli have, in their own particular ways, taught me whatever I may know about friendship and scholarship, even though I often fail at both. Ann Pellegrini has patiently seen me through fits and starts, given me opportunities to present this work as it developed and found value in this project from the beginning. Omri Elisha, whose friendship and intellect make me a better person, has talked me out of the blues or off the ledge whenever I've needed it. If I know any wise thing, it is because of these wise people. Also Kali Handelman (whose editing of my column at the *Revealer*, "The Patient Body," has immeasurably enriched this work), Anthony Petro (who has reminded me again and again what questions I should be asking), Janine Paolucci, Genevieve Yue, Geoffrey Pollick, Francesca Bregoli, Pooja Rangan, Josh Guilford, Quince Mountain, Blair Braverman, Pegi Vail, and the indefatigable, amazing Faye Ginsberg. For years of patient friendship, productive conversation, direction, and support, thank you.

My dynamic and steadfast writing group has read almost every word in this book, even when it wasn't worth reading. Kathryn Joyce, Kiera Feldman, Nathan Schneider, Joseph Huff-Hannon, Lindsay Beyerstein, Robert Eshelman, Brook Wilensky-Lanford, Mark Engler, Erica Pearson, and Audrea Lim have tirelessly offered astute edits, comments, and cheerleading. Thank you, Dania Rajendra and Meera Subramanian, for the patience to read the entire manuscript in draft. Every one of these writers, with their own talent and focus, is doing work you should seek out.

I owe special thanks to the editorial and writing communities that have sustained me over the years and schooled me on what it means to write. Jina Moore first published my article on William Coleman at *Guernica* magazine, and Michael Archer, Hillary Brenhouse, Rachel Riederer, and Katherine Rowland have since made a welcoming place for me in their talented ranks. *Killing the Buddha* gave me some of my first clips and fast writing friends; and the Religion Drinks gang make sure I have a good reason to occasionally leave the house. Thanks also to the staff at the *New York Law School Law Review*; Ron Scapp and Brian Seitz for including my essay in *Living with Class: Philosophical Reflections on Identity and Material Culture*; Jessica Lustig and Roberta Zeff at the *New York Times*; Chris Lehmann at the *Baffler* and *Bookforum*; Diane Winston at the Annenberg School for Communication and Journalism at the University of Southern California for the fruitful leap of faith; Lewis West at *Cosmologics*, a publication of the Science, Religion and Culture Program at Harvard Divinity School, and Ahmed Ragab, the program's director; Patton Dodd at *OnFaith*; the folks at *Waging Nonviolence*; Tiffany Stanley at *Religion & Politics*; Angela Serratore at *Lapham's Quarterly*; and Wendy McDowell at *Harvard Divinity Bulletin*.

Also, for giving me outlets to discuss this project as it developed, I want to thank Stephen Prothero and Laura Harrington at Boston University; Ayesha Tanzeem and Rashmi Shukla of *On the Line* at Voice of America; David McCabe at the Lampert Institute for Civic and Global Affairs at Colgate University; the staff at the Age Boom Academy, a joint project of the Mailman School of Public Health and the Columbia University Graduate School of Journalism; Barbara Glickstein, who hosts *Healthstyles* on WBAI; Lauren Epstein at the Roundtable on Aging of the Jewish Community at the UJA-Federation; Julie Byrne at Hofstra University; and Michael Steinmann at Stevens Institute of Technology. The students brave enough to take my journalism class, The End Is Near, at Drew University, through their earnest writing and conversation, helped shape the material in this book for the better.

Thanks also to those who have listened to me as I felt my way through this material, including Helaine Olen, Jason Vest, Peter Bebergal, Mary Valle, Steven Lukes, Maurice Chammah, Peter Manseau, and Meghan White. In 2005, Jeff Sharlet read the long e-mails I was writing from the hollow as my father died, then from far-flung places around the globe. He saw something in them that I didn't, even as I kept writing.

I'm indebted to the weird and wonderful neighborhood I live in, Red Hook, Brooklyn, which is perfectly happy to let me come and go as I will. Thanks especially to Gita Nandan, Jens Veneman, George Monos, and Denise Oswald. And thanks to Kimo and Cliff for keeping me in coffee and noodles as I write. It takes a neighborhood, and I'm lucky this one is mine.

Laurie Abkemeier, my talented and tireless agent at DeFiore & Company, found me, remarkably saw my early ramblings as a viable project, and has made me feel as if I'm the only author she's got. As I was holed up in my flat working on the early draft, she combed through each chapter. She knows my tics and abilities better than I do.

My first interaction with Amy Caldwell was a phone call in the summer of 2008 when I pitched her some nascent version of this book, roundly off the top of my head. Then years of research, doubt, full-time jobs, related articles, and life intervened, but our conversation stuck with me. Which makes it fitting that this book ended up in her good hands, at Beacon Press, one of the best independent publishing houses around. Her insightful edits have saved me from myself and made it infinitely better than I could have done. Susan Lumenello's and Jane Gebhart's superb copyediting have made it readable. Thanks to everyone at Beacon, including Beth Collins, Will Myers, Tom Hallock, Alyssa Hassan, Nicholas DiSabatino, and Pamela MacColl, for making this book an object and putting it into your hands.

My family has entertained endless questions and inquiries with the tolerance that only family can. Thank you, Jim and Elva Weaver, Dave and Tami Harnish, and Marlin and Ruth Ann Harnish; and Mark Clatterbuck and all my cousins. This book is dedicated to my sister, Malinda Clatterbuck, who is the only person who knows what I know, and who has always been my confidante, and fiercest fan. But it's with my nieces, Alena and Hannah, in mind that I've written it.

I have met and mourned so many during the course of this book; my list of the dead is long and beloved. Although I don't believe they hear me when I talk to them, what do I know? Still I talk, and I am forever changed by the time we spent together. My father's long illness and death launched this project. If he is anywhere, he's in the hollow I call home. I'll say my thanks to him, as always, when I'm there.

Works Cited

Abbott, Matt C. "Remembering Terri Schiavo: Bobby Schindler Comments on Pope Francis, Bishop Robert Lynch, and Working on Behalf of the Severely Disabled." *RenewAmerica*, April 13, 2014. http://www.renewamerica .com/columns/abbott/140413.

American Civil Liberties Union. "Court Refuses to Hear Case Brought by Pregnant Woman Denied Care at Catholic Hospital." June 30, 2015. https:// www.aclu.org/news/court-refuses-hear-case-brought-pregnant-woman -denied-care-catholic-hospital.

Appel, Jacob M. "Beyond Guantánamo: Torture Thrives in Connecticut." *Huffington Post*,
March 18, 2010. http://www.huffingtonpost.com/jacob-m-appel/beyond -guantanamo-torture_b_360082.html.

———. "Rethinking Force-Feeding: Legal and Ethical Aspects of Physician Participation in the Termination of Hunger Strikes in American Prisons." *Public Affairs Quarterly* 26, no. 4 (October 2012). http://paq.press.illinois .edu/26/4/appel.html.

Barina, Rachelle, and Devan Stahl. "Blowing Up Bioethics: A Response to Atrium's Bad Girls and Head Nurses." Bioethics.net, April 17, 2014. http://www.bioethics.net/2014/04/blowing-up-bioethics-a-response-to -atriums-bad-girls-and-head-nurses/.

Baxter, Roberta. "Fighting to Keep the Right to Die with Dignity." *Missoulian*, July 6, 2010. http://missoulian.com/news/opinion/columnists/fighting -to-keep-the-right-to-die-with-dignity/article_3c94ecfa-8905-11df-9851 -001cc4c002e0.html.

Beauchamp, Tom L., and James F. Childress. *Principles of Biomedical Ethics*. Orig. 1977; New York: Oxford University Press, 2013.

Beauchamp, Tom L., and Robert M. Veatch. *Ethical Issues in Death and Dying*. Upper Saddle River, NJ: Prentice Hall, 1996.

Biographical Annals of Lancaster County, Pennsylvania: Containing Biographical and Genealogical Sketches of Prominent and Representative Citizens and of Many of the Early Settlers. Chicago: J. H. Beers & Company, 1903.

"Brain Dead Teen Moving to New Facility, Family Says." ABC News. January 2, 2014. http://abcnews.go.com/US/video/brain-dead-teen-moving -facility-family-21398022.

Butler, Katy. *Knocking on Heaven's Door: The Path to a Better Way of Death.* New York: Scribner, 2013.

———. "What Broke My Father's Heart." *New York Times Magazine,* June 18, 2010. http://www.nytimes.com/2010/06/20/magazine/20pacemaker-t.html.

Caplan, Arthur. "The Time Has Come to Let Terri Schiavo Die." NBC News. March 18, 2005. http://www.nbcnews.com/id/7231440/ns/health -health_care/t/time-has-come-let-terri-schiavo-die/.

Cather, Willa. *My Ántonia.* New York: Houghton Mifflin. 1995. Orig., 1918.

Centers for Disease Control and Prevention. "Leading Causes of Death," *Fast-Stats.* http://www.cdc.gov/nchs/fastats/leading-causes-of-death.htm.

Chammah, Maurice. "The Many Lives of a Death Drug." *Texas Monthly,* June 10, 2014. http://www.texasmonthly.com/story/many-lives-death-drug.

Clarkson, Frederick. "Christian Right Seeks Renewal in Deepening Catholic-Protestant Alliance." *Political Research Associates,* July 23, 2013. http://www .politicalresearch.org/2013/07/23/christian-right-seeks-renewal-in -deepening-catholic-protestant-alliance/.

Colby, William H. *Unplugged: Reclaiming Our Right to Die in America.* New York: AMACOM/American Management Association, 2006.

Coleman, Diane. "Disability Rights Community Responds to Tucker Hire." Not Dead Yet. September 13, 2014. http://www.notdeadyet.org/2014/09 /disability-rights-community-responds-to-the-tucker-hire.html.

———. "Diane Coleman's Response to Institute of Medicine's Committee on Approaching Death Online Survey." Not Dead Yet. October 31, 2013. http://www.notdeadyet.org/diane-colemans-response-to-institute-of -medicines-committee-on-approaching-death-online-survey.

Conley, Mikaela. "Elderly Couple Refuse Food, Water to Die; Get Evicted from Facility." ABC News, "Good Morning America," August 18, 2011. http://abcnews.go.com/Health/couple-stops-eating-drinking-end-life -son-launches/story?id=14327416.

Connell, Mark. "*Baxter v. Montana* Oral Argument." YouTube, uploaded September 2, 2009. https://www.youtube.com/watch?v=Y82Qg27bLaw.

Coulehan, Jack L. "Deep Hope: A Song Without Words." *Theoretical Medicine and Bioethics* 32, no. 3 (June 2011): 143–60. DOI: 10.1007/s11017-011-9172-2 2011.

Davis, Karen, Kristof Stremikis, David Squires, and Cathy Schoen. *Mirror, Mirror on the Wall: How the Performance of the US Health Care System Compares Internationally.* Executive summary. Commonwealth Fund, June 2014. http://

www.commonwealthfund.org/publications/fund-reports/2014
/jun/mirror-mirror.

Death Penalty Information Center, http://www.deathpenaltyinfo.org.

DeBolt, David, and Rick Hurd. "Jahi McMath: Judge Denies Petition to Keep
Girl on Ventilator Past Dec. 30." *San Jose Mercury News*, December 24, 2013.
http://www.mercurynews.com/breaking-news/ci_24787952/jahi-mcmath
-neurologist-present-test-results-at-closed.

Denno, Deborah. "The Lethal Injection Quandary: How Medicine Has Dismantled the Death Penalty." *Fordham Law Review* 76, no. 1 (2007). http://
ir.lawnet.fordham.edu/cgi/viewcontent.cgi?article=4294&context=flr.

Derrida, Jacques. *The Work of Mourning*. Edited by Pascale-Anne Brault and
Michael Naas. Chicago: University of Chicago Press, 2001.

DiBardino, David. "Hoping Within Reality." *Journal of General Internal Medicine*
27, no. 7 (October 2011): 884–85. DOI: 10.1007/s11606-011-1896-1.

Dominican Sisters of Hawthorne, http://hawthorne-dominicans.org/.

Dotinga, Randy. "Slowly Dying Patients, an Audit and a Hospice's Undoing."
Kaiser Health News. January 16, 2013. http://khn.org/news/san-diego
-hospice/.

Dowbiggin, Ian. *A Concise History of Euthanasia: Life, Death, God and Medicine*. Lan-
ham, MD: Rowman & Littlefield, 2005.

Drake, Stephen. "Robin Williams and the Hypocrisy of Suicide Prevention
Organizations." Not Dead Yet. August 24, 2014. http://www.notdeadyet
.org/2014/08/robin-williams-and-the-hypocrisy-of-suicide-prevention
-organizations.html.

Durkheim, Émile. *The Rules of Sociological Method, and Selected Texts on Sociology and Its
Method*. New York: Free Press, 1982.

Eckholm, Erik. "'Aid in Dying' Movement Takes Hold in Some States." *New
York Times*, February 7, 2014. http://www.nytimes.com/2014/02/08/us
/easing-terminal-patients-path-to-death-legally.html.

Emanuel, Ezekiel J. "Why I Hope to Die at 75." *Atlantic*, October 2014. http://
www.theatlantic.com/features/archive/2014/09/why-i-hope-to-die-at
-75/379329/.

End of Life Care in Corrections: The Facts. National Hospice and Palliative Care
Organization. April 2009. http://www.nhpco.org/access-outreach/end
-life-care-corrections.

Ertelt, Steven. "ProLife Groups Elated After Abortion Doc Gosnell Convicted
of Murder." *LifeNews*, May 13, 2013. http://www.lifenews.com/2013/05/13
/pro-life-groups-elated-after-abortion-doc-gosnell-convicted-of-murder/.

Fox, Maggie. "Diane Rehm: My Husband's Slow, Deliberate Death Was Unnecessary." NBC News, July 8, 2014. http://www.nbcnews.com/health
/health-news/diane-rehm-my-husbands-slow-deliberate-death-was
-unnecessary-n150096.

Gafni, Matthias. "Jahi McMath: Terri Schiavo Group Secretly Leading Transfer Efforts." *San Jose Mercury News*, December 31, 2013. http://www.mercury news.com/breaking-news/ci_24825161/jahi-mcmath-terri-schiavo-group -secretly-leading-transfer.

Garasic, Mirko Daniel. "The Singleton Case: Enforcing Medical Treatment to Put a Person to Death." *Medicine, Health Care and Philosophy* 16, no. 4 (November 2013): 795–806.

Goodstein, Laurie. "For Philadelphia Archdiocese, a Powerful Conservative Voice." *New York Times*, July 19, 2011. http://www.nytimes.com/2011/07/20 /us/20chaput.html.

"Guidelines for the Determination of Death: Report of the Medical Consultants on the Diagnosis of Death to the President's Commission for the Study of Ethical Problems in Medicine and Biomedical and Behavioral Research." *Journal of the American Medical Association* 246, no. 19 (November 1981): 2184–86. http://jama.jamanetwork.com/article.aspx?articleid=364199.

Hallman, Ben. "Hospice, Inc." *Huffington Post*, June 19, 2014. http://projects .huffingtonpost.com/hospice-inc.

Heinlein, Sabine. *Among Murderers: Life After Prison*. Berkeley: University of California Press, 2013.

The High Cost of Low Risk: The Crisis of America's Aging Prison Population. Osborne Association. August 7, 2014. http://www.osborneny.org/post.cfm ?postID=431.

"House Debates Terri Schiavo's Fate." CNN.com, March 20, 2005. http:// www.cnn.com/TRANSCRIPTS/0503/20/se.04.html.

Humphry, Derek. *Final Exit: The Practicalities of Self-Deliverance and Assisted Suicide for the Dying*. Eugene, OR: Hemlock Society, 1991.

Jacoby, Susan. *Never Say Die: The Myth and Marketing of the New Old Age*. New York: Pantheon, 2011.

Jakobsen, Janet, and Ann Pellegrini. *Love the Sin: Sexual Regulation and the Limits of Religious Tolerance*. New York: New York University Press, 2003.

Jamison, Leslie. "The Power of Grace." Review of *Lila*, by Marilyn Robinson. *Atlantic*, October 2014. http://www.theatlantic.com/magazine/archive /2014/10/the-power-of-grace/379334/.

Jones, Jeffrey M. "Americans' Support for Death Penalty Stable." Gallup, October 23, 2014. http://www.gallup.com/poll/178790/americans-support -death-penalty-stable.aspx.

Krieger, Lisa M. "Cost of Dying: Discovering a Better Way for Final Days." *San Jose Mercury News*, December 29, 2012. http://www.mercurynews.com /ci_22278023/cost-dying-discovering-better-way-final-days.

Kübler-Ross, Elisabeth. *On Death and Dying*. New York: Macmillan, 1969.

Leff, Lisa, and Terry Collins. "Jahi McMath's Brain Death Ignites Difficult Debate." *Huffington Post*, January 2, 2014. http://www.huffingtonpost.com /2014/01/02/jahi-mcmath-brain-death_n_4531000.html.

Le Guin, Ursula K. *The Other Wind*. New York: Berkley, 2001.

"Letter from Jahi McMath's Mother Gives Latest on Calif. Teen." *Atlanta Journal-Constitution*. February 20, 2014. http://www.ajc.com/news/news/national/letter-jahi-mcmaths-mother-about-recent-developmen/ndWLw/.

Lynn, Joanne. "Rethinking Fundamental Assumptions: SUPPORT'S Implications for Future Reform." *Journal of the American Geriatric Society* 28, no. S1 (May 2000). http://onlinelibrary.wiley.com/doi/10.1111/j.1532-5415.2000.tb03135.x/abstract.

Lesy, Michael. *The Forbidden Zone*. New York: Farrar, Straus and Giroux, 1987.

Lewin, Tamar. "Nancy Cruzan Dies, Outlived by a Debate over the Right to Die." *New York Times*, December 27, 1990. http://www.nytimes.com/1990/12/27/us/nancy-cruzan-dies-outlived-by-a-debate-over-the-right-to-die.html.

Martin, Adrienne M. *How We Hope: A Moral Psychology*. Princeton, NJ: Princeton University Press, 2014.

———. Audio interview with Robert Talisse. *New Books in Philosophy*, April 1, 2014. http://newbooksinphilosophy.com/2014/04/01/adrienne-martin-how-we-hope-a-moral-philosophy-princeton-up-2013/.

McCarter, Dorothy. Montana district ruling in *Baxter v. Montana*. http://www.compassionandchoices.org/userfiles/Judge-Dorothy-McCarters-Decision.pdf.

McCarthy, Justin. "Seven in Ten Americans Back Euthanasia." Gallup, June 18, 2014. http://www.gallup.com/poll/171704/seven-americans-back-euthanasia.aspx.

Menzhuber, Eric. Description of "The Bride," a painting of Terri Schiavo. http://menzhuberartstudios.com/works/434994/the-bride.

Mitford, Jessica. *The American Way of Death*. New York: Simon and Schuster, 1963.

Mohrmann, Margaret E. "God Will Find a Way." In *On Moral Medicine: Theological Perspectives on Medical Ethics*. Edited by M. Therese Lysaught, Joseph Kotva, Stephen E. Lammers, and Allen Verhey. Grand Rapids, MI: Wm. B. Eerdmans, 2012.

Nash, Nan G. Second district court of New Mexico ruling in *Katherine Morris v. District Attorney*. January 13, 2014. http://www.compassionandchoices.org/userfiles/Morris-Trial-Court-Opinion.cc.pdf.

National Hospice and Palliative Care Organization, http://www.nhpco.org/history-hospice-care.

National Institute of Neurological Disorders and Stroke, http://www.ninds.nih.gov/disorders/coma/coma.htm.

Nicholl, David J., et al. "Forcefeeding and Restraint of Guantanamo Bay Hunger Strikers." *Lancet* 367 (March 11, 2006). http://www.thelancet.com/pdfs/journals/lancet/PIIS0140-6736%2806%2968326-8.pdf.

Nohlgren, Stephen, and Tom Zucco. "Schiavo Case Has Myriad Fund Sources." *St. Petersburg (FL) Times*, March 28, 2005. http://www.sptimes.com/2005/03/28/news_pf/State/Schiavo_case_has_myri.shtml.

Not Dead Yet. http://www.notdeadyet.org.

Nuland, Sherwin. *How We Die: Reflections on Life's Final Chapter*. New York: Vintage, 1995.

Peace, William J. "Comfort Care as Denial of Personhood." *Hastings Center Report* 42, no. 4 (July-August 2012). http://onlinelibrary.wiley.com/doi /10.1002/hast.38/abstract.

———. "A Deer Hunter Is Dead: Humanity and Life Needlessly Ended." *Bad Cripple* (blog). November 7, 2013. http://badcripple.blogspot.com/2013/11 /a-deer-hunter-is-dead-humanity-and-life.html.

———. "Disability Rights and Opposition to Legalizing Assisted Suicide." *Bad Cripple* (blog). March 17, 2010. http://badcripple.blogspot.com/2010 /03/disability-rights-and-opposition-to.html.

———. "'Head Nurses.'" *Atrium: The Report of the Northwestern Medical Humanities and Bioethics Program*, no. 12 (Winter 2014). http://bioethics.northwestern .edu/docs/atrium/atrium-issue12.pdf.

People. "Tim Bowers, Newlywed and Dad-to-Be, Dies After Taking Himself Off Life Support." November 7, 2013. http://www.people.com/people /article/0,,20753329,00.html.

Periyakoil, Vyjehanthi S., Eric Neri, Ann Fong, and Helena Kraemer. "'Do Unto Others: Doctors' Personal End-of-Life Resuscitation Preferences and Their Attitudes Toward Advanced Directives." *PLOS One* 10, no.1371 (May 28, 2014). http://journals.plos.org/plosone/article?id=10.1371/journal .pone.0098246.

Petro, Anthony. *After the Wrath of God: AIDS, Sexuality, and American Religion*. Oxford, UK: Oxford University Press, 2015.

Porter, Sue Dessayer. "Unintended Consequences: Obstruction of Patient Choice." Blog of the Bioethics Program, Union Graduate College, Icahn School of Medicine of Mount Sinai, May 19, 2013. http://bioethics .uniongraduatecollege.edu/blog/2462/Unintended-Consequences -Obstruction-of-Patient-Choice.

Potts, Michael, Paul A. Byrne, and Richard G. Nilges. *Beyond Brain Death: The Case Against Brain Based Criteria for Human Death*. Netherlands: Kluwer Academic Publishers, November 2001.

Powers, Doug. "What Would Terri 'Want'? Not a Cheating Husband." *World Net Daily*, March 21, 2005. http://www.wnd.com/2005/03/29442/.

Priest for Life, http://www.priestsforlife.org.

"Q & A Regarding the Revision of Directive #58 in the Ethical and Religious Directives for Catholic Health Care Services." Catholic Health Association of the United States, November 23, 2009. https://www .chausa.org/docs/default-source/general-files/final_qa_d58-pdf.pdf.

Scarry, Elaine. *The Body in Pain: The Making and Unmaking of the World*. New York: Oxford University Press, 1985.

Schindler, Bobby. "My Sister Terri Schiavo Was Alive like Jahi McMath." *Washington Times*, January 16, 2014. http://www.washingtontimes.com/news/2014/jan/16/schindler-my-sister-terri-schiavo-was-alive-like-j/?page=all.

Schindler, Bobby, and Mark P. Mostert. "Remember the Humanity of Jahi McMath." *Time*, January 7, 2014. http://ideas.time.com/2014/01/07/remember-the-humanity-of-jahi-mcmath/.

Schneiderman, Lawrence J. *Embracing Our Mortality: Hard Choices in an Age of Medical Miracles*. New York: Oxford University Press, 2008.

"Sexual Victimization in Prisons and Jails Reported by Inmates, 2011–12." US Department of Justice, Bureau of Justice Statistics, May 2013. http://www.bjs.gov/content/pub/pdf/svpjri1112.pdf.

Shershow, Scott Cutler. *Deconstructing Dignity: A Critique of the Right-to-Die Movement*. Chicago: University of Chicago Press, 2013.

Silver, Mara. "Testing Cruzan: Prisoners and the Constitutional Question of Self-Starvation." *Stanford Law Review* 58, no. 2 (November 2005). http://www.stanfordlawreview.org/print/article/testing-cruzan-prisoners-and-constitutional-question-self-starvation.

Silvers, Anita. "Disability Discrimination: Risky Business for 'Consenting' Adults." Hastings Center Bioethics Forum, July 16, 2012. http://www.thehastingscenter.org/Bioethicsforum/Post.aspx?id=5916&blogid=140.

Smith, Fran, and Sheila Himmel. *Changing the Way We Die: Compassionate End-of-Life Care and the Hospice Movement*. Berkeley, CA: Viva Editions, 2013.

Smith, Wesley J. "Assisted Suicide Cheats People of Time." *National Review*, October 14, 2011. http://www.nationalreview.com/human-exceptionalism/322793/assisted-suicide-cheats-people-time-wesley-j-smith.

Sontag, Susan. *Regarding the Pain of Others*. New York: Picador, 2003.

Stone, Katie, Irena Papadopoulos, and Daniel Kelly. "Establishing Hospice Care for Prison Populations: An Integrative Review Assessing the UK and USA Perspective." *Journal of Palliative Medicine* 10 (October 2011). http://pmj.sagepub.com/content/early/2011/10/12/0269216311424219.

Street, Jon. "Philadelphia Archbishop on Abortion: 'We're Catholics Before We're Democrats . . . Before We're Republicans.'" *Christian News Service*, October 26, 2012. http://cnsnews.com/news/article/philadelphia-archbishop-abortion-we-re-catholics-we-re-democrats-were-republicans.

Sullivan, Winnifred Fallers. *Prison Religion: Faith-Based Reform and the Constitution*. Princeton, NJ: Princeton University Press, 2009.

Thernstrom, Melanie. *The Pain Chronicles: Cures, Remedies, Spells, Prayers, Myths, Misconceptions, Brain Scans, and the Science of Suffering*. New York: Farrar, Straus and Giroux, 2010.

Todd, Douglas. "Accommodations for Disabled Have Taken Root." *Vancouver Sun*, March 13, 2010. http://www.canada.com/vancouversun/news/westcoastnews/story.html?id=9a8f0033-443a-4cd2-9cb1-c7b828abfe65.

Tomeo, Teresa. *Extreme Makeover: Women Transformed by Christ, Not Conformed to the Culture.* San Francisco: Ignatius Press, 2011.

—————. *Noise: How Our Media-Saturated Culture Dominates Lives and Dismantles Families.* West Chester, PA: Ascension Press, 2007.

Trachtenberg, Peter. *The Book of Calamities: Five Questions About the Meaning of Suffering.* Boston: Little, Brown, 2008.

Vickers, Robert J. "Pro-Life Group Warns of Assisted Suicide, Euthanasia Agenda." *Patriot-News* (PA). August 13, 2013. http://www.pennlive.com /midstate/index.ssf/2013/08/pa_pro-life_group_wary_of_assi.html.

Wallace, Jonathan. "What Sybil Knew." *Ethical Spectacle* 15, no. 3 (March 2009). http://www.spectacle.org/0309/sybil.html.

White, Tracie. "Most Physicians Would Forgo Aggressive Treatment for Themselves at the End of Life, Study Finds." Stanford Medicine News Center, May 28, 2014. https://med.stanford.edu/news/all-news/2014/05 /most-physicians-would-forgo-aggressive-treatment-for-themselves-.html.

Wiggins, Ovetta. "Maryland Weighs 'Death with Dignity' Legislation." *Washington Post*, March 6, 2015. http://www.washingtonpost.com/local/md -politics/maryland-weighs-death-with-dignity-legislation/2015/03/06 /187fa3b6-c3a0-11e4-9ec2-b418f57a4a99_story.html.

Williams, Florence. "Adam's Rib, van Gogh's Ear, Einstein's Brain." Review of *Anatomies*, by Hugh Aldersey-Williams. *New York Times Book Review*, August 9, 2013. http://www.nytimes.com/2013/08/11/books/review/anatomies-by -hugh-aldersey-williams.html.

Zimmermann, Mark. "Candidates for Maryland Governor Differ on Education Support, Assisted Suicide." *Catholic Standard*, October 24, 2014. http:// cathstan.org/Content/News/News/Article/Candidates-for-Maryland -governor-differ-on-education-support-assisted-suicide/2/2/6282.

Zoroya, Gregg. "Death Penalty Spurs Wild West Scramble for Drugs." *USA Today*, March 17, 2014. http://www.usatoday.com/story/news/nation /2014/03/09/executions-lethal-injection-drugs-prisons-death-penalty /5866947/.

Index